The Ethics of Water

Also available from Bloomsbury

The Bloomsbury Handbook to the Medical-Environmental Humanities,
edited by Scott Slovic, Swarnalatha Rangarajan and Vidya Sarveswaran

Practicing Empathy, by Mark Fagiano

The Ethics of Climate Change, by James Garvey

Why Climate Breakdown Matters, by Rupert Read

The Ethics of Water

From Commodification to Common Ownership

Cameron Fioret

BLOOMSBURY ACADEMIC
LONDON • NEW YORK • OXFORD • NEW DELHI • SYDNEY

BLOOMSBURY ACADEMIC
Bloomsbury Publishing Plc
50 Bedford Square, London, WC1B 3DP, UK
1385 Broadway, New York, NY 10018, USA
29 Earlsfort Terrace, Dublin 2, Ireland

BLOOMSBURY, BLOOMSBURY ACADEMIC and the Diana logo are trademarks of
Bloomsbury Publishing Plc

First published in Great Britain 2023
This paperback edition published in 2024

Copyright © Cameron Fioret, 2023

Cameron Fioret has asserted his right under the Copyright, Designs and Patents Act,
1988, to be identified as Author of this work.

For legal purposes the Acknowledgements on p. viii constitute an extension
of this copyright page.

Series design by Charlotte Daniels
Cover image: The Water Bearer (1808–1812), Francisco de Goya
(© Album / Alamy Stock Photo)

All rights reserved. No part of this publication may be reproduced or transmitted in
any form or by any means, electronic or mechanical, including photocopying,
recording, or any information storage or retrieval system, without prior
permission in writing from the publishers.

Bloomsbury Publishing Plc does not have any control over, or responsibility for,
any third-party websites referred to or in this book. All internet addresses given in
this book were correct at the time of going to press. The author and publisher regret
any inconvenience caused if addresses have changed or sites have ceased to exist,
but can accept no responsibility for any such changes.

A catalogue record for this book is available from the British Library.

A catalog record for this book is available from the Library of Congress.
Library of Congress Control Number: 2023939537.

ISBN:	HB:	978-1-3503-4880-6
	PB:	978-1-3503-4884-4
	ePDF:	978-1-3503-4881-3
	eBook:	978-1-3503-4882-0

Typeset by RefineCatch Limited, Bungay, Suffolk

To find out more about our authors and books visit www.bloomsbury.com
and sign up for our newsletters.

To my parents and my sister, with whom everything is possible.

Contents

Acknowledgements	viii
1 Introduction	1
2 Water, Rights-based Arguments and Social Entitlement	25
3 An Explication of Common Ownership and Common Territory	53
4 Water Justice as Socioenvironmental Justice	89
5 The Protection of Rights to Water Through Law, Politics and Social Movements	109
6 Conclusion	141
Notes	151
Bibliography	183
Index	199

Acknowledgements

It is the realization of a dream to publish a book of my doctoral research, and I owe an incalculable amount to so many people. To begin, this book exists because of Monique Deveaux's guidance and dedication; her belief in me *made* my time at the University of Guelph and helped give life to the research within this book. I want to extend thanks to Omid Payrow Shabani, Tim Hayward, Karen Wendling and Avery Kolers for their steadfast commitment to making the project as best as possible with their comments through the writing process and at my doctoral defence. Jade Grogan and Suzie Nash at Bloomsbury, too, made this book a reality with their acceptance of my proposal. I am deeply appreciative.

I am grateful to the Social Sciences and Humanities Research Council, the Government of Ontario and the Latornell Family for granting me funding in support of this project. I am thankful for the support for research and enlightening opportunities that Jen Read and the Water Center at the University of Michigan, and Nidhi Nagabhatla at the United Nations University Institute on Comparative Regional Integration Studies, have provided in helping to guide and inspire research within this book.

I want to acknowledge my friends and colleagues who supported me through this process, offering their time to read drafts and provide thoughtful comments. Thank you, especially, to Zack Abrams, Katrina Bahnam, Brady Fullerton, Ben Gillies, Josh Grant-Young, Kyle Novak, Ronald Parmanand, Lindsay Rose, Kyle Schneider and Frank Venter for your encouragement.

A deepest thank you to my family who have given me endless love and support. Those closest to me were always there to uplift me whenever I had doubts and lost my will; I will carry and remember what they have done for me, forever.

The highest good is like water.

Chapter 8, Tao Te Ching

1

Introduction

1.1 Preface

Water is the fulcrum on which life pivots – it is nonpareil in its importance for life on Earth. The necessity of water provides it with intrinsic value, a value that some actors (e.g., private interests, supporters of commodification of water) posit must have a price, while others posit that it must be priceless. Various and sundry nefarious actors, companies, laws and policies compose the latticework of a structure which financializes water. Humanity is ensconced in a period of severe consequences regarding fresh water in environmental, economic and sociopolitical senses. Issues of freshwater commodification and subsequent privatization are pressing matters of life and death.

Such issues call for normative analyses that heretofore are underdeveloped, and I aim to not only analyse but also to develop normative arguments and proposals for more equitable and just principles governing the distribution, consumption and governance of water. Water is a necessary element for life, and fundamental to a community's ability to function; lack of reliable access to clean water is, therefore, a problem of extreme urgency. Human-generated climate change, which has become a focal point for much environmental political philosophy and theory in the past two decades, is a critical contributing factor to water shortages. Yet the commodification and privatization of water by corporations, and municipal and national governments, has received comparatively less attention, despite posing urgent threats to people's ability to access this vital resource. These issues, which are pervasive and global in scope, raise important questions regarding 'ownership' and fair access to water; the rights people might have to this crucial resource; whether (and which) principles of distributive justice might be justifiably applied to adjudicate disputes over water resources; and the role of both government regulation and civil society activism in ensuring reliable access. I situate this book within the knowledge-gap of human activities related to the commodification and privatization of water because such areas of study have received little attention by philosophers and political theorists; moreover, they can fortify moral claims to water.

Climate change and the ever-expanding sphere of freshwater commodification raise important sociopolitical questions and ramifications. I pose and address the following five questions in this book:

1. What right, if any, do people have to water?
2. What are the putative harms of privatizing and commodifying water?
3. Should naturally occurring necessities for human life, like water, be considered owned in common as common territory or property?
4. If so, what are the most compelling normative and ethical grounds for justifying common ownership of water?
5. How might people's rights to access to water be protected through legal and political means, and what role might local and transnational political activism play in hastening the implementation of such protections?

In answering these questions, this work will provide normative analyses of freshwater governance, freshwater injustice and concomitant socioenvironmental injustice, while incisively critiquing the harms of freshwater commodification.[1] I hope to contribute to the burgeoning study of water ethics and justice within academic philosophy while working through the lens of non-ideal theory and a hybrid engaged philosophy. As the book deals with a variation of engaged multi- and interdisciplinary water issues, the arguments and analyses put forth might be used to inform policy decisions and water activism outside of the academy, too.

1.2.1 Methodology

The argument unfolds over six chapters and employs engaged philosophy and non-ideal theory in developing the arguments. To start, I must provide justification for this choice of theory before I outline the forthcoming chapters and arguments. Non-ideal theory 'should develop the constitutive parts of a theory of justice that are needed to bring us one step closer to justice assessments and policy design'.[2] As I consider it necessary that any normative analysis of water justice should lead to action, or 'justice assessments and policy design', I need to address non-ideal circumstances to bolster my methodology.

The arguments put forth in this book represent a form of engaged philosophy seen through the lens of non-ideal theory. I approach this project's questions from an initial abstracted theoretical stance, but transition and incorporate that theory into philosophy that grapples with real-world issues. My experiences as a researcher with the United Nations University – Institute for Water, Environment and Health (UNU-INWEH), the United Nations University – Institute on Comparative Regional Integration Studies (UNU-CRIS), and the Arrell Food Institute at the University of Guelph, as well as my personal service work as a cofounder of the Canadian national non-profit organization Shake Up The Establishment and a board member of the Guelph chapter of the Council of Canadians, significantly influenced the direction of this project.[3] The transformative power of community, deliberative democracy, and multi- and interdisciplinary research should shine through in my arguments because of the influence of the engaged method I utilize.

I can best advance the study of freshwater ethics and justice by offering proposals ultimately derived from environmental theory, but which draw on my experience working on water justice. Such non-ideal theory is pluralistic in terms of openness to a variety of research methodologies; furthermore, it is diametrically opposed to standard non-ideal theory (utilized by scholars such as Simon Caney[4] and Henry Shue[5]) which uses a principles-first method, beginning from ideal Rawlsian principles and applying them to the non-ideal, imperfect world. The standard method is insufficient because, just like ideal theory, it pays little to no attention to power asymmetries and takes the *status quo* as objective.[6] This book, on the other hand, delves into power asymmetries in water governance and ownership and sees the *status quo* as fluid.

The structural character of water injustice necessitates a non-ideal theory lens; these issues are too complex to be traced to merely one person, group, or action. Contemporary examples of water injustices, derived from water commodification and privatization, show that this issue is urgent and current. The 'water wars' in Cochabamba, Bolivia, symbolize such a struggle for water, where fresh water was privatized and denied to the public. In 2000, the IMF and World Bank enabled the privatization of water in Bolivia that led to massive inequality in water access.[7] Further denial of water to those in need has occurred in Detroit,[8] where water has been denied to the poorest members of society,[9] and in Erin and Aberfoyle, Ontario, Canada, where water has been financialized and commodified by private interests (e.g., Nestlé) on expired permits.[10] Cochabamba, Detroit and Erin and Aberfoyle illustrate clear-cut instances of the commodification and privatization of water and the public resistance that followed, and they will play an important role in normative analyses in this book.

The first criticism of this engaged approach of non-ideal theory (or non-ideal theory overall) could be that it will not result in generalizable principles. How could my normative suggestions (such as recommoning in Chapter 5) be taken up if they are stringently context-specific? Why must we shirk ideal theory altogether? As political theorist Zofia Stemplowska has argued, ideal and non-ideal theory are compatible since 'they can deal with different aspects of the same problem and, as such, can be combined should the need arise'.[11] To this assertion, I add that theorizing about structural injustice can certainly be applicable to multiple contexts and problems. Furthermore, as will be explained shortly, ideal theory runs the risk of 'idealization', not generalism; generalism can help generate achievable and desirable recommendations from a fact-sensitive and abstract, not idealized, stance. Philosophers Onora O'Neill[12] and Charles Mills[13] have explained that generalism is necessary if one is to focus on the most important elements of a problem, but idealization differs in that it involves *false* assumptions of a problem.

Non-ideal theory first emerged as a critique of ideal theory but has gradually evolved into a more defined normative approach – partly in response to the arguments offered by central defenders of ideal theory. Proponents of ideal theory say it can provide us a goal to strive for, as well as fundamental principles to ground theory regardless of real-world compliance.[14] Theorists such as Stemplowska[15] and Laura Valentini[16] have argued that ideal theory can be appropriate as long as it gets to recommendations from an *abstracted* standpoint, not an idealized one. Abstraction 'consists in bracketing off some complexities of a given problem, without assuming any falsehoods about them ... simplification undertaken to focus on the most important aspects of the problem at hand', while idealization makes false assumptions about serious parts of the problem at hand.[17] Political theorist Pablo Gilabert argues that ideal theory can be saved as a broadened approach utilized in an 'ongoing deliberative reflective equilibrium … in which we revise both our short- and long-term aims and commitments'.[18] Ideal theory and non-ideal theory exist in tension, then, regarding facts and actions in the real-world. Ideal theory is fact insensitive and, thus, does not provide achievable and desirable conclusions.[19] On the other hand, non-ideal theory is usually fact sensitive (it is cognizant of real-world circumstances), gives recommendations that are achievable and desirable, and sometimes focuses on highlighting structural power inequities. I submit that theorists can use abstraction in helpful ways provided they avoid false idealizations, just as the cases and normative analyses in later chapters will show. We can and should avoid idealization or 'ideology', in Mills' words,[20] of ideal theory to obtain broad, pluralistic and grounded action-guiding principles. As political philosopher Adam Swift argues, non-ideal theory is compatible with action-guiding principles, and 'fundamental, context-independent, normative philosophical claims to guide political action' are needed in the real world.[21] Such is the strength of non-ideal theorizing in water ethics and justice: we *can* step back from the problems or situations at hand and determine the most just actions, such as recommoning of water (as I argue in Chapter 5), but this determination can be informed by engagement with real-world experiences and case studies. Non-ideal theory is not reducible to feasibility alone; its greatest benefits are in describing and grappling with the world as it *is* – the injustices and harms.[22] In this way, I am attempting to use philosophy to produce a normative ethic of water justice grounded in the reality of water injustices and harms, which I consider the key strength of non-ideal theory.[23]

A second criticism of this non-ideal approach to problems of water injustice may be that the theorist cedes their objective, non-partisan position and prescribes weak moral theory as an activist, instead.[24] To this critique, social and political theorists Tommie Shelby[25] and Ben Laurence[26] sum up my retort perfectly: there are categorical theories of justice (which I apply to water norms and social movements for water), but these theories are useless without identifying motivated agents of change, and such identification cannot happen without an engaged method. As Laurence notes, we must avoid the 'technocratic posture' that the political philosopher is neutral and non-partisan, above conflicts and abstracted from grounded moral issues.[27] Instead, in my view, non-ideal political theorists must embrace their work as necessarily political and partisan.[28] Ethical political work, like all standpoints, is inherently unobjective and carries risks of biases and myopia which can be mitigated by epistemological and methodological practices.[29] My approach aligns with Mills' argument that ideal theory is ideological, entrenching and obfuscating existing power dynamics, especially and specifically regarding race.[30] Since racialized communities and social groups that are structurally subordinated bear the brunt of water injustices (e.g., poor water quality and pollution, inequitable water pricing, big dam projects, and commodification),[31] it would be unhelpful to reach for ideal theory to get to action-guiding principles regarding just access to, and governance of, water. Ideal theory shows us a mirage of actions and conclusions that are, in political philosopher Ingrid Robeyns words, a 'Paradise Island' of a seductive theory that we can never get to and is unreal in the sense that it can never be actualized.[32] Instead of putting faith into getting to this 'Paradise Island', perpetually waiting for the fruits of ideal theory to ripen, we must instead run with the inherent grounded nature of water issues. This book is a work in taking a side against water injustice, in supporting community and democracy, and I embrace the necessary partisanship of working against those agents with vested interests in commodified and undemocratic water.

1.2.2 The book as engaged philosophy and non-ideal theory

It is important to not overstate the type of non-ideal theory I have worked with, or collapse engaged philosophy with either applied philosophy or grounded normative theory. For my research, I worked in some activist and research roles that enriched my own understanding of these issues. Although I have performed a method of engaged philosophy framed by non-ideal theory, I have not done the kind of engaged research explained by Robeyns as empirically-supported 'action design and implementation', or as an extensive and direct engagement between theorist and agents of change as conceived by climate policy ethicists Fergus Green and Eric Brandstedt.[33] Instead, I have done engaged research that aligns closely with political philosopher Jonathan Wolff's explanation, that is, I have found a problem in need of attention – water injustices seen the world-over – and created theories to deal with the messiness of the world.

Wolff's account of engaged philosophy echoes the critiques of ideal theory and more grounded normative approaches of thinkers such as Iris Marion Young, Amartya Sen and Elizabeth Anderson.[34] This method of philosophy, as developed by Wolff, consists in a systematic dissection of world issues, the identification of a real-world problem in need of philosophical attention and the construction of theory in six steps:

1. The engaged philosopher identifies the issue and the current state of affairs, taking care to represent the field of concern accurately and learning about how people act in accordance with existing laws and regulations;
2. next, the engaged philosopher identifies the arguments and values in the existing state of affairs; and the,
3. analyses practices in other times and places, to see how they stack up to the ethic or policy the theorist is building, and identify where similar theory has failed before;[35]
4. once past failures have been identified, the theorist constructs new or augmented possible solutions; and
5. evaluates options, culminating in
6. policy recommendation.

In contrast to this engaged philosophy approach, one does merely 'applied philosophy' when one creates, in Wolff's words, a 'grand theory' (i.e., universalizable) and then applies it to the world; John Rawls' theory of justice, Peter Singer's animal ethics, and the effective altruism movements are examples of such philosophy.[36] Wolff explains that the problems with this method are numerous: applied philosophy can suffer from dogmatism, undermine policy outcomes and offer implausible outcomes that cannot be implemented in policy; in addition, partial, incomplete instantiation of applied philosophical policy might make a situation worse, and there might be blind spots in the applied philosophical theory due to being abstracted and 'grand' or universalized (as Mills and Laurence explained).[37] Finally, applied philosophy can suffer from conceptual inadequacy; Wolff targets effective altruism, 'a classic example of applied philosophy in the sense of starting with a theory and looking for problems to which to apply it'.[38] One's conceptual framework, instead of being rigorous, might be superficial; when one is a hammer, everything is a nail.

All of this is not to say that applied philosophy is useless; indeed, applied philosophy can influence public opinion on issues over a long period of time (Wolff poses Mary Wollstonecraft and John Stuart Mill as examples that presaged the passing of liberal legislation in the UK in the 1960s).[39] Applied philosophy can prime the public to a certain policy that might seem, at first, implausible or absurd. However, I do not think this attribute is the sole domain of applied philosophy. Engaged philosophy, too, can develop radical theories and proposals while not being under the guise or 'myth' of abstracted, generalizable applied philosophical principles.[40] Iris Marion Young, Amartya Sen, Elizabeth Anderson and James Tully are a few of the engaged scholars whose theories attest to the transformative power of such philosophy, and my research continues that engaged tradition.

This book is in the spirit of Wolff's idea of engaged philosophy. I take care to explicate the existing water justice landscape, in issues of property, environmental philosophy, national and transnational laws and agreements, politics and social movements. Then, in their respective sections and chapters, I dissect the arguments pertaining to water. Further, I compare approaches to water governance, justice and social movements (e.g., in Chapter 5 in five cases of freshwater activism against what I identify to be injustices), and then I construct possible solutions and evaluate options which problematize and yet map on to the existing water justice landscape (e.g., human rights, pluralistic governance and water recommoning as opposition to economic and technical framings of water governance). The final policy recommendation should be 'supported by reasons that can be readily communicated' and understandable to a wide audience and not only academics.[41] This book tries to live up to this standard of rigorous, broadly intelligible philosophical scholarship.

My approach also resonates with some of the methodological commitments of an emerging approach in political theory, that of grounded normative theory (GNT). Ackerly and co-workers identify four main commitments of GNT:

1 *comprehensiveness* of the inputs for normative arguments through original empirical research or analysis;
2 *recursivity* in creating normative claims;
3 *attentiveness* to epistemological inclusion;
4 epistemological *accountability*.[42]

Although this book is not a contribution to GNT as such, it aligns in a few respects with the values of a GNT approach: the book's normative arguments engage with comprehensive, broad yet local (what will be termed, to borrow from political philosopher James Tully, 'glocal') and empirical case studies of water activism, and the normative arguments are pluralistic and developed in part by heeding an array of voices and ways of knowing (in relation to water justice). I see GNT as existing on a spectrum or continuum; in relation to Ackerly et al.'s criteria for fully developed GNT, this book is thus best understood as offering a thinner variation of the grounded approach (insofar as I did not undertake my own fieldwork).[43]

Due to the admixture of Wolffian engaged philosophy and thin or partial GNT, I shall characterize this book as, in my own terms, a work of *hybrid engaged philosophy*. The world is imperfect and in that same way engaged normative theory and my very execution of it is imperfect – it does not try to convince itself of perfection or objectivity as ideal theory does. My arguments do not come from an exalted ideal stance; let future freshwater ethicists ignore or discard them if they do not adhere to the commitments of GNT, or to the tenets of engaged philosophy and non-ideal theory. *Ad astra per alia porci.*

Engaged philosophy can stipulate what would be needed for justice in non-ideal, real-world circumstances because it can show *why* it is unjust that some forms of ownership prevail and become instituted. A conception of water ethics and justice grounded in non-ideal theory could help guide policies, laws and individual actions.[44] I will use non-ideal theory as a mirror to accurately show the injustice present and the justice needed in our treatment of each other, as a portrayal for how we ought to treat each other with respect to the environment and water governance. As such, I will provide action-guiding principles for the achievement of socioenvironmentally just 'recommoning' of water in Chapters 4 and 5.

1.2.3 Description of the chapters herein

In the remainder of Chapter 1, I examine existing rights to water and the question of whether people have a right to water at all.

In Chapter 2: 'Water, Rights-based Arguments and Social Entitlement', I consider the main philosophical views on whether water is a public or private 'good'; who or what 'owns' water; and how access to it should be distributed and governed. I ask: What do current representative views from the literature and discourse in common ownership and human rights theory say about the issue of who owns natural resources such as water? By answering such questions, I establish that there are serious normative harms of privatizing and commodifying water. I also examine 'soft-law' rights – various UN instruments in which rights to water are claimed as rights or social entitlements – and investigate the basis of such rights. In examining such rights and establishing the basis for water as a human right, I explain in Chapters 4 and 5 of water's important role in community, collective control and deliberative democracy.

In Chapter 3: 'An Explication of Common Ownership and Common Territory', I assess arguments from Avery Kolers and Taiaiake Alfred that treat natural resources as things that treat natural resources as things that are a public trust, as things that ought to be considered common territory and not common property. I give a brief history of common ownership, property and territory, as compared to other forms of ownership, followed by a close look at Mathias Risse's 'common ownership of the earth' argument. I argue that principles of common ownership and territory are best understood as resistances of pathological path dependencies stemming from capitalism and liberal democracy. With respect to water justice, these principles are best realized within deliberative democratic political processes at the local, state and global levels. A critic of common ownership may pose concerns of the tragedy of the commons or hoarding, and I address such concerns with reference to work from Baylor Johnson, Elizabeth Kahn and Anna Stilz. Finally, I build on Risse's Egalitarian Ownership approach to common ownership of the earth by explaining more fully the relationship between water ownership and deliberative democracy.

In Chapter 4: 'Water Justice as Socioenvironmental Justice', I develop my argument that the commodification and privatization of water must be understood as a multi-layered form of socioenvironmental injustice. I argue that the most just distribution of water will be one which stems from, and promotes, socioenvironmental justice. However, water justice is too often reduced to the matter of distribution in the current literature; in contrast, I identify and focus on the non-distributional aspects of environmental injustice, which I characterize as relational *social and political harms*. Does the importance of water for human life make it unsuited for certain types of ownership or notions of justice? Is water actually special at all, and does it fall into a prescribed ethical structure? I examine these questions in relation to literature by Tim Hayward, David Schlosberg and other contemporary political and environmental philosophers. Most significantly, I put forth the normative conclusions that water injustice, such as commodification, is a harbinger of receding democracy and signals democratic deficits.

In Chapter 5: 'The Protection of Rights to Water Through Law, Politics and Social Movements', I argue that the ways in which social movements resist, and counter, water commodification in their communities are important tools for protecting rights to water. I ask: What does it look like when a community works through different social movements? I answer that anti-water commodification activist groups are similar in their uses of 'human rights' language, but they differ in what they identify as water injustice and in what they fight against (i.e., water activism centred against bottled water, or refusal of water to those unable to pay, or dams). Anti-water commodification movements use human rights language but are also frequently driven by immediate concerns (i.e., distribution) which do not lead to success. I draw on 'commoning' research done by scholars such as Cristy Clark, Silvia Federici, Elinor Ostrom and Vandana Shiva. At its simplest, commoning is a process by which 'community action [galvanizes actors] to both protect and reassert the water commons and to engage in broader emancipatory political struggles'.[45] In brief, I use the insights of 'commoning' thinkers to show why a 'recommoning' of water should be the normative focus of anti-water commodification movements. As a concept, 'commoning' is the communal, public governance and management of a natural resource. *Re*commoning of water, then, is similar to that of 'commoning', a process that David Harvey defines as the resistance and potential reversal of 'accumulation by dispossession' executed by water commodifiers.[46] I use the term 'recommoning' instead of 'commoning' to make more explicit the 'taking back' of water from private actors by citizens through legal and political mobilization, exemplified by cases in Chapter 5.

I shall argue in Chapter 5 that water activist organizations can resist and reverse water injustices such as commodification through building organized opposition. Furthermore, I establish that some of the most promising popular democratic initiatives in water justice are ones that aim to bring deliberative democratic processes into community-level governance and decision-making about water. To be explicit, I define 'deliberative democracy' as political theorists Andre Bächtiger, John Dryzek, Jane Mansbridge and Mark Warren do, as people '[coming] together, on the basis of equal status and mutual respect, to discuss the political issues they face and, on the basis of those discussions, decide on the policies that will then affect their lives'.[47] Deliberation over the political issue of water governance, then, consists of 'mutual communication that involves weighing and reflecting on preferences, values, and interests regarding matters of common concern'.[48] Thus, deliberative democracy is 'any practice of democracy that gives deliberation a central place' in governance of clean fresh water.[49]

Water justice movements ultimately seek to democratize water and put it under common control, which is part of a broader goal to have direct say over the water governance matters that deeply affect them. As such, these movements share many of the same goals expressed by deliberative democratic theory and practice. Just as I use real-world examples throughout the book of water commodification to flesh-out the injustice present in such situations, I provide cases in this chapter of resistance to commodification and privatization of water; to wit, Guelph-Wellington, Detroit, Grenoble, Cochabamba and Kerala offer striking examples of people-centred, public resistance to water commodification.

In the concluding chapter (6), I provide a synopsis of the arguments presented. I briefly explain why it is not morally acceptable to commodify water, why water should be considered common territory, the political harms of water injustice, how people's rights to access to water can be protected through legal and political means, and what role local and transnational political activism play in hastening the implementation of such protections, most notably recommoning. I also assert that this book underscores the need for environmentalists (theorists and practitioners) to be as concerned about deepening *democratic* processes and governance as they are about the realities of environmental degradation. Thus, this book contributes to the deliberative democratic literature concerning environmental norms, a field that I argue requires deeper multi- and interdiciplinarity between academics and non-academics. Finally, I highlight questions that researchers in freshwater ethics and justice must ask going forward, with reference to real-world governance and organizations.

1.3 Do people have a right to water? An analysis and explication of the existing literature on the ethics of water commodification

This introductory chapter begins by examining the question of whether people have a right to water. My moral intuition is that there is a *human* right to water, and this intuition informs my analysis; furthermore, after much analysis, I will conclude that a human right to water is a tool within the prescriptive apparatus for remedying water injustice.[50] In addition, I provide an overview of the literature concerning the ethics of natural resource commodification and privatization, with a focus on water. Closing the chapter, I provide a synopsis of forthcoming arguments. I reiterate the five questions listed in Section 1.1 and my answers to each question appear throughout this book.

The discussion concerning water as a right is young, coming to prominence over the past few decades. This burgeoning discussion of water as a human right, territorial or property right, environmental right, or another type of right will be explicated in this section. By enumerating different types of rights that water is claimed to be subsumed under, I hope to clarify my own stance concerning water and rights.

At the level of international organizations, the United Nations (UN) enshrined water as a human right in 2010 through General Assembly Resolution 64/292, explicitly stating that access to water and sanitation is a human right 'essential for the full enjoyment of life and all human rights'.[51] The importance of water not only for life but, seemingly, flourishing provides the base on which the UN places water as a human right. Moreover, the UN echoes the importance of water in its Sustainable Development Goals (SDGs), placing access to clean water and sanitation in SDG 6.[52]

Contemporary political theorists present a variety of arguments about environmental governance, as well as political and moral claims to water that are grounded in water's essential role in supporting basic human needs and capabilities. Water is generally treated by theorists as one among many natural resources to which people have a moral claim. Some contemporary political theorists, such as Chris Armstrong, have identified access to water as a moral entitlement because of its importance for 'basic functionings' and supporting life, while insisting that there is nothing 'special' about natural resources in the distribution of justice.[53]

Rights-based approaches to justice in natural resources within political theory and philosophy vary widely. Armstrong[54] and Risse[55] argue for an egalitarian approach to natural resources, defending a form of ownership that privileges an equal distribution of water across all populations. Risse presents a secular and globally focused egalitarian theory of ownership: 'common ownership of the earth'.[56] Such a globally centred lens to view water ownership and governance is cosmopolitan, that is, water ownership and rights should be instituted and executed without restrictions from extant nation-states. Cosmopolitan water governance overlaps with arguments by proponents of distributive justice, such as theorists Charles Beitz[57] and Simon Caney.[58] Cosmopolitan theories of natural resource governance run counter to nationalist theories expounded by political theorists such as David Miller, who argues that the nation-state ought to be the sole framer and arbiter of environmental or natural resource rights and ownership.[59] Concerning the importance of water and the state, political theorist Tim Hayward argues for constitutionalizing environmental rights.[60] In addition, Hayward broadens the scope of environmental theory by developing a critical framework of 'ecological space' that considers all relations, time and effort attached to natural resources – not only the resource itself – to illuminate our human relationship with the planet – our single 'biophysical reality'.[61]

Other contemporary theories do not focus as much on the nation-state-law nexus, and instead focus on how natural resources contribute to human flourishing. The progenitors of the capabilities approach, Martha Nussbaum[62] and Amartya Sen,[63] provide a lens through which to theorise about water governance, but their work does not have an explicit and specific focus on the environment and water. Normative theory with regard to politics, the environment and, specifically, water has been developed by David Schlosberg, who expands the conversation of rights to include participation and recognition (beyond merely distributional concerns).[64] These different approaches to the problem of water justice – egalitarian ownership, cosmopolitan and nationalist theories of natural resource governance, the constitutionalizing of environmental rights and the critical framework of 'ecological space', the capabilities approach, and the inclusion of recognition and participation (beyond only material distribution) in water governance – have particular strengths and shortcomings, and it is through engaging with them that I develop and clarify my own positions.

One of the most important contributions of normative work on water is the identification of water as a human right. However, some researchers are concerned that merely designating water as a human right does not suffice to block private water ownership and control. For one, geographer Karen Bakker argues that water should be considered as something separate from 'rights talk', as part of 'alter-globalization'.[65] For Bakker, human rights talk and a human right to water conflate human rights and property rights; do not make a distinction between property rights and models of delivery of said resource; and do not rule out the possibility of the private sector increasing their foothold in the distribution of water.[66] Identifying water as a human right does not necessarily rule out, and so cannot effectively prevent, the involvement of private corporations in water ownership. However, in Bakker's book *Privatizing Water: Governance Failure and the World's Urban Water Crisis*, she clarifies that human rights can have value in water justice campaigns as aspirational goals that raise expectations and place responsibility on both private and public actors, all while centring vulnerable groups.[67] Similarly, legal theorist Radha D'Souza criticizes water as a human right because it can be abused by private interests, but she does not throw out 'rights talk' entirely; instead, she argues that we must 'interrogate' those who want to make water a human right. We must be skeptical of their possibly facile interest in human rights and attempt to get to the heart of their interests.[68] We must also, on her view, 'reaffirm human rights' while ensuring stronger implementation through an expansion of democratic principles.[69]

D'Souza and Bakker offer insightful and incisive challenges to the limits of water as a human right; they resonate with my own arguments in Chapters 4 and 5, where I contend that the focus of those concerned about people's access to water should instead be on the broader democratic principles and institutions needed to secure goods needed for life. However, I maintain the language of rights with a critical eye to it being subverted by actors who support commodification. Overcoming water injustices such as commodification and establishing justice in water access and governance will involve, in David Harvey's words, 'confronting the fundamental underlying processes (and their associated power structures, social relations, institutional configurations, discourses, and belief systems)' of such systems while still seeing the attributes of rights.[70] Using human rights language and the UN's human rights system is fraught with risk, but such language can also legitimize and invigorate social movements for water justice.[71]

One prominent concern of critics of water as a human right is that it unreflectively grounds rights in private property. However, recent political theorists have challenged this stance, showing how territory, instead of property, provides a better basis for communally supportive, democratic water governance. To define terms, I conceive 'property' as political philosopher Anna Stilz does in her book *Territorial Sovereignty: A Philosophical Exploration*, where she writes that property 'confer[s] on the state a discretionary right to exclude outsiders from these [natural] resources, and to enjoy the full stream of income from exploiting them'.[72] To ensure resource access, Stilz embraces *jurisdiction* because it 'confers only a conditional right to exclude outsiders from resources on the territory, instead of property'.[73] According to this conception of property, as well as overlapping and illuminating definitions from Kolers[74] and Alfred[75] in this chapter, and Deborah McGregor[76] and Aimée Craft[77] (to be discussed in Chapter 2), property has necessarily liberal (i.e., individualized) and exclusionary stipulations.

Kolers explains the difference between territory and property in *Land, Conflict, and Justice: A Political Theory* which could aid in the improvement of water justice. He notes that property rights do not entail a notion of stewardship, and they also permit eviction from land and the denial of certain aspects of a land.[78] He also explains that territorial rights entail that 'the state may not evict tenants *en masse*; the state may not wantonly destroy objects of great worth; the state has positive obligations to outsiders and future generations that property owners lack'.[79] The 'limitations on territorial rights ... are due to the addition of consideration of non-owners, including those who do not consent to the state and do not own land in it – in some cases, because they do not yet exist'.[80] Kolers' conception of territorial rights makes explicit the importance of land and its resources; so, it is logically consistent that water is 'territory'. The state 'may not wantonly destroy' water, and the state 'has positive obligations to outsiders and future generations' because water is crucial for life.[81] Kolers contends that, if systems that are built on access to natural resources and waterways are disrupted, 'the social systems built on them are at risk of collapse'.[82] On this account, water's importance elevates it above property and into territory.

For Kolers and Alfred, property inherently includes the possession and *dispossession* of the earth and its resources; therefore, to augment political harms associated with property (e.g., domination and anti-democracy, as I identify and explain in Chapters 3 and 4), we should instantiate anti-property conceptions of *territory* (e.g., non-domination, stewardship and non-anthropocentricism which will be explained in Chapters 2 and 3). Alfred supports water as a right with accounts of stewardship and responsibility based in Indigenous traditions and thought. In *Peace, Power, Righteousness: An Indigenous Manifesto*, Alfred explains that the Western conception of property is dominative and exploitative, and territory intersects better with Indigenous ideas of stewardship. He holds that humanity is not responsible for the creation of the earth or of its resources, so people have no right to 'possess' it or dispose of it wastefully or abusively; effectively, 'possession of land by humankind is unnatural and unjust'.[83] For Alfred, questions about water justice and ethics, territory and the social and political nexus in which they exist are best approached through Indigenous ideas, not Western/European ideas.[84] These Indigenous ideas promote responsibility and stewardship of the earth while living in peaceful and respectful coexistence with other humans and the natural world.[85] Water sustainability is of the utmost importance, then, and denying access to water, let alone commodifying water, is normatively unacceptable.

Equitable access to clean fresh water might be secured through broader environmental rights concretized in formal constitutions. In *Constitutional Environmental Rights*, Hayward writes that the right to an adequate environment ought to be constitutionalized because it is a human right; in addition, human rights are so important as to be considered fundamental rights, and so they must take 'the most stringent form of normative commitment, in a state's constitution in order that they can be given full effect'.[86] According to Hayward, 'all human rights ought to be provided as fundamental rights in the constitution of any modern democratic state; the right to an adequate environment is a human right; therefore, the right to an adequate environment ought to be provided as a fundamental right in the constitution of every modern democratic state'.[87] On this theory, the right to an adequate environment requires the full force of being constitutionalized.

Hayward's argument for constitutionalizing hinges on the 'fundamental right' of ecological space.[88] For Hayward, people ought to have a globally equal *per capita* right to the ecological space they need.[89] Climate justice 'implies a fundamental right of each individual to an equitable share of the planet's aggregate natural resources and environmental services that are available on a sustainable basis for human use', and it is this 'aggregate' that is ecological space.[90] Hayward broadens the scope of environmental political theory by asserting that framing rights to ecological space 'capture[s] the basic fact that all human interactions with the nonhuman natural world – all our use of resources and all our environmental impacts – occur within a single biophysical reality'.[91] With regard to ecological space, going beyond our fair share of a resource, such as water, incurs an ecological debt, and inequalities of space utilization are 'unjust'.[92] Thus, in Hayward's framework, a global right to water could be established through *environmental* rights, but not specifically through the identification of water as a human right.[93]

Broad international declarations and statements, such as the 2010 UN General Assembly declaration of water and sanitation as human rights, 'do not create binding international law, but affirmation of a human right to water can be taken to imply that such a right should be recognized in international agreements and institutionally enforced through suitably stringent obligations on states and other parties'.[94] The difficulty with such declarations, for Hayward, is that they are vague in ascertaining who has what goals and obligations to meet, and they do not preclude private interest control of water; hence, enshrining water as a human right does not mean there are agents to enforce it.[95] I will clarify and argue, though, that there are political mechanisms, namely critical and ecologically reflexive deliberative democratic mechanisms, that could prevent private interests from hoarding water or from profiting from water. The human right to water implies an obligation that, in my view, could and should be realized through democratic processes at multiple geopolitical scales, including the contributions of social movements (as I explain in Chapter 5). As I will argue in later chapters, the valid concerns of critics of the notion of a human right to water, such as Hayward and Bakker, are best addressed by couching such rights as part and parcel with socioenvironmental justice and deliberative democratic politics.

Water as a human right can, in my view, encompass the importance of water in the context of environmental and territorial considerations. The fear that considering water as a human right opens the possibility for private interests to control water is not unfounded; however, I argue that human rights framing is the best lens for water justice because it accounts for the political and legal obligations of water governance, namely the need for deliberative democracy and as will be explained in Chapter 5, the support of water justice through the radically political praxis of recommoning. A human rights framework accounts for specific types of justice that we need to keep in mind when thinking of water justice, namely socioenvironmental justice (as explained in Chapter 4). As has been explained in this chapter, and will be explained further in Chapters 3, 4 and 5, much international law already recognizes water as a human right, but such laws might consider water as property, as a resource to be dominated by technocratic and élite undemocratic actors. As the book progresses, it will become clearer that actors can shift the myopic view of water as property to, instead, seeing it as a resource to be managed democratically. The human right to water can, then, be made meaningful and litigable through strengthening democratic practices of community participation and activism – recommoning water – and through institutions that use a model of 'human rights from below'. Furthermore, as will be explained in Chapter 5, deliberative democratic systems that are critical and reflexive, undergirded by the moral force of human rights, provide the best way to resist water commodification because they capture the power that deliberative democratic processes and structures give to citizens to transform structural injustices.

1.4 The author's argument

This book attempts to answer five central questions:

1 What right, if any, do people have to water?
2 What are the putative harms of privatizing and commodifying water?
3 Should naturally occurring necessities for human life, like water, be considered owned in common as common territory or property?

4 If so, what are the most compelling normative and ethical grounds for justifying common ownership of water?
5 How might people's rights to access to water be protected through legal and political means, and what role might local and transnational political activism play in hastening the implementation of such protections?

To start, I frame water injustice with a definition of structural injustice that accords with Young's definition in *Responsibility for Justice*. Young explains structural injustice in relation to the harms of poor public housing: power is exercised and maintained by durable and persistent societal *structures*, and the harms of structural injustice cannot be attributed to a single individual act or policy.[96] Consequences (i.e., harms) of individual actions and specific actions or policies of the state or institutions still produce harm, but they do not encompass the pervasive and deep-seated nature of expansive structural injustices.[97] A confluence of factors can transmogrify a just system into an unjust one, due to 'actions and interactions of a large number of public and private individual and institutional actors, with different amounts of control over their circumstances and with varying ranges of options available to them'.[98] Some agents act individually wrong, while others act individually right, contributing to injustice. For Young, structural injustice exists when social processes put large groups of people under systematic threat of domination or deprivation of the means to develop and exercise their capacities, at the same time that these processes enable others to dominate or to have a wide range of opportunities for developing and exercising capacities available to them.[99] A prominent point in this book will be that water injustice, such as commodification, is a form of domination, a signal of a lack of (deliberative) democracy.

There are many agents and institutions responsible for water injustice; responsibility cannot be traced to merely one person or institution. Water injustices such as commodification can be the result of, in Young's words, 'unintended consequences'.[100] Regarding unintended consequences in the definition of structural justice, Young writes, 'Social structure, then, refers to the accumulated outcomes of the actions of the masses of individuals enacting their own projects, often uncoordinated with many others'.[101] The 'uncoordinated' actions of the masses create injustice, as Young writes that most people attempt to follow rules and do what is best for themselves.[102] As will be observed, Young's ideas of structural injustice and collective responsibility are important for my argument for the recommoning of water in Chapter 5 because we can ameliorate issues of water inequality by empowering agents to *change* structural injustice. The empowerment of agents (as, and through, water justice movements) arises when members engage in a dialogue with each other and overcome their individual powerlessness by acting collectively. A collective effort of 'vocal criticism, organized contestation, a measure of indignation, and concerted public pressure' can instigate change.[103] As I argue, resistance to water injustice begins in, and is promoted by, deliberative democracy that is self-critical and reflexive.[104] I shall present and examine a multitude of cases which will flesh-out the structural nature of water injustice.

I argue that freshwater commodification and privatization are fundamentally undemocratic in their effects. I justify this claim by developing a normative argument for the common ownership of fresh water, where the resource ought to be considered common territory because it can align with democratic principles. The struggles of communities, organizations and transnational networks to protect people's right to water should be participatory and organized bottom-up if they are to succeed in resisting water injustices, so the relationship between democracy and water justice is tightly intertwined. By way of these actual struggles, I argue in Chapter 5 that people's rights to access to water can be protected through political and legal means that are supported by democratic principles, especially deliberatively democratic ones. Such legal and political means vary, as there are different legal and political protections (e.g., environmental laws and human rights laws; democratic political processes at the local and national levels for citizens to have a say over water regulation and use). People can resist and counter commodification in their communities through an empowering political activist strategy that harnesses the power of structure. This strategy emboldens the voices of victims and those of marginalized socioeconomic standing. It is an injustice to deny water to those who cannot afford to access it, and those victims of such injustice play a valuable role in the process of transforming the structure which has caused them grave harm.

My argument shows that water governance is a matter of socioenvironmental justice; however, there is also an instrumental component to the argument. My focus on democratic principles is primarily moral/normative yet is also practical insofar as it recommends action (e.g., recommoning); furthermore, I envisage the moral/normative component supporting the instrumental aspect of democratic principles, whereby normativity gives thrust to instrumental laws, politics and social movements.[105] The moral gives force to the instrumental, existing in a symbiotic matrix.

Securing people's right to access water free from commodification and privatization will require that we conceptualize and develop democratic processes and mechanisms for governing common access to water. The impetus for such development might be in water as a human right. Critics might raise important issues with water as a human right, but private interests could be nullified by way of democratic mechanisms and bottom-up water activist movements which are supported or infused by moral legitimacy and the acknowledgement that commodified water is morally illegitimate. To eschew 'rights talk' and refuse to label water as some sort of right is naïve; water can still be financialized and privatized regardless of whether it falls under a type of right, but 'rights talk' provides normative, moral import that would be lost without such discourse. Refusing to speak of rights in relation to water and its distribution is nothing more than an unsatisfying nepenthe to overcome some understandable, yet conquerable, issues associated with rights. In Chapter 3, I couch, and fully explain, such water rights within a formulation of 'common ownership of the earth', as Risse terms it.[106] I build on Risse's popular conception of common ownership by connecting it with water stewardship and the use of normative, democratic principles to support such ownership. Risse supplies a cogent defence of global responsibilities to *each other* grounded in our existence together in a 'global order', and his approach offers a strong base for my argument for water recommoning in Chapter 5,[107] though I depart from the popular version of common ownership by distinguishing property and territory which, as I argued above, is needed to establish democratically governed water. Such a lack of distinction between property and territory does not address responsibility and stewardship of water, thereby muddling the moral importance of distributing clean water equitably and without financial restriction. Finally, my main claim is that theories about the common ownership of the earth fail to sufficiently anchor their arguments in democratic (especially and specifically deliberative democratic) norms and principles.

Where my view departs significantly from Risse's and Hayward's dominant normative arguments for rights to water is in the implementation and recognition of common ownership, and the resistance to commodification schemes, through deliberative democracy. I will emphasize that bottom-up political movements can resist and reverse such schemes successfully because they harness the power of a plurality of actors, not merely a privileged few. The type of resistance that I propose is inherently democratic and is the antithesis of anti-democratic water commodification; in addition, it is positive and forward-looking. This local and transnational activism that I describe is a resistance, fomented by and grown in deliberatively democratic, people-centred principles which support uncommodified water. Furthermore, this type of activism/resistance protects against the possible transmogrification of a *prima facie* beneficent human right to water. In Chapter 5, I support my argument with reference to real-world, people-centred cases of resistance to water commodification, such as in Guelph-Wellington, Detroit, Grenoble, Cochabamba and Kerala.

Such global water issues are structural injustices that extend to individuals who buy and consume water that has been commercialized and sold for profit, to institutions and governments who issue contracts and allow for privatization, and to companies that perpetuate and steer the water industry. Young gives an account of how responsibility for collective harms could be shared conceptually and politically. Ideas of *recognition* and *political participation* map onto the structural model.[108] Vocal criticism, public pressure and distribution are not enough to spur change; there should be recognition of agents and issues, as well as political participation by all agents who create injustice in a structure. Contemporary political theorists such as Young and Schlosberg note that changing an unjust structure into one that is just is a political action; this idea offers a hopeful and forward-looking method of change that revolves around empowerment, the recognition of all relevant agents and issues, and the promotion of political participation. Young and Schlosberg offer a scheme of change that is active, and their theories buttress my normative, pro-democratic arguments in Chapters 3 and 4.

There is no single person responsible for current water injustices; instead, there is a confluence of actions, stemming from a variety of people, laws and companies that has led to our shared, unjust *status quo*. Structural injustice compels recognition that multiple structures and processes contribute to the problems of water commodification and privatization, and that responsibility for ensuing shortages is dispersed and shared. Furthermore, I endorse and establish the moral case for common ownership of water, an arrangement that is more just than one that commodifies and privatizes this vital resource. In part, I argue that this is because privatization deprives people of control over water and is, thus, arguably incompatible with robustly democratic processes in which citizens determine questions about natural resource distribution and management.

2

Water, Rights-based Arguments and Social Entitlement

It is not anodyne to say that water is a human right, and this assertion does not restrict water from being commodified and privatized. In this chapter, I canvass the current literature on human rights theory and water, as well as commodification and privatization. From this explication of current representative views, I move to explain the harms – both putative and of my own assertion – of commodifying and privatizing water within a human rights framework. Within these discussions, I ask about whether water is a private or public good and develop my argument, from Chapter 1, that water is a human right which includes non-anthropocentric, environmental concerns. I will explain in this chapter that 'rights talk', when done haphazardly, can lead to the conclusion that human rights do not further justice or equity. However, 'rights talk', and specifically environmental rights as an extension of human rights, undergird people's ability to access water equitably and justly. The collective populace supports, and brings to the fore, such rights in a deliberative democratic way.[1] Water ought to be considered a public good aligning with democratic ideals and institutions, acknowledgeing the unsubstitutability of this invaluable resource.

Privatization and subsequent commodification can be seductive, luring a state in with promises of efficiency and profit. This seduction may lie in theory, as their practice proves less enticing. Water injustice issues are rife, with people – mostly racialized, minoritized and of lower socioeconomic status – the world over suffering from such injustices.[2] In this chapter, I will argue that commodification fundamentally changes how people in a community are viewed; people are no longer citizens, they are customers. The harms of commodification and privatization stem from the shift of perspective from people being citizens to consumers or customers; moreover, in this shift, water's value changes into one that is strictly economic (i.e., market-based). Consequently, I shall argue that commodification and privatization harm and seriously undermine democracy and democratic institutions. The crux of this harm, which I explain and support in following chapters, is that commodification is anti-democratic and a form of unfreedom manifested as domination due to a lack of citizens' recognition, participation and deliberation.

2.1 Current representative views on water ownership, and the putative harms of water commodification

Before giving an overview of current debates about water ownership, it is helpful to characterize, in broad strokes, the movement of water from public to private ownership. Privatization is the act of making a commons, such as water, no longer commonly held. It is an 'enclosure' of a commons.[3] Privatization does not necessarily entail commodification, which is the treatment of water as a commodity, as something to be bought and sold for profit.[4] Privatization, however, generally sows seeds of commodification. Privatization thus precedes commodification and, while it does not always progress this way, puts in place the conditions for commodification. Henceforth, the term 'commodification' in this book includes the term 'privatization' within it. Privatization might not necessarily entail commodification, but commodification necessarily requires privatization – the private ownership and possession of water as a commodity. Commodification involves profit-seeking which privatization does not necessarily involve; therefore, I focus on commodification as it is a more inclusive term than is mere privatization.

Water commodification is a crucial element of market-based, normative theories of clean freshwater ownership. Arising at the turn of the millennium, market environmentalism was first widely promoted in the Kyoto Protocol of 1992, the most important environmental agreement supported by neoliberal, market-based solutions. Market environmentalism seeks to secure 'economic growth, efficiency, and environmental conservation' through private property rights.[5] According to advocates of this approach, the free market would solve environmental problems through conscientious free market policies. Proponents of market environmentalism believe that environmental goods are more efficiently distributed if they are considered economic goods and think that doing so would address concerns of environmental degradation and the inefficient use of resources.

Market environmentalists, such as philosopher and economist John Broome, argue that the free market can facilitate necessary restitution to those future individuals who will face the harms of present-day greenhouse gas (GHG) emissions and environmental exploitation.[6] A central tenet of market environmentalism is the importance of individualism, which is consistent with the free market (going back to the first modern explication of economics by Adam Smith).[7] The responsibility of restitution lies with the individual, just as the market itself rests on the self-interested rationality of individuals. This responsibility, for proponents of market environmentalism such as Broome and Nicholas Stern, can be filled in part by implementing low discount rates on goods and scrupulous government regulation, all while the market is driven by individual consumption changes.[8] Such responsibility and restitution are materially driven *and* of moral inspiration because harms (e.g., GHG emissions) are caused by the individual; to add, these significant harms are purposely done with the aim of benefiting said individuals. Thus, for market environmentalists, the relatively inexpensive action of paying restitution in the form of, for example, conservation, tree growing or carbon markets regulates GHGs and the greater market, opening up methods of regulation.[9]

Market environmentalism draws from the field of welfare economics and maintains a utilitarian view of individual consumption which challenges my own assumptions of structural socioenvironmental injustices (e.g., water injustice).[10] The free market, guided by the rational self-interest of the 'invisible hand', does an efficient job of calculating our individual, measurable consumption, automatically creating a costs-and-benefits market which obtains for any product (e.g., commodified water).[11] As William Nordhaus writes, the invisible hand theorem 'means that a person's actions in a well-regulated market are ethically neutral or positive because they generally leave unaffected or raise the welfare of others'.[12] The market is open because of negative freedom, and such openness 'simplifies our ethical lives' by reassuring actors that their actions are ethical as long as they are responsible members of the market (i.e., actors do not steal or cheat).[13] I will explain, though, that such simplification of the market carries with it epistemological harms that leave communities vulnerable to being taken advantage of by water commodifiers.

Knowledge and information efficiency is a key principle of market environmentalism which opens up more appropriate discount rates for water due to the efficiency of the 'invisible hand'. On the market environmentalist account, the market itself 'bakes in' the 'self-love' (self-interest) of actors, ensuring fairness and equitability. As Adam Smith writes in *An Inquiry into the Nature and Causes of The Wealth of Nations*, 'It is not from the benevolence of the butcher, the brewer, or the baker, that we expect our dinner, but from their regard to their own self-interest. We address ourselves, not to their humanity, but to their self-love, and never talk to them of their own necessities, but of their advantages.'[14] Thus, the market is amoral and fundamentally individualistic, making space for 'self-love' of actors driven by survival.[15] In accordance with self-interest and individualization of market costs and benefits, the 'invisible hand' internalizes externalities, that is, in Nordhaus' words regarding carbon pricing:

> One of the requirements for a well-managed society is to ensure that externalities are internalized, and this is one of the powerful arguments for full-cost pricing of externalities – or in this instance, of having a carbon price that fully reflects the social cost of CO2 emissions. From an economic point of view, if everything we buy has an appropriate embedded carbon charge, then that would alleviate our concerns about our carbon footprint. When carbon is properly priced, we can go about our daily lives confident that our actions are ethically acceptable and that ... carbon emissions are in the ethical neutral zone.[16]

The benefit of this informational efficiency, for market environmentalists, is that we do not need to devote extensive time and effort to adjudicate the morality of the market because the market is self-interested, rational and amoral or possibly beneficent; accordingly, we can give more thought to other moral questions concerning, for instance, the meaning and value of natural resources themselves.[17]

How does the market environmentalist approach treat the topic of fresh water? Those who endorse market environmentalism – those in favour of water commodification such as companies and states that work in tandem due to mutually-beneficial relationships – argue that water is a scarce resource that demands market control for efficiency and price; water must be priced at a level that enables its highest value distribution and efficiency.[18] Moreover, the market is inherently beneficial for individual actors, say market environmentalists, and is a boon to informational efficiency. Opponents, though, argue that water is without substitute and essential for life, so there must be a human right to water. Based off this right, responsibility would be placed on the state, and not the private sector, to get water to people.[19] Market environmentalists therefore consider commodification beneficial for justice in water ownership and distribution. For them, publicly owned and distributed water has failed; public sector water is inefficient, costly and does not get water to everyone in need. The private sector is the best route to overcome such obstacles, they argue. Against this view, I shall argue in the coming chapters that commodification causes clean fresh water to be dispossessed, and the resource becomes something held by those 'above' others as a form of 'globalization from above'.[20] Profit is the *idée fixe* of market environmentalists to the detriment of relevant societal issues such as equitability and justice. Citizens are no longer of concern and are not answered to; instead, shareholders are the primary actors of concern.

One reason that commodification tends to go hand in hand with a politically weakened citizenry is that it does not value citizens' freedom – and may even seek to undermine it when it is inconvenient for the ends of private corporations. An additional reason is that commodification fundamentally does not account for structural injustices and non-utilitarian concerns, such as morality, norms of altruism and non-anthropocentrism, or recognition and participation in environmental governance. Overall, there is a shifting of responsibilities from the public to the private realm. As water development scholar Kate Bayliss observes, the commodification of water as part of a broader financialized structure turns water into a private asset.[21] Such privatization entrenches the vulnerability of marginalized people and emboldens the position of the privileged commodifiers by making the marginalized ignorant of the quality of their water and how clean water may be accessed. Bayliss argues against commodification on descriptive grounds, saying water is not a good investment because 'capital costs are high and the payback period is long; the resulting infrastructure is fixed and there are commercial and political risks associated with the strategic nature of water'.[22] Despite these drawbacks, governments push for public–private partnerships (PPPs) by enabling environments for private firms to fill the 'financing gaps' between lack of access to water due to infrastructure. These partnerships are a selling of public sovereignty, a privatizing of gains and a publicizing of losses. What used to be the responsibility and purview of the state is now within the grasp of private interests, facilitated by corruption. To resist corruption, Bayliss argues for uncommodified, collective control of water, writing that there is growing evidence to support the claim that natural resources can be managed 'collectively by users through diverse systems of collective action'.[23] As such, she argues for strengthening the state, and that state control is necessary and been shown to effectively resist private, corporate control of water.[24]

We must, then, think about a more robust normative theory of water justice that requires tangible structural change, including political reforms. Some political theorists, such as Chris Armstrong, see such reforms as largely distributive and descriptive. Armstrong's descriptive egalitarian theory is particularly important in understanding current representative views.[25] Natural resources are 'nothing special' for egalitarian justice in the sense that such justice requires equal access to well-being as a whole, instead of the equal distribution of, say, water itself.[26] Natural resources such as water are arbitrarily naturally distributed and held unequally, so ascribing them a normative description, for Armstrong, misses the mark of what they are and cannot lead to egalitarian justice.

In contrast to market environmentalists' attempts to portray water as a commodity, water is 'raw' or 'original'; it exists apart from human activity yet is central to human life. Justice might dictate redistributing the resource itself (i.e., physically moving fresh water to those in need); however, in most instances it is better to help others develop infrastructure to provide them with said resource than it is to transport a resource. Indeed, physical redistribution of resources might harm the environment.[27] Armstrong adds that there are three classes of benefits of natural resources, and water would fall under the category of being a private good because its benefits are excludable and subtractive. In addition to private goods, there are pure public goods, where benefits are non-excludable and non-subtractive; furthermore, collective goods are non-excludable and subtractive. Remember that Armstrong posits a descriptive definition of natural resources instead of a normative one, so he is not endorsing water as something to be commodified.

The question of where water's value lies is important for addressing the issue of water justice because such normative values of water will inform the norms of water justice policy. I aim to attack water commodification from a normative standpoint; therefore, my analysis of the moral and political harms of water commodification provides the grounding for my argument for the normative value of water. As such, I must explain the prominent arguments in the current water-value discourse, while identifying the strengths and weaknesses of existing theories and putative harms, to see what gaps should be filled. For example, Armstrong and Kolers contribute to the literature on water ownership, but they do not engage deeply with democratic, especially deliberatively democratic and activist, mechanisms and norms relating to water and the instantiation of 'recommoning'. The filling of these gaps and the identification of harms are two of my tasks for this chapter that will inform succeeding chapters as well (i.e., I explain the process and normative importance of recommoning in Chapter 5).

Armstrong cogently connects the relevance of human rights to water by way of *use* and problematizes Kolers' view. Armstrong identifies water as a non-substitutable resource and a fundamental pillar of human rights because it is 'in and of [itself] necessary to human survival'.[28] Water is an 'indispensable' element which supports basic functioning of life and represents 'vital supports for anyone's life, no matter which projects they happen to be committed to', and so it is identified as a universal necessity attached to the universality of human rights.[29] Moreover, the value derived from natural resources must be more than monetary or economic but, instead, connected to culture and history. He proposes that value and ownership of natural resources ought to be connected to *potential* use, in contrast to Kolers who asserts that value must be derived from *intentional* use. Armstrong and Kolers agree that the value of water is more than economic or monetary, but they differ on valuations of use. Kolers argues that natural resources should be conceived as something 'intentional', meaning something cannot be considered a natural resource unless it is used in certain ways by the community that holds/uses it; therefore, the value of natural resources is context specific.[30] Armstrong argues that Kolers leads us 'astray', as natural resources hold importance with their potential benefits.[31] To restrict the label of 'natural resource' to only those things that are being used already is too dependent on the actions of individuals or groups. Such restrictions do not account for the entirety of the value of natural resources which extends to culture and history. In Kolers' account, one would be morally justified to deny those in need of access to water that is 'unused' (water not being used intentionally) because 'unused' water would not count as a natural resource at all.

Minimalism or, more specifically, right-libertarianism contrasts with Armstrong's global egalitarian perspective. Minimalists are concerned with how people's lives go in an absolute sense, whereas egalitarians are concerned in a comparative sense. Egalitarians view equality non-instrumentally; inequality is something that can never be tolerated, either because of effects/outcomes or because of inequality itself. Armstrong unequivocally rejects right-libertarianism and minimalism in general.

Different conceptions of equality will translate into different egalitarian approaches to water justice. For Armstrong, beyond endorsing global egalitarianism, he endorses a 'humanist' or 'non-relationist' approach where humans are the ultimate unit of equal moral respect and concern; human's value certain things, and it would be arbitrary to distribute advantages unequally.[32] Failing to account for why water is not reasonably distributed equally also 'fails to treat moral persons with sufficient respect'.[33] He contrasts the relationism and anti-global egalitarianism of Miller[34] and Risse,[35] who say inequalities can be tolerated as long as they work to the advantage of all.[36]

Of critical note is Risse's 'common ownership of the earth' theory. For Risse, water is 'original', meaning it is of no one's accomplishment and so no one has accomplishment-based claims to water ownership.[37] Thus, it would be arbitrary and unjust to allow water to be owned in any way other than in common. Water as commonly owned 'generates a set of rights, namely membership rights in the global order'; it is the existing state system – the global economic and social structure – connected to the UN and its charter, along with Bretton Woods Institutions.[38] So, water, as commonly owned and facilitating rights in the global order, is a human right and, although its use is private, its distribution ought to be made as equitable as possible. Instead of focusing only on water and its distribution, I shall argue in subsequent chapters that we should consider human rights and egalitarian justice in relation to socioenvironmental justice and the support of democracy. How we conceptualize water, as an ownership structure that is individual (property), or communal (territory), will determine what harms we are able to identify. As will become clearer in this section, we will identify more than economic or instrumental harms when we see water as something more akin to territory instead of property; there will be (political) harms attached to environmental, political, cultural and historical life.

Let us begin by comparing and contrasting potential and intentional water use, as well as water ownership due to territorial, instead of property, rights. Kolers argues that territory rights and natural resources should be conceived as something 'intentional', meaning a land cannot be considered to have a claim to a territory right, or something cannot be considered to have natural resource rights, unless it is utilizes in certain ways by the community that uses it. Territory's meaning is culture and context specific, so it is a's highly particular good and a universal good'.[39] Territorial rights are intimately related to resources such as water:

> Land is composed of resources that we need in order to survive, prosper, and express ourselves; literally, the land constitutes both our physical bodies and virtually every material good we can find or fashion. Hence, secure access to good land, land we can use to do things we care about, is essential to our capacity to make our way in the world ... land and its properties – its location, its material composition, who or what lives on it – are essential to a vast array of world systems, such as nitrogen and carbon cycles, water purification and storage, ecosystems, and the production of oxygen, without which we would not exist.[40]

For Kolers, eligibility, attachment and normativity are three criteria that determine who rightfully claims a territory; on what basis their claim rests; and why such a claim should be one of justice.[41] He argues that territorial rights exist if a legislated, governed land's people develop intentional use of the land.[42] A territorial right exists as an 'attachment approach' to territory, similar to liberal-nationalist and some Indigenous views; these special connections between people and lands carry moral weight. As such, we should look after land and its resources (i.e., 'constituent parts') when it is considered territory not only because of the significant connection with the land, but because stewardship benefits all.

This section has presented the current range of views on water ownership while laying the foundation for the argument that stewardship of the earth will be a necessary element of a water justice ethic, and that stewardship is most appropriately imbued by territory that values the rights of non-owners. This clarification is relevant for my argument for the recommoning of water in Chapter 5, but it has more immediate relevance for the forthcoming argument that water should be commonly owned. An ethic of water ought to move us towards greater justice in water access and governance centred on anti-property, pro-territory philosophies. Avery Kolers, Taiaiake Alfred, Deborah McGregor, Aimée Craft and others have explained territory as distinct from property, and water as an entity wholly separate from private economic ownership, so these existing formulations may support a recommoning ethic as the fuel for water justice movements. We can retrieve a notion of territory regarding water that has been obfuscated by overly rational, technical and utilitarian governance over water.

2.2 The water commons, and a tension in recommoning

The idea that water is held in common for collective use is well established within Indigenous knowledge and belief systems. Deborah McGregor, scholar of Indigenous environmental justice, writes that stewardship is an Indigenous relation to the 'living force' of water which generates morally binding obligations that benefit humans and non-humans that are alive and yet-to-be-born.[43] The Western conception of the natural world is one of property – economic, anthropocentric, and imbued with instrumental value. In contrast, McGregor, Whitaker and Sritharan state that 'Indigenous understandings are based on regarding the Earth as alive and imbued with spirit', generating 'reciprocal' duties between humans and the natural world in a harmonious relationship that is antipodal to property.[44] Water has spiritual and ancestral value for many Indigenous peoples.[45] Indigenous scholars such as Susan Chiblow and Aimée Craft have expounded on the worldview that Indigenous epistemology, ontology and the dynamic with the natural world in Indigenous Environmental Justice (IEJ) is non-anthropocentric: non-humans and the Earth have agency, they are alive and stipulate duties and obligations of care.[46] As Craft notes, water justice requires more than equitable distribution; in addition to distributional concerns, justice demands that water be understood and respected as a being that is alive with its own duties, responsibilities and rights.[47]

Closely connected to the IEJ approach is stewardship. Taiaiake Alfred explains a theory akin to stewardship of the earth, wherein natural resources are not so much 'owned' but 'available' in common. Water, for Alfred, has deep intrinsic value, contrasting the paradigm of the West which ascribes instrumental and economic value. Alfred explains that Indigenous governance systems promote 'harmony, autonomy, and respect' of nature and natural resources, while Western systems promote dominion.[48] Therefore, he proposes a radical shift away from the Western paradigm of ownership; questions of water ownership, for instance, and environmental justice broadly must be confronted not with Western/European ideas, but with traditional Indigenous ideas. Such questions of justice 'are best considered outside the framework of classical European thought and legal traditions' because they do not focus on domination of nature and other beings.[49] In Indigenous philosophies, power and justice stem from respect for the natural world and its resources, but dominant Western philosophical reflections on the natural environment encourage the control of nature through 'coercion and artifice' which alienates us from nature and the resources we use.[50] Alfred adds that Indigenous traditions are opposite from traditional Western thought of materialism and consumerism, and they have always been a 'repository of vast experience and deep insight on achieving balance and harmony'.[51] He writes that, before contact with Europeans, Indigenous societies had achieved 'true civilization', living in harmony with the earth while promoting communal responsibility, equality in gender relations, respect for individual freedoms, and observing natural resources, such as water, as being commonly held.[52] From this harmony sprung forth justice.

For Alfred, water ought to be respected and used in such a way as to promote harmony and, by extension, justice. The lynchpin of this system is stewardship, but Kolers and Alfred differ in their reasons for adhering to stewardship of the earth. For Kolers, we are to be stewards for future generations of people; it is an anthropocentric, grounded and secular theory. For Alfred, we are to be stewards for non-anthropocentric and unsecular reasons; to elaborate, the West devalues nature and reduces it to profit and commodity. The distinction here is crucial for understanding the connection between water and rights: anthropocentric stewardship of the world exists, *ipso facto*, for humans and aligns with human rights arguments, while non-anthropocentric stewardship ideals in Indigenous traditions do not necessarily link up with human rights. As will become clearer later in this chapter, as well as the next, I endorse a human right to water with deliberative democratic protections. Alfred's approach has invaluable elements that can be maintained in a human rights approach (e.g., stewardship and anti-property), and such strengths should be utilized secularly, to be as pluralistic as possible.

A human right to water, though, comes with risks, one of which is anthropocentrism.[53] This is because human rights instruments treat environmental goods as resources to which human beings have rights, but do not recognize the intrinsic value of water and non-anthropocentric life. However, I hold that we must push against this framing of humanity against ecological good; we need not be in opposition. The privileging of human needs does not have to be a destructive privilege because the satisfaction of water as a human right is impossible without stewardship and non-anthropocentrism. Human rights can exist in concert with stewardship (i.e., care and concern) of the non-human world because of the intrinsic value that water has in sustaining human and non-human life. Such intrinsic value and importance of water transcends any dispute between anthropocentric human rights and non-anthropocentric stewardship. I cannot deny that human rights are anthropocentric and exalt humanity over non-humans – we *are* put first – but non-humans are a critical factor in water justice. The relationship between human and non-human need not be exploitative when 'human' rights are present, but instead symbiotic, and progressive for both. This is not a relationship between parasite and host, but of mutual betterment. The human and non-human is in mutual 'work'; when we act amongst ourselves (humans) and with non-humans, our moral actions *make us*. We prune the branches of trees to offer us shade while strengthening those very same branches. When we do such work, we inevitably must deal with the instrumental and anthropocentric issue of commodification, that form of water ownership that I will identify and explain in Chapter 3 as especially harmful to humans and non-humans alike.

A second risk in identifying human rights to water, specifically through the discursive democratic framework that I develop more rigorously in Chapters 4 and 5 (and made real through water justice movements for recommoning), is the danger of majority settler interests overwhelming Indigenous voices in deliberative democratic forums. A critic may identify the tension between deliberative democracy, autonomy and majority settler interests that might be contrary to the just and rightful interests of Indigenous peoples. Should 'new' structures of water recommoning, and local governance, be brought in where

Indigenous communities claim that they have sovereignty over a particular river, for example, because it is their traditional territory? I acknowledge the reality of such a tension – deliberative democracy theorists working in water governance must be vigilant – but I contend that the deliberative democracy I argue for and will posit as being at the forefront of social movements for water recommoning in Chapter 5 should be *movement-based*. This means that various social movements for water justice should work alongside and defer to Indigenous social movements for governance of fresh water, and the United Nations Declaration on the Rights of Indigenous Peoples (UNDRIP) ought to undergird such rightful deference. I do argue that local communities should be centrally involved in decision-making and water governance, and I think this can be consistent with Indigenous sovereignty claims when the deliberative democratic processes are deferential.

I shall explain territorial sovereignty, autonomy and competing interests for water further in Section 3.2.2.1, but expansion on the potential second critique above is warranted here; my response should be in the back of the reader's mind throughout this book. I endorse deliberative democratic framing of water justice movements, and I contend that shortcomings might be redeemed by UNDRIP. Rights alone cannot ameliorate water injustices. For instance, water development scholars William Nikolakis and R. Quentin Grafton, in their rights-based analysis of Strategic Aboriginal Water Reserves (SAWR) in the Northern Territory, Australia, conclude that a rights-only approach is unsatisfactory in achieving water justice; instead, people must be empowered to use their capabilities to instantiate rights.[54] The SAWR and other human-rights led legislation and treaties pose a potential grave risk of entrenching dominant, majority settler values of water (i.e., economic and extractivist),[55] though resolutions such as UNDRIP are an invaluable steering mechanism for water governance.

Consider the following central articles within UNDRIP for water governance and the appropriateness of deference to Indigenous social movements:

Article 3: Indigenous peoples have the right to self-determination.
Article 5: Indigenous peoples have the right to their own political and
    cultural institutions.

Article 18: Indigenous peoples have the right to decision making pertaining to issues that might affect their rights.

Article 24: States ought to recognize the rights of Indigenous peoples over their traditional lands.

Article 25: Indigenous peoples have the right 'to maintain and strengthen their distinctive spiritual relationship with their traditionally owned or otherwise occupied and used lands, territories, waters and coastal seas ...'

Article 26: Indigenous peoples have the right to use, own and control waters within their traditional territories.

Article 32: 1. Indigenous peoples have the right to create strategies of development and use for their lands, territories, and other resources.[56]

These articles concretize the deference that is necessary, appropriate and just in any water ethic and governance supported by deliberative democratic principles. Water science and governance scholars Katherine Taylor, Sheri Longboat and R. Quentin Grafton have argued that UNDRIP is the human rights standard for conceptualizing Indigenous water rights and is indispensable for instantiating water justice.[57] UNDRIP supports Indigenous peoples' right to manage their water in accordance with their own systems of water governance, so a human right to water does not necessarily run the risk of the second critique above – privileging established settler voices above Indigenous voices. UNDRIP can be used to frame water justice issues; it can be used as a reference for crafting water justice policy. Furthermore, UNDRIP recognizes some rights of Indigenous peoples to water, but systems of law differ; thus, Taylor, Longboat and Grafton argue that water governance must evaluate policy on a case-by-case basis concerning which policies should be applied to Indigenous peoples, derived from Indigenous systems of law for Indigenous peoples.[58] Overall, rights still play a crucial role in actualizing water justice, and potential risks can be mitigated with thoroughly deliberative (i.e., democratic and UNDRIP-deferential) movements.

2.3 Water and the question of commodification

In the previous section, I explained the differences between property, territory and common ownership of water according to the existing literature. I also proffered and responded to potential risks of common ownership and territory framed by rights. Ownership of water exists on a spectrum, and on the opposite end from common ownership is commodification. Political scientist Michael Sandel and political philosopher Debra Satz offer compelling critiques of commodification in general and although they do not speak specifically about water, I believe their arguments can be fittingly extended to include the resource. Sandel and Satz are skeptical of market-controlled water and promote anti-commodification efforts. For Sandel, there are some goods which cannot be bought, such as friendship, while there are some goods which can be bought but arguably should not, such as organs.[59] Creating markets for any good – in the instance of this argument, fresh water – smothers any room for morals, usurping the place of morals for profit. 'Buying and selling [something] changes its character and diminishes its value', transforming water from something necessary for life and charged with non-monetary and non-anthropocentric value into one entirely economic and driven by profit.[60]

There are two kinds of normative arguments about what money should and should not buy. The first is the fairness objection, and it points to unfairness or injustice in the selling of something due to dire economic situations and focuses on inequalities in markets. In this objection, actors might be 'unfairly coerced' by their dire economic situations, forcing their questionably (im)moral decision to sell a good. Here, market exchanges are not free or voluntary; they occur under a sword of Damocles. The second argument is the corruption objection, and it speaks to commodification's deleterious effects. Sandel writes that the central 'insight of the corruption argument is that markets are not mere mechanisms; they embody certain values. And sometimes market values crowd out non-market norms worth caring about.'[61] Certain moral and civic goods are degraded, 'diminished or corrupted' when commodified; moreover, this objection is normative because it rests on the moral implications of buying and selling a good. Thus, we can assert that market-driven transformation of water rips the resource from its intended use, bastardizing water *qua* water and the moral import attached to water. In sum, for Sandel, markets are corruptive.

Satz concurs with anti-commodification arguments; however, she focuses on the moral limits of markets on fairness instead of corruption. For Satz, commodification does indeed hurt the object being commodified, but it also 'corrupt[s] us by crowding out our altruistic motivations for performing certain actions'.[62] At the heart of arguments against commodification is *inequality*. As will be exemplified later in this chapter and throughout this book through specific, real-world examples, inequality is begat by water injustice such as commodification.

Sandel's focus on corruption goes beyond common distributive justice arguments against markets and commodification, and political philosopher Elizabeth Anderson offers an amendment to his work. Anderson's analysis of the corrupting effects of markets can help us to see why the creation of a market for water, by way of commodification, corrupts the normative realm that water might be considered to be in. Anderson argues that markets corrupt in two ways: constitutively and instrumentally. Constitutive corruption occurs when a good's 'value is at least partially an expression or embodiment of the reasons and motives for providing it in the first place'; financial incentives corrupt practices in this way.[63] More relevant to fresh water is instrumental corruption, where the 'value of a good is independent of the reasons and motives people have for providing it'.[64] Instrumental corruption of fresh water occurs when resource providers 'have a financial incentive to compromise the quality of the good, or to inflate its price unnecessarily'.[65] For instance, bottled water and other forms of commodified water (e.g., water sold for profit) have been instrumentally corrupted. We can infer that, for Sandel, Satz and Anderson, private ownership of water, coupled with commodification, would be wholly corruptive. Thus, an anti-commodification route, by way of recommoning, might be the most just and normatively appropriate form of ownership.

Deep ecology literature can help us build a normative argument for common ownership of water. Deep ecologists such as Val Plumwood echo the claim that markets pervert natural resources. Plumwood explains that the commodification of nature, and of natural resources, is framed by neo-Cartesianism.[66] The ethics of commodification has a moral dualism: there are those of higher moral worth ('persons') and the rest ('things') which are objectified and become property. These 'things' are of no moral worth, they do not count ethically, and they can be used as instruments of the 'persons' rationality. Plumwood, and the greater deep ecology discourse, is not descriptive but decidedly normative and speaks against the exploitation that commodification has wrought. Global capitalism and its duality of persons and property entrenches exclusions and promotes the rational instrumentalism of commodification.[67] The dualism of neo-Cartesianism is one of domination and it is embedded in commodification.

Admittedly, a critic might raise the concern that domination is a quite general harm. According to Plumwood, there are more concrete structural harms connected to '*remoteness*', that is, 'a high-level … dissociation between costs and benefits, between elite consumption benefits and ecological damage'.[68] 'Remoteness' is not only reserved to deep ecology, it is shared in the language of human rights scholars such as Philip Alston, who refers to a coming 'climate apartheid' where the rich and privileged pay to abscond from climate catastrophes (e.g., droughts, extreme heat and hunger).[69] Remoteness separates us from immediate, before-your-eyes consequences, exacerbates commodification and feeds the ultra-rational, economic, neo-Cartesian dualism which seeks water commodification. This remoteness is geographical and epistemic, and both types are the children of a courtship between liberal capitalism and radical inequality.[70]

Remoteness can give us a fuller picture of the harms of commodification and how commodification arises. The remoteness of which Plumwood speaks is a reactive 'ecological irrationality' that fosters 'systematic opportunities and motivations to shift ecological ills onto others rather than to prevent their generation in the first place'.[71] A profusely myopic consequence, we are made remote, or abstracted, from the consequences of our resource use, from the resource itself and from each other. We make ourselves 'remote' by buying or hoarding our way, at least superficially and in the short-term, from the consequences of our ecological destruction; we are then blind to 'nature's vulnerability and limits'.[72] We become obsequious tools of privileged actors and our own desire for over-use and control of water, the ball of our resource and the chain of our remote and irrational desire to over-consume water attached to us. Fresh water can be bought and commodified, and we can flee with it when the wells run dry and all that is left in our former ecological space are drought and pitted patterns of sand and cracked caliche, the sulci and gyri of our abuse.

Socially privileged actors – those that consume the most resources – become remote from the consequences of ecological harm in what Plumwood calls 'environmental classism'.[73] These groups make themselves remote from particular, and even some general, eco-harms by moving away from polluted or drought-stricken areas. Privileged groups have vested interests in redistributing, rather than preventing, eco-harms associated with, for example, the commodification of water because their privilege depends on its maintenance. As such, they are epistemically remote and possibly intellectually dubious to the damage they cause. Their remoteness is usually a façade or 'master illusion', but it is perpetuated by those privileged groups that are politically active; they further their illusory experience through their 'choices and attitudes'.[74] Their remoteness is a mortgaging of the future that will inexorably be due. All the more reason to enact a stewardship of the earth which outlives our mortal finitude.

Exclusion, domination and remoteness are structural harms, and they are consequences of what Plumwood identifies as liberal democracy. Liberal democracies place power and voice in markets, and poor and marginalized actors become invisible if they are unable to participate. Markets are 'information systems about needs' that only register the needs of those who participate in them.[75] Thus, 'Bad news from below is not registered well by any of liberal democracy's information systems, hardly at all by the market, and often poorly by liberal democratic, electoral and administrative systems'.[76] Those who suffer most from eco-harms connected to water are those not heard by society at large due to these structural limitations. Liberalism has an inegalitarian power structure that is ecologically irrational, and a solution will involve those below – those marginalized and least remote from ecological harms – speaking and acting in a thick democratic structure.[77] As will be explained in Chapters 4 and 5, the forms of democracy that enable action and speech from below will not be neoliberal but, instead, deliberative, participatory, radical and reflexive, resisting the dualism of neo-Cartesianism with the voices of all citizens.

For Plumwood, it is in humanity's best interests to reject neo-Cartesian dualism and seek to not dominate, through commodification, the natural world, for 'when we act to reject moral dualism, we can open up ways to reflect critically and sympathetically on the ethical status of the act of exclusion itself, on our own identities, and on ethical practices of boundary-breaking; these meta-lessons are among the most important for human and non-human spheres of ethics alike'.[78] The tendrils of commodification, from the body of neo-Cartesianism, run from capitalism and colonialism. Instead of commodification of fresh water enabled by a rational liberal democracy,

Plumwood's critique supports my argument (expounded on in Chapter 4 as theory and grounded in case studies in Chapter 5) for collective control of water in a deliberative, participatory or radical democracy. Plumwood's position on remoteness or abstraction expands the sphere of environmental democracy, and my assertion of human rights as connected to socioenvironmental justice (in Chapter 4) is supported by her rejection of neo-Cartesian dualism and anti-domination.

We can see that determining just arrangements of water ownership and governance depends on (anti)commodification language and human rights scaffolding. However, there are piquant criticisms of such language and support that must be addressed. Bakker considers the language of '(anti) commodification' and '(anti)privatization' unhelpful in the water ethics and justice discourse. For Bakker, strategies that are centred on arguing against privatization and commodification, and for human rights, are ineffective because they align with the very same neoliberal framework they are supposed to oppose.[79] In addition, she considers the very terms 'neoliberal', 'commodity' and 'anti-privatization' vague, and that more nuance and specificity can be provided by the terms 'commons' (instead of commodity) and 'alter-globalization' (instead of anti-privatization). The term 'commodity' has contrasted 'human rights', but there is no logical framework that casts them as opposites. Bakker posits that one commits a categorical error when equating the two terms, as 'commodity' refers to a property-rights concept applicable to resources, and 'human rights' refers to a legal category applicable to individuals.[80] The term that should replace 'commodity' is 'commons' because it is a more distinct term within the same category as human rights.

We can observe water as a 'commons' instead of a 'commodity' in the drafting of transnational agreements, yet there is trepidation in adopting such rights at the state level. For example, despite UN Resolution 64/292 explicitly recognizing a human right to water and sanitation, formal, binding, legal uptake of the right has not become popular amongst states. Proponents of water as a human right say that such legal justification is implicit within other rights recognized by international law (e.g., rights to food, life, health, dignity) and 'are implicitly recognized through legal precedents when courts support right of non-payment for water services on grounds of lack of affordability (UNWWAP 2006)'.[81] However, an opponent might offer a few counterpoints:

How can we discern who is responsible to implement such a right to water? Who has the capacity, and what about the complication of possible conflict over transboundary water? Additionally, there is potential abuse by governments who would over-allocate water for privileged groups. More generally, water as a human right has been shown, in the real world, to be unsuccessful in a justiciable sense (e.g., water as a human right as enshrined in the constitution of South Africa). Bakker has argued that human rights are an individualistic, libertarian philosophy that is 'Eurocentric' and, because of this, human rights are compatible with capitalist political economic systems; moreover, water as a human right is anthropocentric, and the search for water to satisfy this right could harm non-humans through environmental degradation.[82]

Opponents may offer the critique that a human right to water does not mean the private sector cannot be involved in water supply systems. Full privatization of water is incompatible with human rights, but private sector participation in water supply with regulations aligns with current international human rights, private property rights, and capitalist systems. This is the fatal flaw of anti-commodification and pro-human rights efforts: they can inadvertently support the liberal, capitalist paradigm. For Bakker, pursuing a human right to water as an anti-privatization and anti-commodification endeavour conflates human rights and property rights, fails to distinguish between different types of property rights and service delivery models, and fails to foreclose the possibility of increasing private sector involvement in water supply.[83]

A more precise contrast to alter-privatization movements is alter-globalization. Anti-privatization favours water as a human right; however, this does not necessarily prevent water from being privatized or from aligning with current international human rights law. For Bakker, alter-globalization eliminates 'rights talk' because such talk alienates communities and furthers the public/private divide, allowing for two bad options of either 'state or market control: twinned corporatist models from which communities are equally excluded'.[84] Proponents of alter-globalization argue for a change to property rights with a focus on the commons, contrasting the language of water as a commodity. In sum, 'collective, public oversight of water, based in community, is inevitable and necessary because water is a non-substitutable resource essential for life with important aesthetic, symbolic, spiritual, and ecological functions'.[85] In my view, considering water as a commons, with community-based oversight and decision-making, does a better job of conserving water through an environmentally collectivist method of solidarity, encouraging users to conserve. Furthermore, the commons view is long-term, seeing conservation of water as key, while the commodity view aims for short-term maximization of profit. Water as a commons is a public good, while water as a commodity is an economic good. Water as a commons is either free or priced to break even and managed and regulated by the community in which the water is, while water as a commodity is given full-cost pricing and managed and regulated by the market. The goals of each type of ownership are different as well, as the goals of commonly controlled water are social equity and improvement of livelihoods while the goals of privately held, economically driven water are efficiency, water security and profit.

In contrast to neoliberal forms of ownership and governance, alter-globalization alternatives are mainly community based, collectivist, participatory and in favour of re-regulation by consumer-controlled NGOs or co-operatives. Communities should be leveraged as an alternative to neoliberal policies of water ownership, commodification and distribution. However, as I will explain further in Chapter 5 with reference to sociologist Mangala Subramaniam's work on water activist groups, we should not romanticize communal control of water as there are serious power imbalances and injustices within communities that should not be exacerbated by undo control and regulatory power. Thus, Bakker proposes that a progressive strategy of water ownership and distribution would push for the state's governance to be reformed instead of abolished, while working with local knowledge to work with local models of resource management.[86]

2.4 The harms of water commodification

The harms of water commodification are manifold. I will present resistance strategies to commodification in Chapter 5, but no such strategies can be constructed without knowing the harms of commodification itself.

Current theories in the water justice, rights and ownership literature do not derive the normative import of uncommodified fresh water from the identification of harms of commodification, what type of ownership is most just, the political and legal means by which commodification can be resisted, and how bottom-up community-centred activism can fight commodification from on high. The task of Sections 2.1–2.3 was to explicate some prominent current theories in the water justice, rights and ownership literature – to present the contemporary dialogue. The task of Section 2.4 is to present my own arguments identifying the harms of commodification. Sections 2.1–2.3 were a presentation of current arguments marking distinctions between property and territory from Kolers and Alfred, and Bakker's critique of water as a human right. Such distinctions and critiques are opening up gaps in normative water theory for where I will insert more deliberative democratic mechanisms and communal support for water (i.e., the meta-normative power of water activism itself, as well as water recommoning).

I argue that the commodification of water harms democracy and democratic institutions because it is an inherently exclusionary and privatizing act, occurring apart from the *demos* and, instead, benefitting an élite few. Unequal access to life-sustaining resources follows from commodification. Undemocratic, privately controlled fresh water inevitably leads to such inequality and, as I will identify further in Chapter 3, political harms. Commodification, as undemocratic and anti-democratic, contributes to two other harms that I identify: citizens as being viewed as strictly customers or consumers, and water's value as being shifted from intrinsic to solely economic.

2.4.1 *The harms of citizens as customers and water's value as only economic*

The role of the citizen as a participant in democracy – knowledgeable of and unabstracted from water issues, deliberative about water governance with fellow citizens, conscious of the obligations between the state and citizen – is reduced by private actors when water is commodified. The citizen becomes a customer when the primary motive of water distribution is profit instead of need. As explained earlier in this chapter, commodification necessarily involves a profit motive, and this motive skews how citizens are viewed. Citizens are then no longer primarily considered agents who vote and instruct democratic government but, instead, are secondary to private interests and actors who stand to make a profit from commodified water.

Commodification subsumes the fiduciary mechanism of financialization, that is, the expansion of finance into non-financial arenas which, in this case, is the water sector.[87] Private capital enables the onslaught of commodification, turning that resource which was public into something private. Financialization and commodification of water turn citizens into customers because they are the ones funnelling money into the water-for-profit schematic, providing for themselves but also furthering the cause of private interests. Furthermore, as Bayliss argues, access to information connected to water distribution becomes privately held, instead of publicly known, leaving citizen-customers ignorant of, or abstracted from, their own needs and ways to satisfy such needs.[88]

Water as a commodity attaches the adjective of 'consumer' to citizens, making water a product to be sold at the highest price the market can bear.[89] There is baggage attached to the terms 'customer' and 'consumer', and there are expectations and obligations on the water-provider and the water-user. The water-provider, in a non-commodified scenario, has as its goal the equitable distribution of fresh water to all citizens because the utility answers to citizens. In a commodified scenario, however, the water-provider answers to shareholders primarily or, if commodification of the water is entrenched, entirely. Citizens' questions and demands are left unanswered because they have no control over water, and the needs of citizens are replaced by the need for quarterly dividends. Their needs are reduced to an ancillary obligation that private actors must satisfy for profit, but those private actors place citizens in a vulnerable position; they can charge however much money they want, and citizens must pay because of water's unsubstitutability. It is those citizens who can pay who will gain access to life-sustaining resources while those unable to pay will suffer. Not only is water reduced to its economic and instrumental value; humans are as well. For the private sector and market environmentalists, for investors, executives or anyone who promotes and stands to gain from water commodification, citizens are a standing-reserve of cash. People, themselves, are a *gestell*. And, so, citizens are used for the purpose of private financial gain, their value no longer intrinsic or immeasurable but quantifiable in terms of currency and litres. As we will see further in Chapters 4 and 5 regarding deliberative democracy and water governance, market environmentalism has also maneuvered itself into deliberative systems that purport to be democratic; however, instead, this market privileges private capital and the satisfaction of self-interest over justifying reasons for preferences.[90]

Private actors see citizens as customers and consumers of commodified water, but profit would not be possible without financialization. Water can be the object of speculation when private-financial capital is injected into the water sector at local and global levels which creates wealth for a minority of investors.[91] Social objectives of just water delivery are incompatible with financialization and, broadly, commodification because such objectives are normative; meanwhile, the economic, instrumental, utterly rational profit-seeking objectives of private actors are devoid of such norms because they are amoral. The citizen is not in need of water for life but is, rather, an object that provides money to the water-provider. Moreover, the economic value of water becomes privileged over the intrinsic value of water as a sustainer of life. The economic view, neoliberal and globalized as it is, has a levelling-quality, razing cultural and historical values and ties to water while replacing such values with the purely economic.[92] The consequence is a homogenization of citizens and their cultures by way of the strictly economic view, erasing people and making citizens effectively invisible. Homogenization, as David Schlosberg observes, 'both contributes to the breakdown of the cultural and social networks in local communities and also destroys the essence and meaning of local cultures'.[93] The cultural and historical values of citizens have no value in the face of strictly economic commodification at the behest of private interests.

Recall the 'remoteness' that Plumwood saw as comorbid with commodification. We can analyse the harm of such remoteness through a fitting frame of reference that feminist Marxist philosopher Silvia Federici critiques as the harms of capitalist 'enclosures' of the commons. The process at the heart of capitalism, which Marx termed 'primitive accumulation' and David Harvey developed as 'accumulation by dispossession', encloses epistemologies and experiences; this act cordons off actors, making them remote. Commodification, of course, encloses or makes private physical, geographic locations of water, but it also erects a 'social enclosure' of 'social events and the reproduction of workers shifting from the open field to the home, from the community to the family, from the public space (the common, the church) to the private'.[94] Citizens are not viewed as emotional beings who *need* community participation and socialization which might centre on water (or, more broadly, the natural world); instead, citizens are more similar to Cartesian automatons, grist for the capitalist-water system. By making citizens into customers, any moral or emotional qualms can be squelched when citizens are denied water or provided unclean water. In addition, virtues that Federici identifies in a commons – collective decision-making, co-operation, solidarity and sociality around the water commons – are levelled and homogenized.[95]

To summarize, citizens become customers when water is viewed through the lens of economic value, reducing the responsibilities of the state while increasing those of private interests to make profit. Private corporate interests, though, are supported by a larger network of international organizations. Commodification efforts at local and national scales are buttressed by the concerted efforts of large international development organizations, such as the World Trade Organization (WTO), the International Monetary Fund (IMF) and the World Bank, to assert private control of water. Such efforts have contributed to the growth of water commodification efforts. In the process, they have aided in undermining democracy and weakening democratic institutions. For example, the WTO, in conjunction with the IMF and World Bank, had pressured the Bolivian government to privatize SEMAPA, Cochabamba's municipal supplier of water, to the detriment of equitable water distribution, stoking the flames of protest and conflict which led to the Cochabamba Water Wars. They enabled the commodification of water in Bolivia which led to massive inequality in water access.[96] There is a water élite, including corporations such as Coca-Cola and Nestlé, that are engrained within the World Bank and its private sector division, the International Finance Corporation (IFC), and the IFC's Water Resources Group, furthering private interests at the expense of the public interest.[97]

I will show in subsequent chapters that such relationships between the state and private actors undermine democracy and enable domination. It is my view that political domination follows from market environmentalist proposals, and proponents of market environmentalism are not concerned about such domination (though they should be). Furthermore, market environmentalist solutions fail to deliver just and fair access to, and governance of, fresh water because they focus on individual consumption and self-interest, to the detriment of analysing and critiquing structural and relational problems (e.g., lack of recognition and participation in democratic water governance, intersecting economic, gender and racial lines). Market environmentalism and the 'invisible hand theorem' can account for internalized costs and benefits, but they struggle to account for externalities and concerns beyond individual use or distribution, such as 'altruism, spite, indexes of inequality, or the welfare of other species'.[98] Markets do, indeed, crowd out morals, and in Chapters 3 and 4 I will argue that the vacuum created by such amorality is filled by domination and anti-democratic arrangements, as exemplified by cases in Chapter 5. On my account, market environmentalist solutions to water injustices, manifested as commodification, financialization, or otherwise privatization of water, are unable to account for freedom in a relational sense (as I do) because they fundamentally do not account for structural injustices and non-distributional considerations (e.g., norms of altruism and non-anthropocentrism). As I will explain in the following section, such an epistemic blind spot undermines democratic water governance.

2.4.2 *The harm of undermining democracy*

The will – the voice – of the many is subordinated to the will of the few private actors who aim to instill water commodification. Water as a public good, aligning with democratic ideals and institutions, does not align with the short-term, economic and instrumental goals of the private sector. We can look to examples in the world of water commodification being the antithesis of democracy. Water was privatized in Grenoble, France, by Lyonnaise des Eaux, in a public–private partnership (PPP); we will encounter this Grenoble case in Chapter 5, but it is pertinent to our discussion of commodification harming and undermining democracy. PPPs frequently work against the public by privatizing profits and shifting the burden of losses onto the public.

As Raymond Avrillier observes within his Grenoble community, PPPs give 'full power to the private sector. The [water privatization] contract guaranteed profits worth a few hundred million Euros for the private sector over a period of 25 years (between 1989 and 2014)'.[99] For the public? 'A fee of a few million Euros (later invoiced to the consumer) was paid to the municipality whose budgets were in deficit'.[100] Such partnerships are rife with corruption, further dissolving democratic tenets. In the case of Grenoble, 'dozens of millions of Francs were paid under the table' between elected officials and heads of private companies.[101]

In Grenoble, as will become clear in Chapter 5, water commodifiers are only accountable to themselves. Assemblies of users in a democratic and public system of water-control make decisions for themselves too, but the 'they' here is the public, done in the public interest. In a commodified system for water, company executives and shareholders work to further their own interests which are *outside* of the area or community in which they hold water; they are, as Plumwood would term it, remote or abstracted from water. Private sector control uses as much water as possible in order to make as much money as possible because water is the product; preservation of the resource is of little to no interest. The private sector aims for water use to be as high as possible while the public model wants water to be used responsibly.[102]

Alternative frameworks for water governance have been developed and actualized by social movements against freshwater commodification. I shall argue in Chapters 4 and 5 that this more locally based approach to developing alternative governance regimes is important because it supports deliberative democracy by acting differently; by acting another way contrary to commodification. Groups should fight for the recommoning of water, as will be explained in later chapters, because they should support deliberative democracy by being and doing deliberative democracy; in doing so, they actualize what I identify in Chapter 4 to be a kind of socioenvironmental justice. The harm of undermining democracy resulting from commodification could be faced by expanding democracy, as deliberative and discursive, beyond the political realm into, for example, informal community gatherings. Democracy, especially deliberative democracy, should present itself as an alternative to capitalism, as something that is not only a political system but an economic one as well. Democracy could be, as legal scholar Radha D'Souza and political theorist Ellen Meiksins Wood have argued, an economic regulator beyond merely promoting a greater equality of distribution.[103] The power of democracy, from politics to institutions to civilian day-to-day life in bottom-up activism, is not promoted by pro-commodification actors. Democracy should provide a roadblock to exclusionary control.

2.5 Harms and property: where to go from here?

The harms of commodification erode democracy by making citizens into customers. In addition, commodification erodes deliberation in democracy by favouring those with influence/power over commodification, and, consequently, is not representative of the larger democratic landscape. I have identified problems with commodification and the concept of 'property', but mere problem identification is insufficient in this task to get to a normative solution to freshwater governance. This is the strength of philosophy, as theory *and* practice, as a rigorous and voracious method of questioning our actions and, more centrally, our values. From the value we assign to water and the natural world, we then treat each other according to those values. Where do we go from here? What is the best, or most just, form of ownership of water? I take these questions up in the next two chapters, moving from water as common territory to water justice being a fundamentally democratic endeavour.

3

An Explication of Common Ownership and Common Territory

Commodification is a mechanism of social relations of subordination and domination, as well as a manifestation of such relations. Commodification reflects and reinforces the social relations of subordination and domination made real, reducing us, and making us beholden to those who hold water privately. Those who lack access to clean, fresh water are secondary to the value of the private asset. Capitalism, neoliberalism or commodification cannot solve current water injustices; instead, starkly disparate options must be considered. I argue that alternatives should be found in common ownership (instead of commodification), territory (instead of property), and ecologically reflexive deliberative democracy.

In this chapter, I develop the argument that water should be commonly owned as territory, which aligns more closely with stewardship, rather than property. Further, to extend arguments from Chapter 2, I hold that commonly owned water aligns best with deliberative democratic principles and does not reduce humanity to potentiality of profit. Common ownership and common territory intersect and combine logically and fittingly not only with each other but with democracy; however, this democracy with which it aligns will be more social-focused than individual-focused. The dominant form of liberalism, which political scientist C. B. Macpherson identifies as having a 'possessive individualism' where an individual's skills are one's own and one owes nothing to society, strides in lockstep with capitalism and enables harmful pathological path dependencies.[1] I explained in Chapter 2, and will add in this chapter, that this dominant form of liberalism does not lead to water justice because of the prominence of profit-seeking. To support this claim, I build on Mathias Risse's Egalitarian Ownership approach to common ownership of the earth by applying it to water; in addition, I highlight the democratic commitments of common ownership. Risse's ownership theory provides a sturdy base for me to flesh-out this democracy-common ownership argument, as I argue that common ownership of water can be promoted through deliberative democracy with critical ecological reflexivity, a point I build fully in Chapters 4 and 5. Furthermore, I connect Risse's Egalitarian Ownership approach to common ownership to larger political and justice-related issues tied to water, such as political recognition and participation (in addition to distribution).

3.1 Path dependencies and commodification

I showed in Chapter 2 that common ownership of water stands in stark contrast to commodification insofar as it treats citizens as merely objects for profit, as customers. Commodification and privatization are mechanisms of dominant capitalist systems which perpetuate themselves and block alternative systems through 'path dependencies' which are strong at providing economic growth but anaemic in other areas, especially as they pertain to socioenvironmental justice issues. As political theorists John Dryzek and Jonathan Pickering observe, path dependencies propagated by commodifiers arose in the Holocene, an unusual period of stability that preceded the current Anthropocene, and persist through systems and institutions.[2] Pathological path dependencies of systems (e.g., liberal capitalism) or institutions (e.g., state governmental or international financial organizations) suffocate other avenues and force themselves to be the singular way of water ownership and access; we become reliant on them. 'Excessively strong continuity' of institutions or systems, without reflection and contestation, constitutes the malignancy of 'pathological path dependency'.[3]

Path dependency entrenches itself when states have a material stake in existing systems or institutions, designing themselves in such a way as to make engagement with, say, commodified water inescapable. Democratic states engaged in commodification dealings and practices, then, act contrary to the will of citizens.[4] Indigenous environmental philosopher Kyle Whyte writes that the colonial violence of the state perpetuates such dependencies as 'vicious sedimentation' and 'insidious loops'. He adds, 'The pattern of how environmental changes compound over time to reinforce and strengthen settler ignorance against Indigenous peoples' – vicious sedimentation – and 'the pattern of how historic settler industries ... violated Indigenous peoples when they began [and are] implicated many years later in further environmental violence, such as climate injustice' – insidious loops – work against society's ability to chart new self-determined ways forward to prevent harms.[5] Institutions of the settler colonialist state entrench harms, as Dryzek and Pickering add that 'the ideas and norms generated by an institution's operation can further solidify the path; market institutions are reinforced by the widely accepted idea that economic growth is essential, and that markets are the best way to achieve it'.[6] Individuals in the system, especially those with material stake, might see the 'product' or system as an extension of themselves and identify with it, seeing regulation as an afront to freedom.

How should path dependencies be broken and altered? I will argue in Chapter 5 that the recommoning of water spurred by community-driven, glocal water justice movements will play a large role in democratizing water and forging a different path. As a foray into my later argument, I must present, here, existing epistemologies and ontologies that resist path dependencies. Indigenous Environmental Justice (IEJ), as explicated by McGregor, Chiblow, Craft and others in Section 2.2, understands that humanity alone cannot save itself from the climate catastrophe it has created.[7] They argue that the solution to our ills is in non-anthropocentric relations which Indigenous knowledge, governance, justice and laws have long understood.[8] McGregor, Whitaker and Sritharan identify this solution in the philosophy of *buen vivir*, or 'living well', within community and the natural world. This 'living well' with the Earth decentres humans as the sole valuators of the natural world, bridging the divide between humans and nature and decolonizing valuations.[9] IEJ scholars see 'living well' in this sense as an active resistance against the established colonial state.[10] Whyte makes clear that Indigenous peoples have centuries of experience in surviving the cataclysmic harms of ongoing imperialism, capitalism and colonialism, and such knowledge can be harnessed in the face of climate change or other injustices of the natural world, including water.[11] Centring IEJ can break the path dependency of colonial settler state valuations of water (i.e., economic) by showing a different way to live.

Water commodification leads to path dependencies of undemocratic water governance because of a lack of inclusion of citizens in decision-making about water resources and uncritical and passive public discourse, symptoms of commodification I explained in Chapter 2. Private actors, such as Nestlé, take advantage of passivity and try to make actors wholly dependent on their privatized water. For example, Nestlé's water extractions have led to dried riverbeds and drained springs in California's Strawberry Creek due to syphoning 45 million gallons in 2018.[12] Nestlé Waters' 2018 worldwide sales were $7.8 billion yet they pay a pittance for rights to bottled water.[13] To clarify, though, Nestlé does not act unilaterally; they come to these agreements with government actors such as California's Forest Service. The path dependency here is faith in the marketplace and in the 'efficiency' of private enterprise. Water commodifiers such as Nestlé induce demand and curry support through donations. For example, in Michigan and Maine, two states where Nestlé has wells, they have paid for new ambulances, fireworks, and baseball diamonds for struggling communities, donated to the local boy scouts, bought high school teams new ski equipment, and sponsored a fair.[14] In Flint, Michigan, residents have paid higher rates for lead-tainted water than Nestlé has for clean water, while Nestlé donates their bottled, clean water to Flint residents.[15] In Detroit, water has been shut off to those residents unable to pay their hydro bills, forcing residents to pay for cheaper bottled water.[16] Even though many states in the United States have varying degrees of public trust doctrine pertaining to water, this does not preclude Nestlé and other water commodifiers from privatizing water. Despite legal arguments against water privatization supported by public trust doctrine,[17] water privatizers are enabled by the path dependency of commodification and liberal capitalism.

In Canada, hundreds of thousands of people have been exposed to unsafe levels of lead in their drinking water,[18] and water issues in Indigenous communities, such as Grassy Narrows, are persistent injustices.[19] Such examples are not directly the fault of water commodifiers, but they point to a path dependency and a serious deficit and deficiency of democracy, both deliberative and representative, on the part of municipalities and the state. Here, path dependencies and those in 'empowered spaces' (e.g., government, or corporate settings with connection to government) do not allow for questions to be asked concerning the ethics and justice of water ownership and distribution, resulting in suffering and want in current democratic states. The conversations being had are not open, honest, critical and reflexive (specifically *ecologically* reflexive), and those racialized and minoritized groups most affected by water injustices currently do not have much meaningful weight in the water discourse. This is a failure of the current liberal representative capitalist democracy that, I argue, common ownership and common territory, along with deliberative democracy, should rectify.

The examples of path dependencies explained above show the reality of consequences of commodification and water injustice in general, and also how vast and structurally baked-in these path dependent policies are. They reveal how path dependencies have made us remote or abstracted from water issues such as ownership and governance. Furthermore, they highlight a growing need to buttress community support and deliberation through democratic methods that act contrary to the liberal capitalist paradigm of individualism, domination and anthropocentrism. We must confront different ways to act by considering different types of water ownership, most notably common ownership, which I take up now.

3.2.1 Common ownership

Global common ownership, developed by Mathias Risse, is a cosmopolitan theory that can help inform demands to end water commodification. Risse's position provides a starting point for my own conception of common ownership and its instantiation through recommoning, spurred by glocal social movements, that I assert in Chapter 5. Explaining Risse's position will help to clarify my own, revealing where I pivot from his popular view. The common thread between us is our support for a common ownership of the earth model, but I depart from his view in a few ways, most notably in considering water as a common territory and in arguing for dramatically reformed and new political institutions and processes, to render them more deliberatively democratic.

Risse grounds human rights to natural resources, such as water, in their importance for human survival and, most originally for Risse's account, humanity's existence in a 'global order'. He writes that 'resources of the earth are valuable and necessary for human activities to unfold and ... those resources have come into existence without human interference'.[20] Thus, common ownership is the most equitable form of ownership, where all citizens of Earth have a 'symmetrical claim' to original resources.[21] Moreover, resources such as water come into existence without human interference and, therefore, 'nobody has claims to them based on any contributions to their creation'.[22] On Risse's account, Earth's natural resources 'are the accomplishment of no one, whereas they are needed by everyone'. Thus, Risse endorses Egalitarian Ownership manifested as common ownership of the earth.

For Risse, natural rights – human rights – are preserved by associative rights, meaning 'membership rights in the global order' (associative rights) maintain the human right of 'common ownership of the earth' despite the existence of nation-states putting such rights in jeopardy.[23] Risse sees three main strengths to this approach to human rights:

1 It rests on a universally acceptable foundation;
2 It can readily demonstrate why the language of 'rights' rather than goals is appropriate here;
3 It entails a genuinely global responsibility for these rights.[24]

Risse's global membership approach to human rights grounds common ownership of the earth, rights pertaining to water, in both needs *and* in the symmetrical claims all people have to resources for life – the greater global order. The overarching strength of this formulation of rights is that it makes *global* rights plausible, as he explains:

> A benefit of this conception of rights held in virtue of global-order membership is that it makes plausible one common intuition about human rights, which is that they can be of *global reach* – and therefore justify actions even against societies whose culture does not support them and, moreover, impose obligations on people to fix particular problems that they had no role in causing. This global-membership approach shows why the language of rights – rather than, say, the languages of goals or value – is appropriate in the context of human rights.[25]

Membership in this cosmopolitan global order, for Risse, gives rise to collective responsibilities concretized as natural common ownership rights that generate associational rights in the global order.[26] Risse explains that 'the flip side of these responsibilities is a set of rights individuals hold vis-a-vis the global order. This is how reflection on ownership of the earth leads to membership rights in the global order, and to human rights.'[27] People exist on Earth together, and they are associated with one another and rely on the same necessities. This global order consists of the responsibility of individuals to not destroy or waste resources, and to abide by collective or common ownership of natural resource necessities.[28] So, water ought to be commonly owned, and common ownership is subsumed by the broader penumbra of Egalitarian Ownership; this is where Risse and I agree. Egalitarian Ownership, a 'shared and equal' ownership of resources, captures human relationships at the global level, along with accommodating concerns about the value of nature and non-human beings.[29]

Common ownership of water involves a right to use while not excluding others from use, and a necessary condition is respect for other co-owners to avoid a tragedy of the commons.[30] Importantly, for Risse, our equal status of ownership is affirmed within common ownership. The Egalitarian Ownership theory of common ownership that Risse proposes ought to be instituted and spurred by, I add, a deliberative, critical and reflexive democratic system. Such a system would encourage all relevant actors to speak about the importance of water and discuss material and normative responsibilities.

Common ownership brings into being a collective responsibility that all people have towards each other as part of the global order. As I will argue in Chapter 5, a 'recommoning' of water embodies the very philosophical ideals that influence activism for water justice. His view of common ownership is simpatico with mine, but I am critical of his conception of global order institutions. Notably, Risse's conception of the global order supersedes states and upholds human rights; the global order usurps the power of an individual state if said state cannot adhere to human rights and secure water for their population. Collective ownership rights have two guarantees: first, states and other powerful governing bodies must ensure that individuals meet their basic needs; second, states and other powerful governing bodies must create opportunities for individuals to satisfy their basic needs.[31] If a state cannot provide for the two guarantees of collective ownership, then the global order steps in to secure such rights. However, against Risse's view, I assert that the global order is not a democratic institution but, instead, an ill-defined hodgepodge of states and economic institutions. A 'global compact' on water, as Risse argues for,[32] is then vulnerable to promoting the *status quo* with the caveat of having an omnipotent watchdog that ensures global rights to water.

Instead, I argue that we should respect and uphold the human right to water through radically augmented state institutions that align more fully with deliberative democracy. It is at the state level that democracy is better managed and realized, not at the global-order level which is similar to existing intertwined economic and state systems. Transnational democracy can be problematic because of the lack of democracy at the global level; as numerous scholars have argued, 'deliberative democracy in system thinking must be normatively strong' or else democracy can be 'diluted'.[33] Moreover, representative democracy is impossible at the global level; such a centralized system would be nearly-authoritarian. Current global environmental agreements (e.g., United Nations Framework Convention on Climate Change) and institutions (e.g., the UN) are inadequately deliberatively democratic yet also inadequately powerful; as I shall put forth in Chapter 5, more deliberation, as a reinvigoration of democracy by way of water recommoning, may provide a successful approach to rectify water injustices.[34] I maintain that deliberative democracy at the state level should necessarily engage with locales, municipalities and requisite local knowledge, fostering new and creative avenues of water governance while also bringing to the fore forgotten strategies.

Many of the shortcomings I have identified in Risse's theory of global common ownership could be redressed by introducing more robust democratic institutions and processes at multiple geopolitical scales. Water is, indeed, 'original' as Risse identifies it, but his subsequent conclusions are problematic for common ownership in a deliberative democracy. Considering water as property, instead of territory, is privational – it cordons water off and makes it the object of privateers and profiteers. Risse tolerates, in a Rawlsian sense, the existence of water inequalities as long as they work for the betterment of all, which is a reasonable stance to take; however, he expands institutions of water oversight (i.e., water 'watchdogs') globally and does not account for the dilution of democracy at the global, instead of the local or state, scale.

In my view, the common ownership of the earth thesis is invaluable for establishing rights to commonly owned water, but I also hold that its focus on equitable distribution of water is at the expense of the political, governance dimensions of water that includes, as Schlosberg writes, recognition and political participation, and what I add is deliberative democracy.[35] Just distribution of water is merely one facet of a triumvirate of necessary parts for justice which includes regulations and agreements about water, as well as democratic governance of water. Political recognition and participation from all agents are required in this augmented and overtly deliberative democracy. The kinds of democratic mechanisms for water governance that I propose fit within a larger framework of deliberative democracy that other thinkers, such as Dryzek, have proposed for culturally plural liberal democracies. For example, the form of deliberation I discuss is reflexive in the manner that Dryzek and Pickering explain, as a specifically *ecological* reflexivity that is proactive, *recognizes* ecological conditions and changes, *reflects* upon past successes and failures, *rethinks* core values, *anticipates* different futures, and *responds* to changes to goals, policies and the values of states, institutions or systems after reflection.[36]

We need more robustly democratic processes inclusive of a wide range of citizens below an international 'global compact'. Risse's proposals of a global compact on water, upheld by a global water monitoring body, would not have adequate representation from locales and states and would, therefore, be inegalitarian and insufficiently deliberatively democratic. Risse's theory of a 'global compact' on water would be monitored by an undefined monitoring body that would determine proportionate use of water by states. This monitoring body would take inventories of global water resources and determine how water contributes to value for human purposes. Furthermore, such a body would identify which populations under-use their water and are water-rich (on a per capita basis). For Risse, those countries that are both under-using their water and water-rich are responsible for ensuring all humans can access water. Such access, for Risse, could be established by either physically transferring water, or allowing immigration from countries that over-use resources and suffer water shortages.[37] Finally, this monitoring body could resolve disputes of water between countries by identifying those states which over-use or under-use their water resource.

I acknowledge that the nation-state model presents a problem for common ownership of water insofar as it justifies states' sovereignty over natural resources within borders. States could refuse to allow others to use a resource or refuse to redistribute it to those in need but, as I shall explain later in this chapter with reference to Anna Stilz's work on territorial sovereignty and the maintenance of a broadly defined state, we can overcome these difficulties. To specify, common ownership rights are natural rights and pre-institutional – they exist before states, laws or institutions. I will argue that the establishment or development of new, deliberatively designed democratic institutions and processes protect such basic rights. Since states (functioning with full, minimally abridged sovereignty) pose obstacles to an arrangement of common ownership rights, it becomes all the more important to ground such rights within a broader framework and apparatus of international human rights.

Risse delves into human rights norms but, in my view, he neglects to explain deeper political, democratic aspects of common ownership of the earth and of water specifically. Ownership ought to be more than instrumental; human rights and respect for deliberative democracy are normative forces attached to water that are more than use rights. It is my position that common ownership is an expression of the rights people have as inhabitants of a space together, and as inhabitants who require necessities within such a space. People have the right to basic necessities for life, as they are individual rights that one holds against others; however, common ownership expresses or represents such rights in a political system or ownership system. To face the multitude of issues related to climate change and the Anthropocene, Dryzek and Pickering argue that a deliberative democratic system must be ecologically *reflexive*, open, ecologically grounded, dynamic, far-sighted and integrated with normative values.[38] The requisite criticality of such a thick deliberative democracy should lead to discussions of different ownership strategies for water.

Reflexive, critical and pluralist deliberation on water governance should involve the most possible relevant actors (i.e., human, and non-human beings alike, as well as existing and non-existing future human and non-human beings). This framework is best captured in commonly owned water not as property but, instead, as territory. One may ask, how might non-human actors, and the environment itself, communicate and add to deliberation in a democratic system? How can water, and the Earth at large, contribute to this discussion? We need only to stop and listen. Non-human beings and the Earth's environment should be represented by Indigenous peoples who have intimate ties to lands and waters, a strategy which has found some success at the level of local – state co-operation. For example, the Muteshekau-shipu, or Magpie River, in Québec is the first river to be granted legal personhood in Canada, by way of co-operative deliberative discourse between the Minganie municipality and the Innu Council of Ekuanitshit.[39] New Zealand's government recognized the Whanganui River and Mount Taranaki as alive and having the same legal rights as humans, with human stewards who represent and protect them.[40] The government of India has also declared the Ganges and Yamuna rivers to have legal rights the same as humans.[41] Lake Erie, too, has had a Bill of Rights written for it by Toledo, Ohio, city councillors.[42] Although the aforementioned bills and declarations are well-intentioned, I hold that the enshrinement of personhood or rights to nature will be insufficient if the structural injustices and underpinnings that enabled use and abuse of water are not fixed. For instance, the Lake Erie Bill of Rights, although voted into effect by most participants in a special election in Toledo, was effectively nullified by Ohio's Chamber of Commerce in a last-minute push by lawmakers and private industry.[43]

3.2.2 Common ownership and the tragedy of the commons

There is much consternation over the question of how much water one ought to take from a commons. A refrain against a common ownership of water model is the issue of the tragedy of the commons. However, is a tragedy of the commons a realistic possibility? Environmental philosopher Baylor Johnson and political theorist Elizabeth Kahn argue that communal destruction of a commons is unlikely.[44] I will add to their analysis by explicitly focusing on freshwater resource governance and ownership, and I will offer the insight that communal depletion of water does not necessarily have to be a worry if proper measures, restrictions and obligations borne by democratic systems and ideals are promoted and maintained. My explanation of the tragedy of the commons (and its unlikelihood) precedes my reply to a possible critique of my argument for water's recommoning. What happens if a local community is able to hoard their water within the broad terms of a recommoning framework? My response in this section sets up deeper explications of deliberative democracy and recommoning in Chapters 4 and 5, showing how my theory overcomes such potential issues, and I engage with political philosopher Anna Stilz's argument for territorial sovereignty.

We can look to ecologist Garrett Hardin's well-known parable, derived from William Forster Lloyd's own work over a century earlier, as an example of a tragedy of the commons scenario, or 'game', where farmers possess a shared common pasture.[45] Each farmer keeps the benefits (e.g., meat, milk, wool, sale price) of the pasture – the fruits of their labour – so the individuals have the incentive to have as many animals on the pasture as possible, though over-use of the land will cause it to degrade and harm their investment long-term. A tragedy of the commons is a scenario in which a shared resource (the common pasture) is significantly or fully depleted by the aggregate use of independent agents. When the resource becomes over-used without a co-ordinated plan, a tragedy of the commons is the result. In Hardin's example, the rational herder would be restrained and put a sustainable number of animals on the common pasture, while others who are less rational (i.e., more self-centred, and less restrained) will use up the amount the rational farmer forgoes.

Hardin's theoretical scenario implies that sharing leads to tragedy, but this is not necessarily the case in the real world. In my estimation, supported by Elinor Ostrom's research on common pool resource (CPR) governance and my investigation of case studies of water justice movements in Chapter 5, Hardin and Lloyd are incorrect in their cynicism: use of a common resource does not necessarily lead inexorably to ruin and tragedy. Later in this section, and in subsequent sections in this chapter, I concede that, on occasion, natural resources have been depleted, but collective agreements are often negotiated; people follow strategies, by way of collective agreements, to circumvent the tragedy that Lloyd and Hardin predict. Such agreements are rarely person-to-person and individually made; instead, they are legislations or treaties between states.

The view that self-governance can avert a tragedy of the commons scenario and be a successful alternative to globalized government is perhaps most associated with the political economist Elinor Ostrom. As will be seen more fully in case studies in Chapter 5, Ostrom's research of the commons, communal control and self-governance provides a critical lens to view social movements for water recommoning. Her research examines conceptual shifts in understanding communal forms of CPR[46] governance and, through the deployment of a pluralist lens, argues that there is a 'middle way' between private, technocratic control and state-led governmental solutions to CPR governance.[47] Ostrom investigates numerous cases of CPR governance in the mid-1900s that exemplify this 'middle way' and a few warrant explanation and closer inspection here: land ownership and farmer-led deliberation and control in Switzerland and Japan; the *huertas* system of water governance in Spain, specifically in Valencia and Alicante, and the similar *zanjeras* system in the Philippines; and water allocation and governance in California.

Switzerland and Japan present an interesting case study in that they show the forged 'middle' path of communal control of a mountain commons that provides forest products that citizens rely on, without top-down technocratic approaches from either the state or private industry. In villages in both Switzerland and Japan, Ostrom observes 'the ongoing, side-by-side existence of private property and communal property in settings in which the individuals involved have exercised considerable control over institutional arrangements and property rights'.[48] Mountain resources pertaining to forests and pastures are maintained, in Ostrom's view, because 'generations of Swiss and Japanese villagers have learned the relative benefits and costs of private property and communal-property institutions related to various types of land and uses of land'.[49] Villagers come together to deliberate on the use and value of the CPR and, from the bottom-up, they '[choose] to retain the institution of communal property as the foundation for land use and similar important aspects of village economies'.[50] These villagers are not 'remote' or 'abstracted' from their resource and, because they are intimately familiar with the CPR and their fellow villagers, they are epistemically grounded and privileged in their use.

The inter-relationships developed around CPRs in these villages, Ostrom notes, foment skills that make CPR governance successful long-term.[51] Such relationships are fluid, similar to those within and between water justice organizations I present in Chapter 5.[52] Further, such flux means that communal property as the crux of CPR governance is intrinsic to CPR governance and not merely vestigial. Ostrom clarifies this point, writing, 'One cannot view communal property in these settings as the primordial remains of earlier institutions evolved in a land of plenty. If the transactions costs involved in managing communal property had been excessive, compared with private-property institutions, the villagers would have had many opportunities to devise different land-tenure arrangements.'[53] Villagers, over centuries, came together to discuss their land tenure claims and the general management of the CPR, and communal control has persisted. Ostrom makes explicit that the institutions used to govern the use of the CPRs consistently have 'appropriators [CPR users] themselves make all major decisions', which have contributed to CPR governance being long-lived and successful.[54]

Ostrom's examination of CPR governance in Swiss and Japanese villages highlights plural forms of communal governance of CPRs, finding a middle ground between private property and state control that is reflected in water recommoning cases in Chapter 5 (e.g., Cochabamba). In Spain and the Philippines, Ostrom turns her pluralistic lens on the CPR of fresh water. In Valencia, Spain, *huerta* irrigation institutions have dealt with water disputes since the Middle Ages.[55] The *huerta* system involves 'irrigators from seven of the major canals... organized into autonomous irrigation communities whose syndic, or chief executive, participates in two weekly tribunals [*Tribunal de las Aguas* or water courts]' that have convened for centuries.[56] These water courts are informal yet bind the community's governance of the CPR, overseen not by lawyers but, instead, 'onlookers'.[57] Syndics participating in the courts are 'executive officer[s] of each individual irrigation unit' and are 'elected every 2 or 3 years by farmers who own lands eligible to receive water from the canals'.[58] In Valencia, those most active and participatory in water governance are, indeed, the farmers or 'appropriators' of water, as 'decisions about when to shut down the canals for annual maintenance and how the maintenance work will be organized are made by the members of this committee of irrigators'.[59] In these cases, instead of decisions being made mostly or solely by private actors, farmers communally and directly make decisions on how much water to use and allocate based on drought or water abundance.

Demonstrating that water can be governed in many different collective arrangements, and that these arrangements are durable and feasible, lends support to the case for water recommoning. As I made explicit with reference to a plurality of governance methods in Chapter 2 and earlier in this chapter, and will show in cases in Chapter 5, water recommoning is but one way to instantiate water justice. How might CPR governance, relating to water, differ amongst separate local communities? Ostrom's research on water governance in Alicante, Spain, enlightens how a specific subset of appropriators (farmers) can successfully manage the CPR of water. She identifies that water governance differs in Alicante because deliberation amongst farmers is narrower than in Valencia. Ostrom writes:

> First, there is only one irrigation community for the entire *huerta*. Second, to vote in the general assembly of the community, a farmer must own 1.8 hectares of land; to vote for the executive commission, 1.2 hectares of land;

and to be eligible to serve on the commission, 3.6 hectares of land.[60] Whereas a farmer must own a minimum of land to participate, the votes of farmers owning more land are not weighted to reflect differences in the amounts of land owned. The executive commission is composed of 12 representatives (*sindicos*) who serve four years each (half rotating every second year). One member from this body is selected as the director.[61]

Although there are elections in both Valencia and Alicante, the criteria for appropriator participation (farmers in Alicante require a certain, larger amount of land ownership) is more exclusive; therefore, rule-making and governance itself is more exclusive and unrepresentative of the larger body of water appropriators. From this difference, Ostrom argues that the *huerta* system in Valencia and, she adds, the *zanjera* system in the Philippines are alike (and differ from Alicante) because of the 'central role given to small-scale communities of irrigators who determine their own rules, choose their own officials, guard their own systems, and maintain their own canals'.[62] However, such communally grounded governance of CPR is limited to landowners (as we shall see in California as well), which limits the expanse of deliberation over such natural resources.

Ostrom's case of the West Basin Water Association further supports my claim that deliberative governance of water can support democracy and fill epistemological gaps opened by a recommoning approach. Around Los Angeles, California, groundwater rights were first tied to overlying landowners and then to 'first in time, first in right' prior-appropriation water rights.[63] Such rights encouraged water users to adopt inefficient strategies for water distribution relating to pumping-cost externalities and strategic externalities. Ostrom notes that these two pressures incentivize over-exploitation, as they 'reinforce one another to aggravate the intensity of the pumping race. Without a change of institutions, pumpers in such a situation acting independently will severely overexploit the resource.'[64] As an answer to such policies that exacerbated continuous water withdrawal, the West Basin Water Association was created as an open, deliberative and transparent community organization to improve sustainability.[65] Ostrom expands on the virtues of the West Basin Water Association:

> The association provided a continuous open forum for discussion of all major steps taken in West Basin by producers and representatives of various

local, regional, and state public agencies. The resources of the association frequently were used to obtain and make available the best possible technical information about the basin. Extensive minutes were kept for all West Basin Water Association meetings, as well as the meetings of the Executive Committee and most of the working committees of the association. Those files were open to all members, as well as to others interested in gaining information about past decisions, technical data, and studies of the benefits and costs of alternatives ... The practice of obtaining the best information available and disseminating it widely increased the degree of understanding and level of cooperation among the participants.[66]

The West Basin Water Association thus made monitoring public and transparent, increasing trust and conformance.[67] 'Watermasters' oversee monitoring, and they have 'extensive monitoring and sanctioning authority. Monitoring activities are obvious and public. Every year, each party reports total groundwater extractions and receives a report listing the groundwater extractions of all other parties (or anyone else who has started to pump).'[68] Authoritative actors made their actions transparent which, on Ostrom's account, helped fill epistemological gaps cleaved by top-down, technocratic methods.

Importantly for my argument concerning bottom-up recommoning, Ostrom argues that pluralistic CPR governance can be successful if people who might otherwise have different positions arrive at a similar understanding of the problems through processes of dialogue and deliberation. She writes, 'Individuals who do not have similar images of the problems they face, who do not work out mechanisms to disaggregate complex problems into subparts, and who do not recognize the legitimacy of diverse interests are unlikely to solve their problems even when the institutional means to do so are available to them.'[69] In Switzerland, Japan, Spain and California, despite differences in CPRs and in the scope of actors who can participate in deliberation, those successful models brought communities together to discuss CPR governance, making communities active (instead of remote, abstract or passive).

A similar conclusion can be drawn from Ostrom's case studies, and the cases presented in Chapter 5: community *autonomy* plays a central role in successful, long-lived communal control of vital resources. She writes, with reference to 'long-term ownership claims' amongst Nepalese farmers, that those 'who can communicate, develop their own agreements, establish the positions of monitors, and sanction those who do not conform to their own rules, are more likely to grow more rice, distribute water more equitably, and keep their systems in better repair than is done on government systems'.[70] Bottom-up oriented environmental and water-focused organizations (e.g., the Council of Canadians explained in Chapter 5) call for more autonomy and democratic deliberation about water governance, which is consistent with Ostrom's argument for dispersed communication between relevant stakeholders in CPR governance. The primary difference between my forthcoming cases in Chapter 5 and Ostrom's cases, though, is that I expand water governance discourse to more than farmer-appropriators. Specifically, I include all those in a populace capable of discussing the various values of water. It is my view that this deliberative expansion not only *can* be done but *should* be done.[71]

We can conclude from Ostrom's analysis that local governance of CPRs can be successful in avoiding a tragedy of the commons scenario without recourse to top-down control from the state or the 'invisible hand' of the free market. Those in favour of free market solutions to a tragedy of the commons scenario (e.g., market environmentalists from Section 2.4.1, such as Broome) might contend that it is the individual, and not the collective, that has the responsibility to reduce use of a commons to a sustainable level. However, Baylor Johnson argues that there would instead need to be a collective agreement to reduce everyone's resource use to a sustainable level, for 'in a tragedy of the commons there is no reasonable expectation that individual, voluntary action will succeed'.[72] I concur with Johnson's view that the claim that one is obligated to reduce one's own use of the commons unilaterally, without regard for the actions of others, is implausible. Rather than requiring that we reduce our consumption of resources, concerns about a tragedy of the commons scenario should enjoin us 'to promote an effective collective agreement that will co-ordinate reductions in commons use and therefore avert the aggregate harm'.[73] As earlier discussion of Ostrom established, people can and do willingly form CPRs for governing natural resources that avoid tragedy of the commons scenarios. A collective agreement is needed to prevent potential depletion. It is important to note that such depletion is not the result of an individual but, instead, of aggregate use.[74] Such depletion by aggregate use can be regarded, in my thinking, as diffused across a range of actors, further supporting my claim in Chapter 1 that water injustice (i.e., commodification) is structural.

Johnson provides context for such potentially democratic agreements, writing that they are collective or co-operative because they 'coordinate the behaviour of individuals to protect the commons'.[75] These collective agreements are most effective when imposed in a democracy because they are likely supported by a majority of citizens.[76] A critic, though, might broach the concern of a tyranny of the majority in such a scenario, despite democratic development and assent, manifested as a concern about hoarding. The tyranny of the majority is a distributive concern from the point of view of global justice, one that Chris Armstrong has similarly raised against political philosopher Anna Stilz's conception of territorial sovereignty.[77]

In my view, the requirement that people take collective responsibility for not depleting CPRs is a compelling solution to the potential (though unlikely) tragedy of the commons scenario; in addition, water recommoning would be founded upon, and give further support to, a notion of collective responsibility to not deplete resources, as Ostrom's research makes clear. The popular Kantian answer to the problem of the tragedy of the commons is to lessen one's individual use of the commons; however, Johnson disagrees, saying individual, voluntary and, I add, liberal action 'is mistaken because it fails to distinguish acting unilaterally from acting as one of many in a co-operative scheme to address a problem'.[78] As I see it, collective action does not face the same structural barriers that individual action does. A collective, co-operative scheme places onus on all people to act collectively and preserve resources, while an individual scheme runs up against barriers of other individuals, which is inconsistent with the complexity and connectedness of water systems. The moral obligation, then, is to come to, and promote, a collective agreement to protect the commons.

A critic might posit that collective, democratic agreements could undermine water recommoning. What happens if a local community is able to hoard their water within the broad terms of a water recommoning framework? Consider the example of a local community that has agreed to democratic control, and they have plausible (but arguably unjust) reasons for wanting to keep more than they 'need' for themselves. At first glance, the hoarding concern presents a thorny issue for my forthcoming argument for recommoning; however, it is not intractable. In the following subsection, I shall address the hoarding concern by using Stilz's examination of the right of occupancy and sovereignty. In brief, I argue that there is no thick form of democratic sovereignty that justifies hoarding water; hoarding is fundamentally undemocratic. Recommoning, as I will explain in Chapter 5, should be fuel for water justice movements, as a way to instantiate a different way of living and valuing water separate from capitalist valuations. I also hold that a distributive concern of global justice is speaking 'a different language' from my recommoning argument because, as I made explicit in Chapters 1 and 2, my project is a normative one, and water justice is far more than distributive.

3.2.2.1 *Common ownership and the hoarding concern*

To build on the claim that the challenge of the tragedy of the commons is not necessarily a problem to be faced by commons control, I must address the concern of hoarding. Can a local community justifiably control more fresh water than it requires, even if said governance and ownership was arrived at democratically? In *Territorial Sovereignty: A Philosophical Exploration*, Anna Stilz starkly differentiates between jurisdiction and property. Stilz's support for territorial rights justified within broadly construed state systems of global reach, as well as her supporting concepts of the Right of Occupancy and collective self-determination, undergird my argument for recommoning in Chapter 5.

One of Stilz's main claims is that jurisdictional exclusivity is a significant feature of territory because the international system of sovereign states exalts it as an ideal. However, the current nation-state system should not be taken as given. Stilz agrees with cosmopolitans such as Armstrong that the current state system must not be accepted as a form of immutable government. Stilz does argue, though, that there are central aspects of the current system that can be defended morally. Crucially for her theory, and in addressing the hoarding concern, territorial sovereignty can be 'served by organizing our political world as a structure of self-governing territorial units' justified by three core values: right of occupancy; basic justice; and collective self-determination.[79]

Although all three core values are pertinent to water governance, the right of occupancy, according to Stilz, is the most relevant for the hoarding concern. To begin, the international state system upholds this 'preinstitutional' claim to specific areas; this right disperses 'political authority in a *spatial fashion*, a mode of political organization that is particularly distinctive of the territorial state'.[80] For Stilz, occupancy rights are use-rights that agree with common ownership of the earth, and occupancy is determined by the use of an area for social, cultural and economic reasons.[81] Important for the hoarding proponent, the right of occupancy stresses how individuals' life plans are intricately tied to a specific geographical location; therefore, any interference between said individual and the location (such as restricting water use) 'undermines the lives people have built'.[82] Violation of the three core values ultimately undercuts autonomy. She concludes that the best way to protect and secure territorial sovereignty is 'through a pluralistic and decentralized order of self-governing territorial units', or states as conceived in a broad sense as any institution that has binding collective rules and can enforce such rules in disputes.[83]

One challenge that Stilz's argument faces is the prospect of hoarding. How can we stave off hoarding if autonomy and territorial sovereignty are so crucial for life plans? Stilz centres her answer on a fair use (minimalist) proviso: Earth happens to be unevenly divided into territorial states, but, as common owners, humans are entitled to fulfill their needs. Needs override territorial sovereignty rights, but 'once everyone's basic territorial interests were satisfied, the minimalist proviso would place no further constraints on the pattern of holdings'.[84] Still, this proviso might be taken advantage of and make hoarding justified. Stilz, though, in an interesting turn makes a distinction between ownership and jurisdiction which gets us closer to addressing the concern.

Stilz defends a *limited* resource principle of sovereignty that has relevance to water governance. This principle maintains that resource sovereignty is a matter of *jurisdiction* instead of *ownership* (i.e., *property*), and that resource sovereignty should be constrained by environmental justice duties structured by international institutions. In Stilz's words, 'Jurisdiction [confers] only a conditional right to exclude outsiders from resources on the territory rather than property which [confers] on the state a discretionary right to exclude outsiders from these resources, and to enjoy the full stream of income from exploiting them'.[85] Beyond distribution, though, Stilz makes a compelling move in her argument that digs deeper against the hoarding principle on moral grounds. Although states are important for instantiating resource sovereignty, she argues that people, instead of states, are the appropriate subject of resource sovereignty.[86] The international state system buttresses basic rights, but people hold the right of occupancy and the right of self-determination; therefore, for Stilz, people have moral claims to resources. Limited resource sovereignty fits in with her broader construal of the state, whereas permanent resource sovereignty is held by the Weberian nation-state. Her limiting of resource sovereignty to jurisdiction instead of ownership constrains the ability of a state to hoard or otherwise use their resource in a harmful way. Hoarding would be justifiable in a permanent sovereignty nation-state system, but that is the very system my argument for water recommoning pushes against.

One retort to the hoarding concern is that we cannot tolerate people's 'right to do wrong' because water is fundamentally important across boundaries. Stilz says we *can* tolerate 'the right to do wrong'; if a people lie, break promises, or are unkind, such are the risks of a minimalist proviso which maximizes autonomy.[87] However, water is a special case. The clear answer is that water is too important for life, and toleration of hoarding would harm others' basic justice and right of self-determination, as well as weaken the right of occupancy. Another retort to concerns of distributive justice is that it is rather consequentialist and outside the scope of this project, so strictly distributive concerns are 'speaking a different language'. I am, first and foremost, concerned with normative and political, democratic harms of water injustices such as commodification and the value of recommoning as 'filling the gaps' in water governance.

I do, indeed, argue that water justice movements for recommoning be deliberatively democratic. To reiterate the definition of deliberative democracy provided in Chapter 1 by Andre Bächtiger, John Dryzek, Jane Mansbridge and Mark Warren, deliberation is 'mutual communication that involves weighing and reflecting on preferences, values, and interests regarding matters of common concern'.[88] Deliberation includes 'reasoned argument, strategic bargaining, experiential testimony, and other kinds of discursive claims'.[89] Deliberative democracy is then the practice of democracy that centres such deliberation.

I also argue, though, that such deliberative movements should not be parochial or provincial; they should be *glocal*, that is, their deliberations are grounded in a local context but with an eye to the larger, global scale of water ethics and movements. To hoard water as a part of recommoning would be inconsistent with the type of recommoning I will explain. Furthermore, I endorse Stilz's claim that the territorial state – that pluralistic and decentralized order of self-governing territorial units – is indispensable for instantiating water justice globally. Also, I see the normative importance not so much in fortifying individualized autonomy and interests (as Stilz does) but in concretizing communal autonomy as glocal movements. To foster deliberative democratic communal movements, I hold that *people* can be the subject of resource sovereignty, instead of states (again, not the nation-state, but the broad conception of the state given by Stilz).

This is all to say that the hoarding concern is not, in my view, as serious a risk for recommoning as some critics have suggested. Global egalitarians such as Chris Armstrong might proffer that hoarding is a risk;[90] however, I will contend in Chapter 5 that deliberative democratic glocal movements can contribute to securing water justice in their communities while not losing the forest for the trees in seeing the borderless, global importance of water.

3.2.3 Commons control in relation to self-governance and state-governance

State institutions are frequently deadlocked by path dependencies that ultimately block significant changes to water or environmental decisions, thus preventing much-needed structural transformation of water distribution and governance. I propose that critical ecological reflexivity at the local and state levels might provide a way to break inertia and thwart processes of commodification. Reflexivity is ecological and proactive; as Dryzek and Pickering explain, ecological reflexivity involves three components:

1 recognition of ecological conditions and changes;
2 reflection upon past successes and failures, rethinking core values, and anticipating different futures;
3 response, as in changes to goals, policies, values of a state, institution, or system after reflection.[91]

The control of a commons should take the form of self-governance of water, moving upwards from local actors that are familiar with water stewardship practices in a specific locale, towards the level of the state and then through newly structured institutions at the global level. Moving towards a more deliberative form of democracy would provide better support for water self-governance than liberal representative systems that have less opportunity for citizen participation, and do not distribute power as widely. For example, deliberative democratic mechanisms have been used to address natural resources such as water through collaborative government initiatives and citizen assemblies in the Canterbury region of New Zealand[92] and in the Prairie Provinces of Canada,[93] two cases I will examine in Section 3.3.

Before I draw a line between Ostrom's research on CPR governance in social-ecological systems (SES) and deliberative democratic mechanisms in such governance, it is relevant to clarify the relationship between deliberation, participation and representation. Deliberation on fresh water requires more than discussion; it intercepts the concepts and practices of participation and representation, as well. Deliberation, participation and representation are not at odds with the deliberative water governance proposed and analysed in Chapter 5; instead, these ideals and practices are complementary with one another and can both be utilized in deliberative water governance. Political theorist Stephen Elstub summarizes how deliberation and participation in a democratic system reinforce one another, which helps clarify their relationship with representation as well:

> [T]he normative and explanatory potential of (both deliberative and participatory democracy) is diminished without the presence of the other, so it is desirable and coherent to pursue a "participatory deliberative democracy" in which citizens make collective decisions through deliberation. Participatory democracy can enhance and facilitate the inclusion of all relevant reasons and assent from all affected, as a deliberative interpretation of legitimacy requires. In turn a specific focus on "deliberative" participation makes participatory democracy less vague, can contribute towards delivering the educative effects that political participation is considered to cultivate in citizens, and help reduce inequalities by promoting public reasoning.[94]

Deliberation necessarily requires discussion and participation via 'non-deliberative modes of engagement such as voting, mobilizing, and protesting'.[95] Thus, deliberative democracy and participatory democracy are, on the view defended here, mutually supportive.[96] The term 'deliberative democracy' necessarily includes a commitment to ensuring wide participation in decision-making and governing processes by those affected.

What might participation and representation in deliberative democratic water governance look like, and what do they promote? I will explain in Sections 3.2.3 and 3.3 that participation and representation can be realized through deliberative minipublics, as seen in New Zealand's Canterbury region and in the Prairie Provinces of Canada, and they promote trust. As political theorist Simon Niemeyer writes, 'The promotion of minipublic deliberation as an exemplary form of political reasoning potentially mitigates non-deliberative cues reinforcing deliberative pathologies' by 'harnessing trust in fellow citizens to carry the cognitive load and work through the issues.'[97] This kind of deliberation in minipublics can be influential because it formulates strong reasons for certain outcomes regarding, for instance, water recommoning (which builds transparency and trust).[98]

Ostrom's research establishes the feasibility of recommoning, and her findings can guide our normative comparisons and appraisals of water governance systems. I draw on her research on CPRs, as well as her writings on SESs, in developing my argument for water recommoning. To explain, these SESs are complex and multi-system, and Ostrom writes, 'In a complex SES, subsystems such as a resource system (e.g., a coastal fishery), resource units (lobsters), users (fishers), and governance systems (organizations and rules that govern fishing on that coast) are relatively separable but interact to produce outcomes at the SES level, which in turn feed back to affect these subsystems and their components, as well other larger or smaller SESs.'[99] These SESs track the structural complexity of what I identify in Chapter 4 to be structural water justice – socioenvironmental justice.

Ostrom's investigations of CPR governance, and her debunking of the tragedy of the commons scenario, further supports the case I make for recommoning water because her findings support the viability of self-governance.[100] For Ostrom, resource collapse (i.e., tragedy of the commons) is not inevitable in a self-governed communal system, but collapse is more likely in a top-down, non-pluralist model. She writes, 'Scholars have tended to develop simple theoretical models to analyze aspects of resource problems and to prescribe universal solutions. For example, theoretical predictions of the destruction of natural resources due to the lack of recognized property systems have led to one-size-fits-all recommendations to impose particular policy solutions that frequently fail.'[101] Thus, popular conceptions of property enable homogenized water governance policies to lack sufficient and necessary local grounding and knowledge, ending in failure.

Ostrom acknowledges that 'resource collapse is supported in very large, highly valuable, open-access systems when the resource harvesters are diverse, do not communicate, and fail to develop rules and norms for managing the resource'.[102] Note the caveats that users 'do not communicate' and 'fail to develop rules and norms'; communication and norm development are two virtues of the conception of water governance I develop further in Chapters 4 and 5 – a recommoning of water that is developed by, and then itself promotes, deliberative democratic mobilization for water justice. We will see in cases from Detroit and Cochabamba that water has been used as a unifying element that binds communities and helps citizens resist commodification. Furthermore, such self-governance and communally-centred water governance, on Ostrom's account, do not necessarily result in collapse because of discussions amongst actors, as she states that resource collapse is 'not supported under conditions that enable harvesters and local leaders to self-organize effective rules to manage a resource or in rigorous laboratory experiments when subjects can discuss options to avoid overharvesting'.[103] Deliberation can break down epistemic walls that might have made actors abstracted or, to recall Plumwood's term, 'remote' from water.

Ostrom identifies a host of criteria for assessing self-governance systems around resources,[104] of which six are especially relevant for self-governance as water recommoning:

1. Resource System (RS3): Very large territories are unlikely to be self-governed because of high costs, and very small territories do not generate considerable value streams; "thus, moderate territorial size is most conducive to self-organization."
2. Resource Unit Mobility (RU1): "Due to the costs of observing and managing a system, self-organization is less likely with mobile resource units, such as wildlife or water in an unregulated river, than with stationary units such as trees and plants or water in a lake."
3. Norms/social capital (U6): Actors "have sufficient trust in one another to keep agreements" when they share norms on how to work together in groups.
4. Knowledge of the SES (U7): Actors "perceive lower costs of organizing" when they possess common knowledge of the SES (i.e., water governance).

5 Importance of the resource to users (U8): "In successful cases of self-organization, users are either dependent on the RS for a substantial portion of their livelihoods or attach high value to the sustainability of the resource."
6 Collective-choice rules (GS6): Actors with full autonomy to make collective choices face lower costs of transactions and defense against invaders.[105]

As will become clearer in Chapter 5, the criteria above can assess collective water governance. Large territories of water (RS3) might be unwieldy and costly to manage, but communal and (to borrow Roland Robertson's and, later, Tully's term)[106] glocal governance may make water more 'conducive' to commonly governed, uncommodified means. Water *is* mobile in the sense that it is always in flux (RU1), but costs of observation and management might be superseded by positive norms/social capital (U6) that water engenders, as well as common epistemologies and ontologies (U7). Water is also important to actors (U8) not only biophysically, but culturally, historically and spiritually, too (U6, U7). Finally, Ostrom's identification of collective-choice rules (GS6) highlights the importance of deliberative governance systems which come through in Granada, Kerala and other locales examined in Chapter 5.

Critically for my argument for water recommoning, Ostrom's research shows that water-system collapse is preventable, and strong communal supports can be erected, through self-determination or 'self-organization'. Commodification and extensive state control would, then, be unnecessary apparatuses which support domination and do not mitigate a tragedy of the commons. To build on Ostrom's critique of Hardin's tragedy of the commons scenario, I add, and shall explain later in this chapter and in subsequent chapters, that such collapse can be avoided when a collective, democratic agreement to preserve a commons is created and promoted through critical deliberative democracy.

To summarize, Hardin's tragedy of the commons 'game' rests on three rules or assumptions:

1 The only incentive players have is to maximize benefits from use of the commons (all benefits and losses are internal to the game).
2 The only way players can communicate is by increasing or reducing use of the commons.

3 Use of the commons is shared, but individual herds are not.

  a. So costs (to the commons) of increased use are shared but benefits from increased use accrue to the individual herder. Benefits (to the commons) of reduced use are shared, but costs of reduced use are borne by the individual herder.
  b. Resources saved by one individual are available for use by any other user.[107]

Baylor Johnson provides compelling refutations of the above assumptions. Assumption 1 might never be true because people usually have many different incentives, and assumption 2 does not hold for advanced communities with sophisticated ways of communication. Assumption 3a is true for use of a commons without a collective agreement, as is 3b; however, in 3b, an individual's reduced use of a commons does not mean others will automatically use more of the commons.[108] Therefore, there are few parallels to be drawn between the tragedy of the commons 'game' and real-world tragedy of the commons scenarios. What remains true for the 'game' and the real-world tragedy of the commons scenario is that individuals get all the benefits while costs are shared amongst all users. The 'game' usually does not hold in the real world because rules 1 and 2 do not hold. People have more than the one motivation of voracious consumption; they have ethical considerations, concern for their standing in their community, aspirations to improve the world, fears that they may be harming the world and worries of retribution from others. In addition, relaxing rules 1 and 2 leads to different circumstances for 3a and 3b because collective agreements in the real world involve sanctions for free riders and over users. Such sanctions build confidence in individuals that using less of the commons is not in vain and that sustainable use is enforced.

For Johnson, collective agreements will be more successful than individual actions in preventing a tragedy of the commons. He holds that, without universal assurance through legislation or collective agreements, voluntary unilateral reductions will fail because individuals will see unscrupulous users go unpunished and, resultantly, be discouraged to use reasonably.[109] There is a lack of incentives in the individual-reduction-of-use model; individuals will see their reasonable use as being in vain.[110] As Johnson argues, our moral obligations run deeper in collective agreements where we have a moral obligation to protect the commons collectively, not individually. One is to inform others of the dangers of over-use, 'appealing to their self-interest as well as their concern for the common good, seeking and suggesting ways of regulating use, of promoting an agreement, and of enforcing one on the reluctant and the would-be cheaters'.[111] Our very moral obligation is to come to a collective agreement that averts a tragedy of the commons.

As I will argue in Chapter 5, activist organizations and social movements can sometimes counteract path dependencies and challenge the 'ambivalence' of the state. To better set the stage, I should make explicit my view that commonly owned water should be protected through a democratic, bottom-up agreement that enjoys wide public support, achieved through deliberative democratic means. Water treaties or legislation that amends existing laws, and which are produced through deliberative processes, are examples of this. Coming to a collective agreement involves communicating with others not through the limitations and excess use of the commons, but through organizing and promoting the agreement. Moreover, in a democratic state, it would indeed be the case that all citizens deliberate on how to share their country's water in forums and, in Stevenson's and Dryzek's terms, discourse which transcends current time and actors.

The democratic representation afforded through majoritarian liberal representative democracy does not adequately represent the plurality of views on water at the state and global levels. Elected assemblies, such as parliament or congress, inadequately account for the need for transnational decision-making just as, for Stevenson and Dryzek, they are too small for the global issue of climate change.[112] It is at the deliberative *systems* level that the structural complexity of water is captured at its fullest, allowing for expression, then listening, and finally reflection.[113] As Stevenson and Dryzek write, 'A system of any kind consists of differentiated yet linked components that can be interpreted in light of some common purpose.'[114] The common purpose at issue – water ethics and justice – is multitudinous and goes beyond current actors, so a deliberative democracy should take into account stewardship and tragedy of the commons concerns. For example, collective environmental agreements include the international agreement Canada signed to prevent unregulated high seas fisheries in the central Arctic Ocean.[115] Also, collaborative water management occurs effectively and meaningfully in the Northwest Territories, where First Nations and the territorial government work together in water sustainability in a strategy which privileges Indigenous knowledge and explicitly recognizes Indigenous rights.[116] People become active participants communicating with each other, continually building a dialogue with those open to reflection, change and criticality.[117]

Such active participation imprints itself on us reflexively.[118] Reflexive participation is reinforcing, provides stability and involves actors looking back onto themselves and their most concrete beliefs regarding, for instance, water ownership; moreover, it involves meta-questioning. Reflexive institutions make themselves into living frameworks which can provide stability for agreements within and between states. Markedly, the Strategic Foresight Group in India found that 'any two countries engaged in active water cooperation do not go to war for any reason'.[119] Furthermore, a global study of 'all potential cases of "water [driven] wars" between states shows not a single example of water as a *casus belli*'.[120] Deliberative, collaborative and collective government strategies to tackle water issues have led to innovative solutions.[121]

My view that collective action on water justice can best be achieved within more deliberative democratic processes of decision-making and governance most resembles work in deliberative democracy from Dryzek and Niemeyer. Niemeyer's focus on deliberative small-scale minipublics and their potential use for shifting public discourse to bring about 'ecological democracy' helps inform my stance on the communal power of water recommoning, and he adds to Dryzek's work on reflexivity. To build on the explications provided in Sections 3.2.1 and 3.2.3, as a definition, reflexivity is a norm within democracy, an ideal that is a 'willingness to reflect upon and act to change unsustainable trajectories'.[122] Such ecological reflexivity, as Dryzek argues, is a crucial feature of deliberative systems, involving reflection on the successes and failures of past methods and adopting new methods to improve.[123] Without such reflexivity, path dependencies can quash recognition of actors, as well as alternative, communal-focused discourses pertaining to water governance.

3.3 Common ownership, common territory and deliberative democracy as complementary

Common ownership *ipso facto* brings about and establishes certain obligations because of the common importance of water. The same is true for common territory, where we are not permitted to evict people from a land or deny people necessities for life derived from a land (e.g., water). Stewardship is a critical factor in territory as well, not only for existing humans but for those yet to be born. Beyond these anthropocentric concerns, it is logical to extend stewardship to non-human beings when considering water as a common territory because it is necessary for more than anthropocentric life. Common territory does not require restrictions on stewardship or access for humans, as Kolers argues. This lack of restrictions should be extended to non-human beings as Alfred and deep ecologists such as Plumwood argue.

Such restrictions do not hold for 'property', a term associated with commodification and exclusion. When water is controlled as private property, it becomes the object of self-interested agents. Property, especially private property, does not lend itself to the commonality and stewardship that water demands; it is inherently non-common and self-interested. The characteristics and assumptions of property do not align with the goal of equitable, democratically controlled water.

On the other hand, deliberative democracy that reinforces local-and-state collaborative water governance can expand democratic water strategies. Let us consider two examples, one from the Canterbury region of New Zealand and another from the Prairie Provinces in Canada, to illuminate the positives and negatives of types of deliberative democracy that could support water governance, such as systemic deliberative democracy and deliberative polls (in New Zealand) and Local Water Councils (or LWCs, in the Prairies). First, political theorists Nicolas Pirsoul and Maria Armoudian propose a systemic approach to deliberative democracy that expands democracy beyond local, specific contexts and tries to bake-in '[the establishment of] mutual respect and creating inclusive and egalitarian decision-making processes beyond the local spheres of deliberation'. As such, they argue for minipublics with sortition to ensure representation to overcome deliberative democratic water governance issues too.[124] After investigating the relationship between the Māori and the Crown in the Canterbury region of New Zealand, they propose that a systemic deliberative democracy instantiated by deliberative polls could be a novel approach to water governance to mitigate 'vertical exchanges between different levels of decision-making and those arising from the socio-economic and ideological diversity of participants'.[125] Local authorities in Canterbury, such as

Environmental Canterbury, take a collaborative governance and deliberative democratic approach similar to Ostrom's 'self-governing communities' explained in Section 3.2.3.[126] To combat 'wallpaper democracy', as Bächtiger and Parkinson term it – a shallow form of deliberative democracy that does not engage stakeholders on structural governance issues – water deliberators must get around self-selection bias by way of minipublics.[127]

Minipublics can boost trust in legislative forums by serving as 'trusted information proxies to guide citizens' political judgments in situations characterized by limited information', and in executive forums as *anticipatory publics* to guide policy-makers in rapidly developing policy areas that may become contentious in the future, but which do not (yet) have public opinion attached to them'.[128] It should be noted, though, that Dryzek shows that minipublics do poorly with regard to justification.[129] So, the systemic approach to deliberative democratic water governance can build trust (as will be further explicated in case studies in Chapter 5), but there can be a lack of epistemic justification, such as grounded or local knowledge, due to said trust, as a variation of the abstraction I explained in Chapter 2.

Consider a second example of locally situated deliberative democratic forums: LWCs in the Prairie Provinces (Manitoba, Saskatchewan and Alberta) of Canada. Social scientists Margot Hurlbert and Evan Andrews analysed LWCs and their effectiveness in growing democracy in watershed governance. As opposed to the largely top-down, hierarchical approach to watershed governance, LWCs attempt to localize governance and bind community relations. The Prairies were evaluated across five concerns – mandate comprehensiveness, mandate significance, resources, representativeness, and reflexivity. Although LWCs generally complement and supplement state functions, they differ in their strengths and weaknesses across locales.[130] For instance, LWCs in Alberta and Manitoba were found to be reflexive, but Saskatchewan's had 'significant reflexivity through valuing ecosystem services; experimentation with other instruments; reflection and reconsideration *built into* [my emphasis] source water protection planning'.[131] Here, the systemic approach to deliberative democratic water governance boosted reflexivity because the model *itself* braided reflexivity. Across the five evaluative concerns, no province excelled in all five categories; specifically, 'Alberta excels at community representation and contested deliberation, Manitoba at mandate and resources, while Saskatchewan at what will be described as interconnected reflexivity'.[132]

Disappointingly, Hurlbert and Andrews found 'very limited representation of immigrants, women, and Indigenous people' in LWCs and source water planning in the Prairies.[133] Evidently, such LWCs are insufficiently democratic. Without adequate representation from all relevant stakeholders, deliberation will track the advantages of only privileged populations. As I explained in Chapter 2 and will build on in Chapter 4 (by identifying water justice best understood in a framework of socioenvironmental justice) such mal- and misrepresentation is a political harm. It is my view that deliberative democracy with sortition, proposed by Pirsoul and Armoudian, could overcome such representation issues in LWCs (despite strengths in reflexivity) because their strategy is systemic, attacking the lack of representation at the root. I do not want to belabour the point concerning the power of deliberative democracy fomented by, and within, water justice movements – that is the work of Chapter 5 – but we shall see that such movements instantiate representation by *being* deliberative and *acting* differently from unrepresentative water commodifiers. I broach LWCs to show the positives that can be taken from them (deliberation and reflexivity) while acknowledging the shortcomings (representation, which should be improved by more systemic and critical methods).

Despite their shortcomings, Canterbury and the Prairies underscore the indispensability of deliberation and reflexivity for critical discourse; that is, deliberation should affect those who are a part of it. Whereas uncritical and passive governance and discourse tend towards pathological path dependencies such as private property, self-interest and maintenance of current sociopolitical and legal/ownership structures, systemic deliberative democratic arrangements presuppose cascading norm shifts that put into place national and transnational legal obligations. The moral weight of water should precede legal obligations of egalitarian distribution – they should fit into common ownership – yet economic and political discourse privileges dependency on the market and eliminates discussion of other options. Stevenson and Dryzek note the privileged position that markets (i.e., private industry and actors) have in PPPs, as 'this privilege squeezes out opportunities for public deliberation, which is considered costly, cumbersome, and counterproductive to the overarching objective of maximizing investment ...'.[134] Markets squeeze out empowered, informal public spaces of non-professionals and privilege private actors in PPPs. Therefore, there is a need to increase effective discourse between empowered spaces which make legal policy decisions (e.g., parliament) and public spaces of non-professionals (e.g., forums consisting of the general citizenry such as augmented LWCs that ensure stronger representation). These spaces can be bridged through discussion of water governance which crosses boundaries, bridging human and non-human beings, as well as existing agents and those yet to exist. Empowered spaces might have civility and common interests, but discourse usually involves market-friendly terms because counterviews currently do not have a meaningful place in deliberation.

Effective deliberative systems need a public space for transmission of concerns to empowered spaces. Yet how can this chasm be bridged? Stevenson and Dryzek argue that it can be done through discursive representation and activism (in this case, activism directed against water commodification). Changes resulting from communication between public spheres and empowered spaces can occur slowly due to norm shifts and subsequent shifting of the balance of discourses.[135] Issues that arise in common ownership of water structures, such as a tragedy of the commons scenario, would be avoided altogether as open, critical and reflexive discourse pre-emptively situates the democratic system to be cognizant of actors (human and non-human, extant and yet-to-be-born) and water scarcity.

I shall explain more fully in Chapter 4 that deliberative democratic water governance is constantly in flux as present and future actors engage in critical reflexive dialogue about ownership and distribution. Such open and critical discussions, as a perpetual process, are similar to Amartya Sen's consideration of justice as something in continual discussion in a participatory and public manner.[136] In *The Idea of Justice*, Sen explains the notion of 'Public Reason', of actors coming together to openly, honestly and rationally discuss all manner of ideas with the outcome being, possibly, a new creative path and conclusion to justice issues, as opposed to 'changing' surface-level issues that do not dent structural injustice.[137] Sen's argument that justice is best actualized in a participatory and public way fits nicely in a scheme of common ownership because it enables actors to be just that – *active*. Common ownership involves actors engaging with each other, be it individuals with individuals, collectives with collectives, institutions with institutions, and all kinds of dialogue in between. Such deliberation is proactive and about instrumental values (e.g., distribution) and intrinsic values (e.g., culture). The discourses within this deliberation would be deemed by Stevenson and Dryzek to be 'Green Radicalism', that is, discourses which elevate human rights, justice and equity over short-term economic values and 'infinite' growth.[138]

3.4 Conclusion

Looking to forthcoming chapters, we need to ask what impedes people's access to this most vital of resources, and we must look at broader wasteful processes that contribute to water injustice. How we govern water is ineluctably political, always bound up with questions of social, economic and political justice. I contend that such questions of socioenvironmental justice, as I identify in Chapter 4, can be helpfully conceptualized in terms of 'ecological space' in the sense developed by Tim Hayward. Ecological space is not only the resource itself, but all the time, space and effort that transformed that prior 'pure natural phenomena' into a resource.[139] In the case of water, we can consider the time, space, effort and energy that makes water safely consumable.

Ecological space captures the whole of human interaction with the environment, space and planet on which we reside. We will see in Chapters 4 and 5 that in deliberative democratic systems created by, and promoted through, discourse in democratic institutions, actors recognize the energy and concomitant waste associated with making a natural resource useable. The egalitarian distribution of water and, at a greater level, ecological space, is then a 'living' system that makes and remakes itself in a critical way. The uncritical economic view associated with property ought to be replaced by, as economist Nicholas Georgescu-Roegen and Hayward explain, a 'biophysical' view. The free market relies on an assumption of an 'indefinite expansion of productive economic activity', or infinite growth, which cannot be accommodated by a finite resource base.[140] This contradiction requires a shift from the economic view to the biophysical view of 'ecological space'.

For instance, whereas an economic view would frame the transformation of coal into energy as production, biophysics frames it as dissipation of natural resources and recognizes the pollution involved in the process. Whereas an economic view considers water as something to be made 'efficient' in the market, regardless of exploitation in a variety of forms, the ecological view considers the need for an *equal* share of natural resources, such as water, of utmost importance. For Hayward, the distribution of ecological space must be of an equal share in terms of opportunity to access, not a share that is, in Lockean terms, 'enough'. One could argue, as David Miller does, that the free-market would determine equal distribution of a natural resource (e.g., water);[141] however, genuinely free markets do not exist – they are all chimerical, all mixtures of demands that determine market pricing.

Common ownership of water as common territory can work against water injustices that intersect with exploitation, distribution, property and politics. Furthermore, using ecological space to frame the complexity of water governance underscores how water injustices are inexorably structural. Building on these insights, I shall develop a systematic relationship between water, justice, collective action and deliberative democracy in Chapters 4 and 5. First, though, I will explicate injustice in the context of freshwater commodification and explain socioenvironmental justice of fresh water in Chapter 4.

4

Water Justice as Socioenvironmental Justice

Humanity will face freshwater scarcity as this century progresses. Water use grew twice as fast as the global human population last century, and an increasing number of regions around the world are facing, or will face, scarcity.[1] Four billion people face water scarcity at least one month out of the year.[2] Scarcity makes water valuable for commodifiers as an investment vehicle; it emboldens the currency of commodification. In this chapter, I build on the critical and normative work done in Chapters 1–3 to make a case for water justice as socioenvironmental justice. The injustices that can and do attach to fresh water are not reducible to merely distributional wrongs or injustices; they are political harms as markers of a failing democracy, and water injustice is a structural harm. I build on the literature of power dynamics from Iris Marion Young and David Schlosberg to argue that water injustice is structural, involving mis- and mal-recognition and political exclusion. Moreover, I introduce the argument that water injustice, including commodification, reflects the erosion of democratic structures because private actors make decisions about the vital resource without any meaningful deliberation from citizens, a relation that manifests itself as domination.

In this chapter, I ask critical ethical questions regarding water justice to serve as a bridge to Chapter 5, where I explicate the protection of rights to water through legal means and political activism. Does the importance of water for human life make it unsuitable for certain types of ownership or notions of justice? Is water actually special at all, and does it fall into a prescribed ethical structure? It is the task of this chapter to clarify such questions while providing a normative and ideological base for the engaged philosophy of water justice movements. As I explained in Chapter 2, water commodification undermines democracy and democratic institutions, and treats people as objects for profit, citizens only as consumers. I will explain in this chapter that water justice frames social and environmental justice as *socioenvironmental* justice. Here, justice is a process and practice of constant improvement through democratic deliberation, instead of a rigid state. Enacting socioenvironmental justice is best conceived as a forward-looking process to address and change pressing matters of water ownership and distribution; however, more importantly, it addresses non-distributional, relational types of injustice that are political harms, and which are not as extensively explicated in the current literature.

In Chapters 2 and 3, I laid the foundation to explain that commonly owned and communally controlled water is the most just arrangement from the standpoint of social and environmental concerns, applying to the human and non-human, extant and not-yet-existing together. In this chapter, I extend this argument to the political realm. I will explain that water justice should be the engagement with, and promotion of, ideas that political philosopher James Tully calls 'glocalism' and 'diverse citizenship', as opposed to 'modern citizenship'.[3] I will conclude that water injustice is a harbinger of receding democracy, of the erosion of democratic rights and a weakening of democratic institutions.

4.1.1 Water justice as socioenvironmental justice

Water justice does not only refer to matters of distribution and access; water justice movements do not cease once water is equitably, physically distributed. In this section, I argue that water justice is best understood and pursued within a broader framework of socioenvironmental justice. In my view, injustices that attach to fresh water are not reducible to merely distributional wrongs, harms or injustices; instead, there are stark political harms attached to water injustice. In Section 4.2, I will identify such harms as domination – lack of recognition, participation and deliberation (i.e., democratic inclusion) of citizens in democratic water governance – which drives water injustice. Although one can identify issues of water deprivation as distributional injustices, a structural injustice approach to water distribution and ownership issues can get to the injustices that entangle and influence such deprivation. Such an approach, akin to those employed by social political philosophers such as Iris Marion Young[4] and David Schlosberg,[5] identifies the fundamental power dynamics and power differences between actors which form power structures. The differences in power dynamics can be traced to water commodification and, broadly, the social and political structures of water control. Young and Schlosberg can offer insight on such structural injustices, but they do not identify water issues specifically, so I will build on their ideas of structural injustice.

Recall Section 1.4 where I posited that unjust water arrangements are structural; responsibility or blame cannot be pinned on one individual, actor, state or institution. Actors form a vast web, as will be evident in Chapter 5 in struggles for public water against local and international actors in Cochabamba and throughout India, fighting water commodification and the construction of dams, respectively.[6] By identifying water injustice as a structural issue, questions over control of water ought to follow.

As I will explain in the following section, as well as with real-world cases in Chapter 5, a more democratic and participatory approach to water justice that utilizes discursive democracy (as Dryzek and Schlosberg have developed) might be able to resist and reverse water injustice. What does 'participatory' mean here, though? For Schlosberg, participation is one of three necessary parts of environmental justice, along with distribution and recognition. 'Distribution' does not necessarily include water itself, but instead the distribution of 'equity … of environmental risk'; 'recognition' involves a 'diversity of … participants and experiences in affected communities' and is pluralistic; 'participation' involves 'political processes which create and manage environmental policy'.[7] Schlosberg's accounts of participation, distribution and recognition are salient in that they must be considered when thinking of water justice, but he does not ask questions related to water, and he does not sufficiently explain the political harm of domination stemming from structural water injustice. I will connect his arguments to the harms of water injustice that I identify, and I will argue that a systemic deliberative democratic approach should be utilized to redress such harms.

4.1.2 Participatory water justice: the importance of recognition and inclusion

Water justice discussions, especially those located within the framework of liberal theory, over-emphasize distribution to the neglect of normative harms, such as the lack of democratic governance in decision-making.[8] Maldistribution is caused by social-structural relations of social power that a 'distribution paradigm' lens cannot capture. By looking at water injustice through a structural lens, we move beyond the 'what' of water justice (i.e., the quantitative, physical distribution of the resource) and get at the 'how' (i.e., the qualitative) and 'why' (i.e., political harms) of the structure. By addressing such questions, we can better see that water justice pertains to socioenvironmental concerns because there are important social and political power relationships which contribute to such justice (or injustice). As such, ownership structures, governance and related decision-making contribute to water justice. As was explicated in Chapter 3, just water ownership frames water as territory, not property; these two terms have different rights and responsibilities attached to them, but the baggage of 'property' is ineluctably instrumental, capitalist and transactional.

Conceiving of water injustice as structural puts the spotlight on power relations that shape decision-making and governance, and it prompts us to imagine and develop more just alternatives to water-as-property. Stewardship, as well as democratic recognition and participation in water governance, are a few alternatives. We can look to critical research of water governance and legislation development in Canada to see the gaps in development, to show where water justice is falling short. Bakker and co-workers argue that exclusion from government processes – as in a paucity of recognition and participation in policy and decision-making concerning water – and a lack of water security are intricately linked.[9] Their research, powerful in its analysis of water injustices against Indigenous peoples, argues that 'justice-as-recognition should underpin justice-as-inclusion (full participation in decision-making processes)'.[10] In the case of a lack of recognition of Indigenous rights, 'Current injustices in regulatory decision-making and water access are likely to persist.'[11] They argue, for example, that the British Columbian government, with regard to its relatively recently published Water Sustainability Act (WSA), has committed an injustice with said act as it did not thoroughly and meaningfully engage with the Indigenous community in its creation.[12] There was no participatory aspect of developing or adopting the WSA, despite regulations in the Constitution of Canada and the UN Commission on Human Rights (2005) (and sub-committee on the Promotion and Protection of Human Rights Working Group on Indigenous Peoples) stipulating consultation and free, prior and informed consent (FPIC), respectively. This example shows that mere surface-level engagement by the state is insufficient for justice, neither supporting recognition nor underpinning inclusion. Bakker and co-workers' analysis underscores the procedural and systemic harms committed by the British Columbian government that should be rectified by deeper deliberative democratic mechanisms. We cannot depend solely on the state to prefigure their consultation and recognition methods, as Bakker and colleagues make clear; instead, concerted pressure by way of deliberative democracy, made real by water justice movements at the glocal level (see Chapter 5), should fill the gaps in water governance.

Water justice requires recognition and participation of all parties and, in circumstances involving colonialist destruction of Indigenous lands and ways of life, traditional, local knowledge ought to be at the forefront of justice.[13] Bakker and co-workers explain that water ownership and distribution, in such cases, must be done exclusively on the terms of the Indigenous community or in a co-management system as is seen in the Northwest Territories, where Indigenous and territorial governments work together in water sustainability, in a strategy which privileges Indigenous knowledge and explicitly recognizes Indigenous rights.[14] Citizens are then recognized as being more than objects of profit, as a commodified mode would have them; instead, people are fully fleshed in their humanity. Recognition and participation exist separately from distribution because they are not 'things' to be distributed like natural resources or wealth and income; they are relationships and social norms. In addition, recognition means the preservation of distinct cultures and peoples, resisting homogenization that erases people's cultures and social networks.

Water justice requires the participatory dimension of deliberative democracy. A critic might contend that representative democracy, which I criticized in Chapter 3, suffices to be participatory and inclusive. However, current systems of governance are reductive in that representation does not fully speak for the plural, vibrant and diverse makeup of the *demos*. Citizens reflexively deliberate in a variety of forums – not necessarily formally in a congress or parliament – which concretely make them active stakeholders in discussions about water. As such, 'representation' is connected to said stakeholders, and to engage in stakeholder discussions such as deliberative minipublics (a forum of 20–500 participants), consisting in deliberative polling and citizen juries is, itself, discursive inclusion.

I argued in Chapter 3 that minipublics may hold potential for democratizing water and overcoming democratic deficits of commodification, in expanding democratic deliberation through active and glocal situatedness and involvement. Deliberative democracy, as political scientists Walter Baber and Robert Bartlett identify, is a 'reflexive practice', and citizen juries might help further the legitimacy of informal and radical deliberation through polarizing, reflexive contestation.[15] They note that 'enclave deliberation', or deliberation amongst and between actors who have been historically unrecognized and excluded from popular discourse, might in fact strengthen deliberative democracy by developing neglected ideas. This group polarization 'promotes the development of positions that would otherwise be invisible, silenced, or squelched in general debate'.[16] Such discourse gaps provide space or 'frontiers of disagreement' for the water justice activism groups that I explain in Chapter 5 to act, manoeuvre and insinuate water recommoning efforts.[17] To add, participatory, deliberative methods have been found to build accountability, trust and community between citizens. Lam and co-workers found that participatory, discursive development between transdisciplinary graduate research students, professional researchers with the Ecological Farmers Association of Ontario (EFAO), and participatory farmer researchers with EFAO, built community and trust, and strengthened accountability between participants to communicate effectively over a common goal: sustainable and ecological farming.[18] There is no reason to think such democratizing and participatory processes cannot be instantiated in water justice too, as water governance is similarly (arguably even more) transboundary as farming.[19]

4.1.3 Difficulties of democratizing water justice: social movements, recognition and human rights

I must acknowledge that democratizing water justice can be difficult to initiate and institute because the state and water commodification companies are powerful, intertwined actors. As such, globally focused and organized social movements must be careful to not be co-opted by ideas which they work to overthrow and replace. I want to acknowledge difficulties posed by and for such transnationally focused organizations to underline my normative turn to deliberation as a more locally, communally situated water governance.

The argument for water to be recognized as a human right, as some globally focused water justice organizations support, is sometimes rooted in their influence by other NGOs and states. The conception of water as a human right, where all stakeholders have a right to water, has led to private interests controlling water because the impetus for creating water NGOs came *after* the formation of the World Trade Organization.[20] The recognition of water as a human right with no meaningful input from the public left commonly owned water vulnerable to commodification. For instance, water organizations such as the World Water Council (WWC) and Global Water Partnership (GWP) had at least 40 per cent of their stakeholders from private corporations.[21] Clearly, participation from all relevant stakeholders is severely lacking. The public sector, as citizens or institutions, does not have enough support, especially at the transnational level; instead, private corporations own and distribute water as they see fit.

Recognizing water as a human right would then be part of the rule of law, which is why industry organizations, influenced by private interests, have generally endorsed this thin human rights approach. Organizations which might have initially been conceived to criticize such liberal powers (e.g., WWC and GWP) found themselves tied up with them. As D'Souza argues, movements and organizations that should be more Marxist in their tendencies (i.e., critiquing universal rights as being tied to an exploitative economy where the state, composed of the bourgeoise, would not do anything despite recognizing such universal rights) are in reality liberal (i.e., in favour of individualized private property, the rule of law, citizenship as conditional on being a member of a state, and the state as a framework for capitalist markets).[22]

Water justice movements must then be critical of structural injustices in property, unrepresentative or non-discursive government or governance, and exclusionary, undemocratic systems and movements. Such movements must inquire about various actors within and around water justice, especially those who might argue for water as a human right without any sense of communal participation, recognition or distribution of water. D'Souza explains that when one argues for anything as a human right, they invoke their moral sentiment to make their argument; however, as she argues, when one then calls for said human right to be recognized as law, one reverts to the liberal principle one started with because human rights law is 'a formal right with little material equality'.[23]

As I have explained in previous chapters, safeguards against commodification and associated harms of water injustices (e.g., weakening democracy, treating citizens as customers/consumers) can be put in place to maintain the integrity of a human right to water. In the next section, I shall explicate the harms of water injustice without such democratic safeguards, beginning with domination and the erosion of democracy.

4.2 The political harm of water injustice: the weakening of democracy

Water injustice is made possible by a context of insufficiently democratic institutions and processes, which allows private interests to commodify water. In this section, I argue that water injustice is a political harm in the form of domination: domination over other humans and non-humans, and domination of the political order by undemocratic systems and actors. My argument about water injustice builds on Iris Marion Young's conception of domination in political systems, as well as political theorist Sharon Krause's definition of environmental domination. I aim to show that water justice is not merely a distributive injustice but is also a political harm insofar as it instantiates a lack of democratic decision-making and democratic governance. This lack of democratic participation (i.e., recognition and inclusion) contributes to democratic deficits, drives water commodification and makes citizens into strictly consumers. Water injustice affects responsibilities between citizens, corporations and the state, and fundamentally changes normative frameworks. Finally, I argue that water injustice as a political harm consists in democratic deficits which foment domination through path dependency and the entrenchment of power dynamics with regard to water commodification through what environmental literature scholar Rob Nixon has termed 'slow violence'.[24]

Young provides a jumping-off point to discuss domination. In Section 4.1 I explained that, for Young, structural injustice exists when social processes put large groups of people under systematic threat of domination or deprivation of the means to develop and exercise their capacities. At the same time, these harmful processes enable others – in the case of this argument, water commodifiers – to dominate or have a wide range of opportunities for developing and exercising capacities available to themselves. Water injustice (e.g., domination through water commodification) denies people the ability to 'exercise their capacities' as democratic citizens in the state whose voices are minimized by water-commodification capital.[25] In other words, those actors with the most capital, such as money or clean freshwater holdings, steer deliberation and drown out the voices of those without such capital.

Young's conception of domination is valuable for establishing political harms of commodification as dominative. Her definition, as well as Val Plumwood's clarification of domination rooted in neo-Cartesianism and Taiaiake Alfred's argument for domination as economic, instrumental and property-based, all add to my argument that commodification commits political harms.

To further pin down a definition of domination that builds on Young's political and capacity dimensions, and Plumwood's and Alfred's analyses of ecological domination from Chapter 2, it is helpful to further cement the term 'domination' according to Krause's recent work on environmental domination. Krause considers environmental domination inseparable from politics, economics and culture and, crucially for an ethic of water that aims for non-anthropocentrism, she extends discussions of domination from humans to non-human beings too.[26] Her definition of environmental domination helps establish a relationship between justice, politics and the environment which informs my argument that water justice is socioenvironmental justice.

Krause establishes a definition of domination with two main features: '(1) being subject to insufficiently checked or *unlimited power* and (2) being subject to *exploitation*, meaning treated as a mere instrument for the profit or power of another without regard to one's own well-being.'[27] As was introduced in Chapters 2 and 3, domination exemplified by commodification (and water injustice in general) is an unlimited power by water commodifiers to control and exploit this most vital resource; in addition, such control and exploitation is political *and* environmental, over humans *and* non-humans. To this point, Krause offers valuable clarification by defining environmental domination as a type of domination that 'transpire[s] in and through human interactions with more-than-human parts of nature. One familiar example in the context of interhuman relations is how poor and marginalized people disproportionately bear the brunt of environmental damage.'[28] Environmental domination on Krause's account is about unfettered 'power that lacks principled, institutional constraints' that lack entitlements to prevent exploitation.[29]

For Krause, environmental domination, which I identify in commodification, is a matter of unfreedom; environmental action does, indeed, do justice to humans and non-humans, but it also helps humans and non-humans live freer lives – lives filled with *choice*, outside the bondage of harms from commodification.[30] Krause identifies harms of environmental domination similar to those I explicated in Chapters 2 and 3, specifically in path dependencies, as she writes of the 'ironlike inescapability of the environmentally damaging practices that sustain daily life for everyone in modern societies'.[31] It will be fleshed-out in Chapter 5 that water commodifiers make themselves out to be the only choice for clean fresh water, despite costs or harms to the environment, citizens or democracy.

Commodification presents a tension between private investment, control and democracy. The more capital one has, the greater their voice in the water ownership and distribution discourse, to the detriment of democratic mechanisms. Capital naturally pools to fewer actors than there are citizens, so the voices and actions of the wealthy (e.g., commodifiers) grow louder, creating a positive feedback loop for privileged actors. Policies are driven by those actors with the most capital (i.e., water holdings and influence) which further embeds inequalities. As Stevenson and Dryzek observe, 'this inequality clashes with the formal political equality of citizens in liberal democracies and the pluralist assumption that groups can equally influence the direction of development; it also clashes with the deliberative democratic ideal principle of equality among deliberating individuals'.[32] Water injustice manifests as undemocratic and, possibly, authoritarian, a political arrangement wholly unsuited for just water ownership.[33] Moreover, when municipalities or states open the door to the injustice of water commodification and sell to private actors, dystopian consequences such as school closures due to water shortages, and the buying back of water from private actors who bought water for relative pennies on the dollar, have occurred. For example, the Tambourine Mountain state school in Queensland, Australia, in December 2019 had to close due to water shortages stemming from the state's sale of water to bottling plants owned by Coca-Cola.[34]

Young's definition adds a deeper political dimension to Krause's, where domination 'consists [of] institutional conditions which inhibit or prevent people from participating in determining their actions or the conditions of their actions'.[35] This definition is helpful to capture structural injustice, but it does not quite capture the state of *unfreedom* of water injustice. Such unfreedom is built on by critical theorists such as Rainer Forst, who contend that justice is non-domination, transnational and discursive.[36] Building on Young and the critical theorist argument, agents are prevented from acting in certain ways, such as changing unjust structures, because a multitude of individuals and groups – government and business institutions, leaders and policymakers, and a generally apathetic populace – perpetuate water injustice.

The account of political domination sketched here, drawn from Krause and Young, helps us to better see the sense in which water injustice signals, ultimately, a condition of social and political domination. Under the umbrella of 'domination', water injustice involves oppression, a 'powerlessness' explained by Young in the 'five faces of oppression'.[37] Powerlessness is characterized by a lack of democratic decision-making, authority and 'sense of self' that the most powerful have.[38] Political domination is thus the underlying condition that leads to water deprivation; a lack of decision-making power at the political level perpetuates domination over citizen's lives and capacities when water cannot be accessed. In an example I analyse further in Section 5.2.2.2, those denied water in Detroit are the poorest citizens who are subjected to water injustice. Such citizens' impoverishment is exacerbated by being unable to participate in democratic processes; considering distribution, they do not have adequate water, but they also do not have adequate or sufficient democratic recognition or inclusion. Therefore, water commodification is also an issue of control. Individuals, families, corporations, or any such actor of a certain monetary worth in control of water become a state unto themselves; in fact, those who control water or possess immense wealth can make themselves 'remote' from the socioenvironmental consequences of water commodification by living far from the source of their wealth – water – and cross the globe totally *unlike* a state. Such actors become mobile states, roving parasitically.

4.2.1 Water and democratic governance

As I explained in Chapter 3, while socioenvironmental justice requires reflexive[39] and deliberative discourse among relevant actors within a location (e.g., municipality, state), water commodifiers such as Nestlé (as will be explained in Chapter 5) belong to no such locations; they are unbound and do not engage in deliberation with all relevant actors in democratic systems. A remedy will require democracy of a more direct and diverse kind that also involves institutional transformation. The forms of democratic activities I propose that can best serve as a bulwark against water commodification are chiefly deliberative and are related to what thinkers such as James Tully identify as 'diverse', not modern, citizenship. Water issues, I contend, are global and without boundaries, but instituting democracy at the global level is unfeasible and undesirable as it does not meet my criteria for inclusive, participatory democratic water governance. Thus, the state level is important as an intermediary between local and global levels. The state system does not need to be discarded; instead, Anna Stilz's broadened definition of the state can be utilized to include any governing body that makes laws and has the power to enforce them.[40] To make explicit, it is reasonable to argue that social movements should work within a framework of water as territory to transform unjust commodification systems. Recommoning could provide a focal point for water justice movements. It is my position that water justice activism should begin at the local level and move bottom-up to the state then global levels.

As will be illuminated through examples in Chapter 5, local movements for water justice typify the collective struggle against commodification. To better see why struggles against water commodification, such as campaigns aimed at recommoning, are necessarily collective in character, it is helpful to consider movements organized around accessing particular social or natural resources. Social collaborations that are known as 'collective consumption movements' offer one such. These movements have to work with the state due to the scale of the resource, the capital investment needed to distribute it to all actors, and the public nature of the resource itself (i.e., need for regulation). However, collective consumption movements are not as expansive or broad as, say, those during the Cochabamba Water War; they are more localized yet still thoroughly political. Movements against dams in India, as well as Indigenous water protector movements, are collective consumption movements because they politicize anti-commodification struggles. Moreover, they make clear the benefits of democratized water governance and reveal the resource *itself* to be something political. The resistance is, then, a political struggle and process. As political philosopher Monique Deveaux succinctly writes of collective consumption movements:

> In their interactions with government over the provision of these goods, collective consumption movements expose and challenge discriminatory practices and other obstacles that prevent particular social groups (such as low-caste individuals, ethnic minorities, and the urban chronic poor) from securing access to social entitlements. In other words, they *politicize* access to public utilities and services, and by extension, poverty-producing social relations.[41]

An example of direct political action that comes from these movements is the illegal reconnecting of utilities for those not receiving water, and the destruction of water meters, in Soweto, Johannesburg, South Africa to circumvent water allotments. Water activist Silumko Radebe, interviewed by Cristy Clark, explains the erosion of the sense of community post-water commodification in Soweto: 'Before the meters, neighbours bonded through mutual hospitality. Now people hesitate to invite people into their homes. What if their visitors flush the toilet and use up the household's last remaining water? Even putting on the kettle is a fraught exercise when you are out of credit.'[42] Commodification erected barriers between citizens, yet these same citizens worked to tear down barriers through direct political action: the destruction of water meters and the installation of illegal, unmetered yard taps by 'Struggle Plumbers'.[43] In these examples, the economic and instrumental view of citizens merely as consumers, as is the case with water commodification, is undermined; the domination by those who control water is directly subverted by those who need the resource.

Collective consumption movements play an indispensable role in instantiating water justice and politically transforming water governance rooted in citizenship. In addition, collective consumption movements, or any effective movement and employed strategy against commodification, operate in the state as mediator and interlocutor between local and global levels. To clarify this position, it is necessary that I explain two types of citizenship explained by James Tully: modern citizenship and diverse citizenship. For Tully, modern citizenship is a 'civil', law-based form of citizenship, and diverse citizenship is a 'civic' *activity*-based citizenship.[44] This kind of civic citizenry is a practice which does not hinge on hegemonic, dominant and exploitative institutions to grant citizenry; one becomes a civic citizen by participating in civic life. Moreover, for Tully, civil citizenship is bound by institutions and exists only within the formal state apparatus, yet civic citizenship is substantive and fluid, always existing within 'relationships' that are developing, interdependent and interactive.[45] Tully's criticism of modern citizenship and markets mirrors those from Plumwood and Schlosberg in Chapter 2, specifically that capital homogenizes pluralistic world views and makes invisible those actors who cannot participate in markets – those without capital.[46]

Tully's account of diverse citizenship, upon which I draw here, 'is associated with a diversity or multiplicity of different *practices* of citizenship in the West and non-West'.[47] Further, this type of citizenship 'is not described in terms of universal institutions and historical processes, but in terms of grass roots democratic or civic *activities* of the "governed" (the people) in the specific relationship of governance in specific locales and the glocal activities of networking with other local practices'.[48] Here, Tully's conception of diverse citizenship supports deliberative democratic principles because this type of active citizenship requires 'listening to the other sides and for silenced voices, of responding in turn, negotiating in good faith and being bound by results, experimenting with the amended or transformed relationship'.[49] When instantiated by water justice movements, this engaged citizenship produces itself by movements' very acts of resistance, deliberatively and reflexively acting against water commodifiers. As Tully explains, modern citizenship is a historical process of modernization and colonization, of moulding states into representatively democratic, capitalistic and technocratic institutions, unwieldy and Argus-eyed towards private property.[50] However, diverse citizenship is not so Western- and Euro-centric; it is a pluralistic amalgam of Western and non-Western practices of citizenship. The practice or *praxis* of this participatory citizenship is not only local or global but 'glocal', a type of citizenship that is a 'local' practice which can take different forms, globally, in different locations.[51]

Tully contrasts diverse citizenship with modern citizenship:

> Whereas modern citizenship focuses on citizenship as a universalizable legal status underpinned by institutions and processes of rationalization that

enable and circumscribe the possibility of civil activity (an institutional/ universal orientation), diverse citizenship focuses on the singular civic activities and improvisations of the governed in any practice of government and the diverse ways these are more or less institutionalized or blocked in different contexts (a civic activity/contextual orientation). Citizenship is not a status given by institutions of the modern constitutional state and international law, but negotiated practices in which one becomes a citizen through participation.[52]

Thus, in Tully's view, modern citizenship 'subalternizes' different pluralist accounts of citizenship and replaces them as *the* standard for citizenship.[53] On the other hand, though, diverse citizenship pluralizes other types of citizenship as 'singular and historically contingent' and critically contrasts different theories in terms of norms and perspectives.[54] According to Tully, diverse citizenship 'de-universalizes' modern citizenship and 'de-subalternizes' other forms of citizenship, circumventing domination.

This more pluralistic understanding of citizenship has ramifications for the relationship between capital and ecology, and they inform the type of citizenship (diverse) in which water justice movements participate. Tully identifies private corporation 'personhood' as the cornerstone of modern citizenship, writing, 'Private corporations in the late nineteenth century gained recognition as "persons" with the corresponding civil liberty of private autonomy (negative liberty). Thus, paradoxically from a civic perspective, the first right of modern citizenship is to participate in the private realm and to be protected from interference by the citizenry and its representatives.'[55] Modern civil citizenship is realized in 'historical dispossession of people from access to land and resources through their local laws and non-capitalist economic organizations; the Enclosure of the commons ... the concentration and the imposition of modern legal systems of property law, contract law, labour law and trade law that constitute and protect the system of free markets and free trade'.[56] The markers of modern citizenship that Tully expounds upon have been realized in instances of water commodification explained throughout this book and will be critically identified in Chapter 5.

In my view, a proper response to modern citizenship and water commodifiers would be to *act otherwise*, to turn away from the not-quite-inexorable gravitational pull of private property and embody one's citizenship.[57] Water justice activism works in such a way against, in Nixon's words, 'slow violence', a gradual yet dynamic violence against humans and the natural world by entrenched actors. Although the slow violence of water injustice might be hard to see, it creeps and replaces democracy, instilling undemocratic path dependencies such as water commodification. Such slow violence, though, has been resisted and reversed in transformative ways of acting otherwise against the path dependent, undemocratic hegemony of some nation-states. Take, for example, the civic citizenry and diverse citizenship of certain environmental activist movements, such as the Green Belt Movement (GBM) in Kenya. Led by Nobel Peace Prize winner Wangari Maathai, GBM resisted Kenya's authoritarianism and environmental destruction through tree planting. Intersectional yet based in Kenyan identity, GBM thrust people into the natural world to plant trees while promoting human and environmental rights and frequently clashing with Kenya's authoritarian regime. Nixon writes that the 'nation-state remains a potent actor, in societies as diverse as Kenya, Venezuela, Indonesia, China, and India ... The struggles and successes of the GBM clearly cannot be understood outside the particular dynamics of Kenya's national authoritarianism [and] cannot be viewed solely within a national frame: local and global geopolitics contributed in complex, often unpredictable ways.'[58] Water justice movements borrow from these other intersectional environmental movements which are local, move through the state and convey their message globally with support from actors around the world.

Water justice movements stimulate new dialogues between activists fighting for water justice, strengthening those actors resisting domination and oppression as a 'consciousness raising collective', in the words of feminist philosopher Amy Allen.[59] Activists show that path dependencies can be resisted; they 'denaturalize forms of social life that have up to now seemed natural and necessary'.[60] Such movements foster dialogues about the inextricable convergence of racial, gender and environmental injustice in water injustice, as seen in, for example, Flint, Michigan.[61] Furthermore, decentralized non-profit community organizations such as The Human Utility in Detroit and Baltimore in the United States, and Wellington Water Watchers and the Council of Canadians in the Guelph-Wellington region of Ontario in Canada, work for such water justice actively and educatively, making explicit fundamental rights to water while working against the structural domination of water commodification.[62] Such organizations work in communities, at the local level, while also working for change at the state level; from the state level, the message of water justice can be dispersed to the global or, more appropriately, glocal level. Crucially, water justice activists show that there is another way to live, in transforming systems of water injustice.

4.3 Conclusion

I made two main claims in this chapter. First, I argued that water justice should be considered as part of broader efforts to secure socioenvironmental justice. Greater socioenvironmental justice requires there to be no structural barriers blocking access, but this is not to say it is a distributional issue alone. Water justice is obtained in deliberative (more than representative) democratic governance systems, while being treated as territory (i.e., stewardship and non-anthropocentric rights and responsibilities) and not property (i.e., myopic, economic and instrumental, and anthropocentric rights and responsibilities). Such water justice reflexively remakes itself over time, qualities that I have explained in this chapter and Chapter 3 as being crucial components of democratic water governance.

Second, I argued that political domination and a paucity of democracy play significant roles in giving rise to water injustices such as commodification. Water injustice augers the weakening of democratic governance mechanisms, and it is a political harm which takes the form of domination. As a political harm, water injustice contributes to a democratic deficit. A lack of decision-making and democratic governance are deliberative democratic deficits (which includes recognition and inclusion), signalling the political harms of water commodification.

Having explained what water injustice broadly consists in, I now turn to the task of bringing water justice into the world. The clarion call for water justice arises from many sources, and the job of Chapter 5 is to provide clarity, and a roadmap, for how to resist water commodification and instill public water ownership and distribution in communities. We can investigate and possibly use established governing bodies that provide suggestions on instantiating socioenvironmental water justice. For example, the Transnational Institute and

Corporate Europe Observatory suggest the following steps to enable a social, political and economic environment conducive to public water:

1. Sustaining and expanding innovative and participatory public water delivery models around the world, for instance through international public-public partnerships.
2. Canceling the crippling debt of developing countries in order to free public funds for expanding access to water.
3. The World Bank and other IFIs must end privatisation conditions for financial support to those requesting it.
4. Wealthy northern governments must increase funding flows and end the pro-privatisation bias.
5. Enshrining the human right to water in international legal instruments, including a UN convention.
6. Exempting water from the GATS negotiations (services liberalization talks within the World Trade Organisation) and other trade agreements.
7. Renegotiating bilateral and regional trade and investment agreements which enable private water corporations to claim undue 'compensation' from public authorities via arbitration cases.[63]

Indeed, in 2010, the UN General Assembly adopted a resolution recognizing water and sanitation as human rights and two months later, the UN Human Rights Council produced a full report on the meaning of this resolution and what it requires of government. However, I stress that the norms which undergird these seven steps may lack legal and political force. Indeed, it has been the aim of this book to provide such groundwork theoretically, but action, through a blueprint, is also required to bring about water justice. The instruments and agreements explained above may potentially undermine socioenvironmental justice and democracy because they can be undergirded by pro-privatization mechanisms.

International agreements that privilege private actors and interests over the needs of the commons, such as investor-state dispute settlements (ISDS) that tie states to private interests and favour commodification, have hastened socioenvironmental injustices. Promulgated through international state and corporate agreements such as the North American Free Trade Agreement (NAFTA) and early versions of its successor, the United States-Mexico-Canada Agreement (USMCA), ISDS were undemocratic because they were initially created by, and worked exclusively for, private actors; additionally, they contributed to the dependence and partiality of states and legal systems in the private sector, to the detriment of the populace – the commons.[64] There is space for communal, anti-corporate, pro-democracy movements here too, though, because the ratified version of the USMCA had its initial Chapter 11 (which hinged on corporatist, privational and commodification language) eliminated completely between Canada and the United States and greatly weakened between the United States and Mexico.

As I explained in this chapter and will continue in Chapter 5, the erosion of democracy, environmental rights, and related safeguards (such as judiciary independence) against commodification by pro-commodification actors is legion and resists water justice movements, but the antidote should be in re-invigorating democracy through reflexive discourse and participatory philosophy and action. In Chapter 5 we will see such strategy in Guelph-Wellington, Detroit, Cochabamba, Grenoble and India. Without implementation, critical analysis and the provision of a partial theory of what socioenvironmental justice in water requires is inert, yet the socioenvironmental justice that has been developed in this chapter is a *living* one. Thus, critical analysis and theorizing about socioenvironmental justice must be married with action. Yet how can such justice be acted on? This is one of the questions for Chapter 5, as law, politics and social movements are the matrix of theory and action that ought to resist water commodification.

5

The Protection of Rights to Water Through Law, Politics and Social Movements

In Chapter 4, I argued that water injustice is a political harm which manifests as domination; therefore, water injustice can spur political protest movements and mobilize citizens opposed to water commodification. I have argued that water justice, understood and pursued in a broader framework of socioenvironmental justice, is structural. As such, the structural nature of water injustice means that there is diminished access to communally owned fresh drinking water, less or no say in governance structures around water, and the commodification of water. I also asserted that we ought to communally work within unjust structures to initiate water justice through reflexive, democratic mechanisms.

Academic analysis in the fields of water rights, justice and activism has burgeoned over the past decade through work done by Karen Bakker,[1] Joanna Robinson,[2] Mangala Subramaniam,[3] and Farhana Sultana and Alex Loftus,[4] amongst many others. I build on their work and contribute to freshwater ethics and justice from the point of view of engaged philosophy, in a more explicitly normative register. My project takes the baton from such research by developing deeper normative analyses about the nature of socioenvironmental injustice and deliberative democracy in water governance. These philosophically political critiques and theories, developed in a different register, complement the existing literature.

In this chapter, I will utilize Jonathan Wolff's form of engaged philosophy to illuminate the normative harms and injustices that water justice movements protest. By engaging with real-world cases, I shall explain that deliberative democratic laws and institutions (informal and formal), and participatory and bottom-up social movements, are needed to protect and solidify rights to water through law, politics and social movements. I draw on commoning research done by Cristy Clark, Silvia Federici, Elinor Ostrom, Vandana Shiva and others to argue that a 'recommoning' of water, as a meta-normative value, should be the driving force of social movements to actualize water justice and resist water commodification.[5] I build on their work to underline more prominently, through normative analyses, how social movements can reinvigorate deliberative democracy through recommoning and, thus, embody the democratic virtues they aim to actualize. I support my arguments with reference to real-world examples of national and transnational water agreements, water justice and activism against water injustice.

We can glean from Chapter 4 that water justice and anti-water commodification activism are *alive*. Social movements for water justice (i.e., recommoning) are precisely like the commons itself: a process.[6] They are an ouroboros. Movements make and unmake themselves, in flux yet unified and challenging the political harms of water injustices explicated most thoroughly in Chapter 2: the instrumentalization of the natural world, the domination of humans and non-humans alike, the political violence of making citizens into consumers, and the undermining of democracy. When social movements work against private actors, interests and water commodification, and *for* the recommoning of water, they work towards socioenvironmental justice and instantiate democracy. Anti-water commodification movements transform unjust structures when they work towards socioenvironmental water justice. In sum, social movements for water justice make themselves real and collaboratively build just structures in which they aspire to live and to, as stewards, pass on.

5.1 Social movements as protections for rights to water

I have explained that water injustice is a political harm which has tended to give rise to social protest movements around the world, as people seek to defend their rights to fresh water. In this section, I argue that social movements which seek to protect access, and the ways in which they resist and counter commodification in their communities, are important tools for protecting rights to fresh water.

In states with democratic institutions, water injustice is, most of the time, due to a lack of democratic (especially deliberative democratic) mechanisms and institutions, environmental rights related to water health and access, and related safeguards such as judiciary independence. I will argue, with reference to Mangala Subramaniam's definition of the 'ambivalent' state, that the antidote should be in reinvigorating democracy through reflexive discourse and participatory, active philosophy which circumvents the political harms of water injustice enabled by the ambivalent state. Alternative, bottom-up structures created by water justice movements can reinvigorate and actualize deliberative democracy.

To support my arguments in Sections 5.1 and 5.2, I use examples of informal public forums for the discussion of water rights and justice (e.g., the Alternative World Water Forum), activism for non-anthropocentric water rights, and co-operation between transnational, non-state, anti-water commodification organizations. Moreover, there are existing national and transnational environmental and water agreements which could provide a springboard for water justice movements. However, the agreements I present should only provide a guided framework for new, more localized agreements. In Section 5.3, I will expand on my argument with a critical evaluation and focus on community activism, social movements and the power of recommoning water. First, I must explain the importance of deliberative democracy, reflexive discourse and participatory philosophy and activism in social movements protecting rights to water.

5.1.1 Deliberative democracy, discursive reflexivity and participatory philosophy

Water injustice (e.g., commodification, the denial of water to those who cannot afford to pay and as will be explained in this chapter, big dam projects) abrades the scaffolding of democratic mechanisms and institutions. In Chapters 2–4, I argued that the political harms of water injustice are the result of private actors working through existing structural injustices. These actors and interests are usually remote and unattuned to the locations in which they operate – they are outside of the community yet sow anomie within the community. The social movements that I examine in this chapter, however, are bottom-up oriented, attuned to the workings of their communities and counter water injustice through reflexive discourse and participatory activism. Water commodification is generally made possible in contexts of eroding democratic institutions.

Accordingly, I argue that a rebuilding or reinvigoration of democratic structures related to the governance of natural resources, often spurred by social movements, can go a long way in shoring up rights to water.

Social movements for water justice and recommoning can (re)build democratic structures, as I will explain in Section 5.2. This process involves extensive discussion between citizens, a deliberative democracy of communication, effective justification of positions, the pursuit of mutual understanding of positions, and criticality towards coercive and deceptive language. Furthermore, sites of deliberation have expanded beyond formal institutions; so, too, as deliberative democracy theorists Selen Ercan and John Dryzek argue, democracy itself must be 'broadened' to involve communication *and listening and reflection* and must be 'deepened' to 'engage participants in ways that are indeed authentically deliberative, involving competent and reflective participation'.[7] In this chapter, I will provide a normative evaluation of different efforts around the globe to secure water justice, and the main criterion is whether such movements align with deepened democratic principles and practices.[8]

Social movements can strengthen rights to water in a variety of ways, especially when they are community-based. Let us begin with one instantiation: community forums and boards. The creation of community forums and boards, such as the Citizen Utility Boards in the United States in the 1960s and 1970s, are an example of participatory, reflexive institutions (along with co-operatives) which democratize water, hold leaders accountable and resist water commodification.[9] Such organizations and collectives – themselves social movements against water injustice – have successfully resisted commodification in the United States; civil society organizations, allied with labour unions, influenced the cancellation and reversal of water privatization in Atlanta and New Orleans.[10] In Stockton, California, a lengthy five-year legal fight instigated by community groups reversed the municipality's decision to sell the operation and maintenance of their water system to the private utility company RWE/Thames.

Social movements that resist and reverse water injustice work against commodifiers who argue that the state is 'less productive, efficient, and effective than markets'.[11] These social movements exalt deliberation and reflexivity; they promote action and the participation of manifold organizations and public interests. Of course, as I will explain further in Section 5.3, social movements against water injustice have varying levels of success. For example, although Stockton's movements eventually succeeded in reversing privatization, it was only after a protracted legal battle and five years of privatized, expensive and sub-standard water service. Sociologist Joanna Robinson contrasts the social movements and organization in Stockton in the early-to-mid-2000s with social movements which resisted proposed water privatization in Metro Vancouver in 2001.[12] Whereas the organizers in Stockton kept their frame of resistance local and narrow, those in Vancouver connected their local issues with broader global struggles against water privatization; they 'glocalized' their social movement and engaged with democratic mechanisms. In addition, they engaged with a multitude of local and transnational actors deliberatively and reflexively in public and political forums. Vancouver had no lengthy legal battles and no interstitial period of water privatization, unlike in Stockton. Robinson argues that, although both social movements reversed water privatization in their communities, Stockton's was not as successful or efficient as Vancouver because its social movements were too myopic and alienated politicians within the city, whereas Vancouver's used locally focused frames which connected with global issues along with legal opinions to frame their protests.[13] Therefore, successful movements (as will be explicated in Section 5.3) should have a glocal lens through which they make recommoning of water the ultimate goal – the embodiment of their movement's ideologies (i.e., recommoning). Furthermore, social movements that engage with deliberative democracy, reflexivity and participatory philosophy should overcome the political harms of water injustice when they actualize recommoning.

    I am not arguing that social movements are a panacea for all the ills of water injustice.[14] What I am arguing is that social movements can make and express themselves in such a way as to resist and possibly reverse water injustices due to the weaknesses or 'ambivalence' of the state opening up doors of influence. A helpful concept for understanding the weaknesses of the state's policies regarding water is Subramaniam's idea of the 'ambivalent state'. The state, as she argues, is at once at the crux of struggles *against* commodification and yet a multi-institutional structure of varying responses to commodification. The ambivalent state is blown by the wind, capricious and paradoxical and unmoored, pursuing conflicting neoliberal goals across various institutional levels of the state. Subramaniam explains that ambivalence is shown in 'the flexible and variable decisions about privatization, between state institutions that may not comply with those advocated by global financial institutions such as the World Bank and the IMF. Some of these expressions have been prompted by people's action.'[15] The ambivalent state is irrational and dynamic, pushed and pulled, hither and thither, by competing interests.

Descriptively, the state acts as the intermediary between local community organizations, actors and movements, and international bodies; moreover, 'this dynamic or ongoing dialogue [as the intermediary] with state institutions across the national and sub-national levels renders the state led neoliberal agenda ambivalent'.[16] The ambivalent state does not always further the interests of neoliberal (i.e., pro-commodification) actors because its obscured focus results in unequal adoption of neoliberal policies. I contend that this ambivalence is not neutral but, instead, works against the interests of the commons and water justice; the nation-state might be ambivalent, yet it still works in a neoliberal structure of domination, exploitation and anthropocentrism. The goal for anti-water commodification social movements should be to fill the gaps of the inconsistency within the ambivalent state and to transform it through the power of discursive democracy. These gaps provide wiggle room for social movements to not only be the wind which blows the sails of the state, but to be the rudder when they work for recommoning. For example, some movements in South Africa have filled the gaps by using recommoning to legitimize themselves in activist and political ways while pointing to the inadequacy of state apparatuses (such as constitutionalizing water rights in South Africa).[17] The cases in this chapter will further the claim that social movements for water justice can use recommoning as normative and political fuel to propel their movements, realize justice and fill the power gaps between themselves and the state.

Social movements for water justice are important in protest and advocacy; they show a more direct and bottom-up form of direct democracy that established government might be incapable or unwilling to bring to the fore due to path dependencies (i.e., commodification and instrumental, economic valuations of water). As Avery Kolers observes, social movements might not be highly integrated with close links between individuals' actions and intentions, as recent weak methodologically individualistic action theory presupposes.[18] In fact, Kolers writes, 'Their highly galvanized core members are often dwarfed in number by networks of activists, constituent organizations, supporters, and sympathizers whose grasp of plans and intentions is vague or divergent but who are nonetheless causally essential.'[19] I propose that local, bottom-up social movements for water justice – an alternative way to act compared to neoliberal policies – ought to operate in the gaps formed by the vicissitudes of the state, and that water recommoning can bridge diverse or 'divergent' social movements. Such social movements will be seen to vindicate Kolers' assertion that social movements 'do essential work in not just revealing attitudes but in alerting others to genuine social problems and spurring creativity both in understanding those problems and in devising win-win solutions'.[20] In revealing sentiments and making citizens aware of socioenvironmental water injustice, social movements shed light on political harms of commodification (e.g., domination and anti-democracy) while underscoring the need for alternative structures (e.g., water recommoning).

Forthcoming examples will make it clearer that these social movements can create alternative structures which, themselves, create space for discourse and participation; however, these social movements can fail, such as in Stockton, California, or in the drawn-out process against the Sardar Sarovar Dam in India. Despite failures, social movements which promote non-anthropocentric water rights and co-operation between transnational, non-state, anti-water commodification organizations through informal deliberative settings can be important tools against water injustice. Despite imperfection, there are strong successes of alternative social movements.

At the glocal level, separate from the established and neoliberal World Water Forum (of the World Water Council) is the Alternative World Water Forum (AAWF), a gathering of the rural poor, peasants, environmentalists and organized labour. The AAWF brings these diverse actors together to discuss participatory, reflexive, democratically discursive and ecologically minded environmental policy. The AAWF and specific declarations promote different, more communal ways to act; for example, the International Indigenous Water Declaration, and the general ethos of the AAWF itself, is anti-nation state because the nation state, in their view, enables water commodification. Alternative forums such as the AWWF and the National Summit on the Human Right to Water are themselves discursive resistances against water commodification.[21]

As I will discuss in this chapter, popular, transnational social movements are dedicated to securing open access to water, such as La Via Campesina, a grassroots organization of 200 million peasant members. La Via Campesina sees the struggle for land as integrally related to struggles against commodification of water supplies – in rivers, seas, local water sources – and agribusiness reforms that harm peasants' abilities to farm and feed their families. As a peasant and worker member organization, La Via Campesina creates and utilizes new spaces and decentres dialogues from formal bureaucratic, technocratic and capitalist forums to make inroads against socioenvironmental injustices through collaboration in similar initiatives.[22] I shall argue that the value of alternative forums, including local social movements seeking water justice, is that they spotlight meaningfully different and radical ways of thinking about water that open up through deliberative democracy, reflexivity and participatory activism.

5.1.2 Advantages and disadvantages of existing formal water agreements

Existing national and transnational water agreements can provide a jumping-off point for water-focused social movements but only as a guided framework for new, more localized agreements which expand the sphere of discourse. Social movements ought to heed Iris Marion Young's advice that they should 'try not only to build on and create global legal and regulatory institutions, but also to expand possibilities for transnational association and public spheres'.[23] Although a critic might assert that my endorsement of deliberative democratic laws and (informal and formal) institutions, *as well as* participatory and bottom-up social movements as being complementary is not radical enough, I hold that they can indeed work from the bottom-up and provide a radical perspective. Civil society engagement with established UN frameworks and human rights language for water makes sense when we endorse legal pluralism, that is, we acknowledge that law is not monolithic and that norms are constructed by many actors, not merely state institutions.[24] As legal scholar Balakrishnan Rajagopal has argued, it is through a legal pluralist lens that we can justify human rights for water and the complementarity of social movements with law and politics as being a radical 'international law from below'.[25]

Water can provide a standpoint shift in policy and decision-making away from instrumental and economic valuations of water. Community-led social movements can leverage this shift with support through the legal realm. International water law, established by the UN Convention on the Law of the Non-Navigational Uses of International Watercourses (1997 UN Watercourses Convention) and the UNECE Convention on the protection and use of Transboundary Watercourses and International Lakes (1992 UNECE Water Convention) are essential building blocks for international, transboundary water justice; however, these agreements are too broad for specifically local use. Existing frameworks for international agreements pertaining to water law may only provide a starting point for discourse on water agreements, especially at the local level. According to the Global High-Level Panel on Water and Peace, the following two basic principles of the 1997 UN Watercourses Convention illustrate the specific nature of international water law: the principle of equitable and reasonable utilization of the watercourse; and the obligation to not cause significant harm (see Articles 5 and 7). Moreover, there is a general obligation of riparian states to co-operate.[26] To strengthen ties through trust-building co-operative action (see Article 9), the co-operative exchange of information between various researchers, actors and disciplines should be emulated by community-based social movements for water justice.

Transnational water agreements can be co-operative yet undemocratic, though, which can result in a struggle for the instantiation of democratic norms and mechanisms. There is no one-size-fits-all approach to social movements for democratized water justice. International agreements such as the Paris Agreement (Articles 7 and 11) speak to the importance of participatory development. However, this is the very drawback of large international water agreements: the involvement of 'tens of thousands of private companies'[27] in the UN Global Compact for Migration and other transnationally formal agreements enables 'protectors' of water to be exploitative. The normative thrust of trust, confidence, transparency, participatory development and democracy – the importance of the local, communal level for actualizing the meta-value of recommoning – are undermined by those actors who are at once remote and global. One of the key obstacles to democratizing water access, as well as community-driven social movements for water, is the prominent role occupied by private water companies in water agreements. The participation of private companies, coupled with a serious lack of on-the-ground participation in water treaties, serves to only extend the dogmatic slumber of neoliberal water management and fails to make water discussions democratic, reflexive or participatory. Then, the terms 'participatory', 'community' and other alternative methods of development and, specifically, water-focused activism and social movements are co-opted by the very actors said social movements work against. As Silvia Federici succinctly writes, 'We must be very careful…not to craft the discourse on the commons in such a way as to allow a crisis-ridden capitalist class to revive itself, posturing, for instance, as the environmental guardian of the planet'.[28] Recall Chapters 1 and 2 and the difficulties D'Souza and Bakker had with identifying water as a human right: this identification does not exclude commodification or water injustice entirely and, in fact, might enable the political harms I identified in Chapter 4.

I explained in earlier chapters that co-operation strictly within and between affluent and élite private actors prevents non-élite stakeholders, including citizens, from participating in decision-making; therefore, active and engaged governance between all actors should come as a solution. More local (yet still state-to-state) water policies and agreements ought to, and do, inform water governance. For example, the Framework Agreement on the Sava River Basin, a transnational policy for countries of the former Yugoslavia, has helped maintain transnational trust and confidence. Some river-basin agreements, such as this, succeeded conflict, while others, like the Shared River Basins Agreements between Portugal and Spain (Albufeira Agreement of 1998) were developed in a time of political stability. These agreements do support democratic water through normative elements of trust, transparency and co-operation; there is a formal, moral strength to entrusting others (i.e., other citizens or states) with water access and security, a delicate push-pull relationship driven by participation and reflection, pillars of deliberative democracy. In addition, they work towards realizing the recommoning of water under the moral understanding of the greater community of water entrustment, largely strengthened by human rights law.

Local water disputes have been alleviated by democratic water governance. For example, in Costa Rica, after years of conflict, dialogue and negotiation, inhabitants of the Turrialba region voted against a hydroelectric dam project in the Pacuare River. The government and president supported this vote, and the water resource conflict was resolved due to strong advocacy and the equal participation of multiple actors involved in the issue. Furthermore, water as a communal resource, with community input, has proven fruitful in the 'Voluntary Code of Practice' for common water management in Mongolia, which is a critical step towards building trust among government authorities, local communities, civil society organizations and the media.[29] Such agreements speak to the power of consultation and participation in initiating or maintaining water justice; as will be seen in the following sections, this particular way of structuring decision-making about, and governance of, water resists injustice.

The examples above show successful water governance within and between states, but local social movements are still essential. Such social movements play a crucial oppositional role in the dialogue between the state, private enterprise and citizens. Therefore, social movements ought to be the leading interlocutor in a water governance dialectic which pressures governments and state bureaucracies to democratize decision-making around water. Bottom-up social movements are still necessary because they consistently demand water rights for all citizens, melding local and global calls into a stronger 'glocal' movement. Importantly, such social movements generate innovative approaches for local and autonomous governance of water, specifically the meta-normative value of recommoning. In the following section I argue that social movements for water justice should leverage their power for protecting rights to water, especially when a 'glocal' lens of protest is used, while promoting recommoning. In the subsequent section, I explain the problem of violence, a possibility that any social movement must reckon with.

5.2 Democracy, resistance and water recommoning

To build on my brief explanation in Chapter 1, I take recommoning of water to be a cornerstone of resisting and reversing water injustice while (re)building community through deliberative democratic politics, activism and institutions. As I asserted in Sections 5.1.1 and 5.1.2, rights-based approaches to realizing water justice can still be radical despite calling for institutionalization if they use recommoning to fill motivation gaps. Despite potential pitfalls of using human rights language, it is important to realize that human rights language, as legal scholar Cristy Clark observes, 'is particularly effective at galvanizing community action to both protect and reassert the water commons and to engage in broader emancipatory political struggles'.[30] Water justice campaigns and activism can be bolstered by rights language because such rights have always asserted these rights 'from below'.[31] The case studies in this chapter attest to the animating power of human rights embodied by recommoning.

Recommoning water instantiates democratic water governance. Many social movements for water recommoning utilize a 'glocal' lens, insofar as they are focused on local water governance achieved through bottom-up social movements connected to the broader global movement for water justice. The actors in social movements promoting water recommoning are local and embedded in the community in which they work for change; they are not abstract or remote, which bolsters their support for, and defence of, rights to water and causes in favour of water justice. As Clark notes, citing critical theorist Max Haiven, rights were '"always taken and defended from below, never given or protected from above"...From within this understanding, rights, such as the right to water, are "constantly animated by struggles from below".'[32] The activist organizations and groups discussed in this chapter, then, more effectively, readily and meaningfully animate human rights through communally and community situated, yet globally relevant, struggles from below. The commons, community and such rights are inseparable.[33] Thus, initiatives to recommon water are also in part efforts to reconstitute community, common ownership and the democratic principles that undergird rights to water.

Recommoning, as we have seen, stands in stark contrast to commodified water. The political harms of commodification (e.g., the erosion of democracy, the turning of citizens into consumers, the myopic and anthropocentric lens of commodification) can be resisted and reversed by the strengths of recommoning (e.g., trust-building between actors and communities). Moreover, informal and formal arenas which are democratically deliberate promote transparency and participation, concepts that are anathema to furtive, undemocratic commodification. These virtues of recommoning (e.g., trust, confidence, transparency, community building), bounded in and building community, could be realized with Ostrom's eight principles for managing a commons:

1 Clearly defined boundaries between users and the commons itself.
2 Compatibility between costs and benefits.
3 Actors have the autonomy to deliberate and change rules and regulations.
4 There is active monitoring of the commons and monitors are accountable to fellow users.
5 Graduated sanctions for violating rules and regulations.
6 Local-based conflict-resolution mechanisms.
7 Minimal recognition of rights to organize, so users can create their own institutions with no challenge from the state.
8 The above rules and regulations are organized in nested enterprises.[34]

We shall see these principles mirrored by the cases in this chapter, such as in Guelph-Wellington, Detroit, Flint and Baltimore. In many cases, actors must have the freedom to deliberate and change rules within a recommoning framework. Furthermore, such groups aim to localize water governance and conflict while working within nested enterprises (since water is globally important). Movements organize naturally, and they sometimes form without challenge from the state.

Commodification is at odds with – and commodifiers actively oppose – these principles. Actors for commodification know no boundary other than where capital (i.e., water) is, and costs and benefits routinely favour the commodifiers and harm the public. The paucity of democracy in the way of commodification shuts avenues for deliberation, and the monitoring of water use is left to commodifiers to self-regulate. Commodifiers face few sanctions for taking more than their allotment of water, and local-based conflict resolution is usually overwhelmed by the power of capital of large multinational corporations and similar actors. This chapter's case studies will show, though, that Ostrom's eight principles are supported in the normative force of recommoning, concretizing water justice in bottom-up, glocal movements.

In the forthcoming cases, organizations against injustices such as big dam projects and water commodification take the form of alter-globalization movements (recall Bakker in Section 2.3) instantiating, in environmental philosopher and activist Vandana Shiva's words, 'water democracy'; that is, these social movements are locally based and varied, yet they consistently offer alternatives to neoliberal water ownership.[35] It is at the glocal level of acting otherwise, against neoliberal water policies, that recommoning can strengthen community, expand democracy and undermine commodification. This is not to say that protecting rights to water happens in this singular way of recommoning; it is to say, though, that recommoning is one such important way to protect rights to water and actualize water justice. Via forthcoming cases in this chapter, it will be clarified that initiatives to recommon water are part of a broader set of popular struggles to give communities greater control over their natural environment, by democratizing decision-making and governance.

Ostrom's research provides a starting point to critically analyse water ethics, justice and governance, but as this chapter progresses, it will also become clearer that I am working within a human rights framework that she does not explicitly endorse. As the actors and organizations in this and previous chapters attest to, the recommoning arrangements and deliberative practices that support water recommoning are always backstopped by a human right to water, and this framework is one of a few key differences between my approach and Ostrom's research. This book is a work of setting up norms that are more abstract than Ostrom establishes, and new arrangements of water governance require theorists and actors to strive for more inclusive and egalitarian power-sharing arrangements that are occluded by some of Ostrom's case studies which focus solely on deliberations between landowners. For example, as explained in Chapter 3, her cases in Alicante, Spain, and in California are invaluable studies pertaining to CPR governance amongst 'appropriators' (resource users), but they are centred on farmer communities, amongst property owners.[36] Instead, my case studies broaden the scope of who counts as an 'appropriator', including all relevant and capable actors who can discuss water governance issues (i.e., ownership, value).

I build on Ostrom's descriptions of CPR governance by developing new deliberative mechanisms and arrangements underpinned by extensive deliberative democratic processes; I am constructing a roadmap for where water governance *ought* to go, yet I ground this process (by way of my engaged-hybrid philosophy) in cases that analyse real-world justice movements. In the following section, we will see that recommoning builds ties between actors and communities, through structural changes which decentre power from the state to a more localized community. In fact, these groups can leverage their privileged epistemic and geographic positions – their lack of remoteness or abstraction from water – in a 'double-pronged' strategy so that the state provides citizens with public water while building on local knowledge and self-organization.[37]

5.2.1 Community activism, social movements and 'recommoning' water

I have argued that social movements themselves are important tools for protecting rights to water, as they can resist and counter water commodification. In this section, I ask what anti-water commodification activism looks like through different communities and social movements. Such activist groups are similar in their use of 'human rights' language, but they differ in what they identify as water injustices and in what they fight against (e.g., water activism centred against bottled water in Guelph, the refusal of water to those unable to pay in Detroit, the privatization of a formerly public water company in Cochabamba, or dams in India). Anti-water commodification movements use 'human rights' language which is frequently driven by instrumental concerns (i.e., distribution); this strategy is not always successful.[38] To fill the gaps in ideological motivation, I argue that a 'recommoning' of water ought to be the normative force for anti-water commodification movements.

To support my argument that a recommoning of water is necessary and is, in fact, the actualization of water justice and the embodiment of a social movement's cause, I will first examine real-world examples of water justice activism and water injustice in Guelph-Wellington, Detroit, Cochabamba, Grenoble and Kerala. I utilize a comparative approach to describe water justice movements that are locally based yet contend with similar global water issues, concluding that recommoning water should be the normative power behind such movements. As water injustices are diverse and global, water activism is diverse and global too, and I intersperse these examinations with parallel examples to show the 'glocality' of the nexus of water justice, rights, and activism. People from diverse socioeconomic strata lead and engage with these movements. Second, I posit that recommoning of water is consistent with discursive democratic principles, with reference to the aforementioned real-world examples.[39] Third, I argue that the recommoning of water is the actualization of the socioenvironmental water justice I have put forward in Chapter 4. As such, the most meaningful and impactful resistances to water injustice are those social movements that construct laws and institutions which uphold the human right to clean fresh water, embolden community water activism, and prevent or outlaw water commodification because each act builds on philosophical ideas of trust, confidence, transparency, participatory development and democracy.

5.2.2 *Water activism and social movements: local-global, or* **glocal***, cases*

This section contrasts the national and transnational agreements in Section 5.1.2 by presenting more intranational and local social movements for water justice, moving from North America to South America, Europe and India. I will begin this section with an examination of the social activism organization Council of Canadians (CoC) to show that the agenda of water justice organizations or broader social groups, such as the CoC, fluctuates depending on the political context (e.g., commodification, or when citizens' rights are jeopardized by policies), but are no less normatively powerful.

5.2.2.1 *Guelph-Wellington, Canada*

Water activism arises as a response to private actors seeking to commodify water, and they generally use human rights to defend rights to water. In Erin and Aberfoyle, Ontario, Nestlé has bottled water on expired permits.[40] The act of bottling water has drawn the ire of local and national water activists. Residents in the Guelph-Wellington area are quite engaged with water justice issues, representing themselves and voicing their opposition to water commodification through local community groups such as Wellington Water Watchers (WWW) and the locally chaptered yet nationally active organization Council of Canadians (CoC). CoC co-founder and pre-eminent Canadian water activist Maude Barlow makes moral, human rights claims against water commodification, as one 'cannot trade or sell a human right or deny it to someone on the basis of inability to pay'.[41] The CoC, and water justice movements throughout the world, argue from the same human rights standpoint with similar language.

Social movements offer different justifications to support their demands for water justice, as WWW promotes water as sacred and appeals to the religious, historical and cultural values of water. The CoC is not wholly focused on water, unlike WWW, and members consider water as intricately bound by political and economic concerns. These organizations work for water justice through community engagement, making space for a broad coalition of people in the Guelph-Wellington area arguing through formal and informal political action against water commodification. Moreover, activists speak before local city councils to, for example, argue against the extension of permits for bottling water.[42] There are, quite explicitly, arguments for the recommoning of water from these local activist organizations, an idea with (obvious) local credence that also points to the 'glocal' situatedness of water issues. Indeed, water activists argue that remunicipalization could lead to satisfying the goals of the UN's SDG 6.[43]

The nature of social movement organizations such as the CoC and WWW are similar to those in the United States, Bolivia and France in that they are focused on the human right to water and the promulgation of said moral rights against water privatization; in India, water-focused social movements are dam-centric and sometimes less efficacious. With the CoC, WWW and other movements in Canada, there is a strong bedrock of democratic ideals that propel social movements to organize, influencing various (formal and informal) forums for social movement activity. A variety of standpoints and forums against water injustice is important because diverse arguments influence productive conflict and are an antidote to apathy. As political theorist Jennifer Dodge argues, multiple viewpoints of disagreement present themselves as 'frontiers of disagreement' which encourage reflexivity and debate in civil society.[44]

I will expand on the usefulness of such frontiers in Section 5.3 in relation to violence, but some framing is helpful here. Frontiers of disagreement might contribute to the din of what Ercan, Hendriks and Dryzek term the 'communicative plenty', that is, the sound and fury from a bevy of arenas (e.g., social media, participatory forums, unrepresentative minipublics) which can homogenize and manipulate deliberation.[45] I contend, though, that frontiers of disagreement need not be harmful if they are pluralistic yet focused on a common goal of recommoning water as a democratic realization. A productive range of views can be maintained in a process of *expression*, then *listening*, and then *reflection* to counteract the possible perniciousness of communicative plenty.[46] Variety and diversity are promoted by way of focusing on recommoning, of building up community while acknowledging the role legal institutions can play in concretizing water justice, while not losing their radicality. In this way, social movements in Guelph-Wellington and upcoming cases contribute to keeping action for water justice 'in productive tension' between forums (e.g., minipublics, legislatures), systems (e.g., federal or provincial legal and health systems), and a polity that has 'particular integrative norms'.[47] These norms, as exemplified in Guelph-Wellington, Detroit, Cochabamba, Grenoble and Kerala, bring actors together into a tessellation that should, and at times does, use water recommoning as their impetus for civic engagement.

Variety can affect the focus of organizations (i.e., activism centred on water as a human right, commodification, or sanitation and health), but this variety is usually still grounded in civicism. Civic organizations do important work in water, sanitation and health (WASH) which points to the importance of recommoning water for immediate health effects as well as trust, confidence and democracy. For example, the US-based NGO Food & Water Watch has implemented a strategy for the rapid mobilization of WASH-related activism. Food & Water Watch canvassed informal (i.e., diverse online and in-person forums) and formal (i.e., the formal political arena of the United States, such as Congress) places of discourse to press for a moratorium on water-shutoffs due to the COVID-19 crisis and pass the Water Affordability, Transparency, Equity and Reliability (WATER) Act of 2019.[48] Here, NGOs, activists and legislators worked collaboratively, engendering trust and transparency through discourse. Such deliberation is not only spoken, but also acted upon by tabling legislation, voting and mobilizing citizens and politicians to collaborate and participate.

5.2.2.2 Detroit, Flint and Baltimore, United States

Community-centred (e.g., anti-corporate), bottom-up public activism can work to protect rights to water through diverse collaborative activism. Ultimately, such activist movements instantiate and actualize community through and *with* the natural world in recommoning. In Guelph-Wellington, we can see that the CoC and other civil society organizations call for recommoning that is consistent with some of Ostrom's principles: actors must have the autonomy to deliberate and change rules because the social movements themselves deliberate and push for recommoning. Moreover, they work to localize water and resolve conflicts, tapping into alternative, anti-capitalist valuations of water (i.e., cultural, historical, spiritual, non-anthropocentric). Such movements also exist due to, and push for (in other locales), no challenges from the state; movements organize organically. We can observe adherence to these principles of managing a commons in community-building and the drive for recommoning water beyond the Canadian context, in Detroit (and other American cities), and beyond continental boundaries, in Bolivia, France and India.

Collaborative and direct activism criticizes and attempts to undo water injustice. In Detroit, water has been denied to those who cannot afford their water bills, entrenching domination, dehumanization and anti-democracy.[49] Water has been shut off from poor and racialized citizens.[50] Collaborative and direct action through, for example, the Detroit Water Brigade, the Detroit People's Water Board, the Detroit Water Project and We the People of Detroit, work to bring water to those in need, identifying and challenging the moral harm of a lack of clean water and the political harm of lacking recognition and participation in water processes.[51]

In Detroit, activists have used rights-based language similar to that used in Baltimore[52] and Flint: water rights are not merely human rights, they are civil rights. The water activism in these cities promotes the community, the inherently civil or, more appropriately, *civic* nature of water. Activists have utilized the universal need for water to enhance communal deliberation, bridging civil society with religious leaders to mobilize and lead the passing of a ban on water privatization in Baltimore. As Alvin Gwynn, president of the Interdenominational Ministerial Alliance of Baltimore, states, 'Banning water privatization gave us the power to enact a more moral and more just law for managing our water billing and addressing our water woes. Across the [United States], water privatization has led to higher water bills, worse service and little transparency'.[53] Activists call for more deliberative democracy and bring to the forefront the highly racialized nature of water injustice stemming from systemic racism.

These social movements call for deeper participation and recognition by those on the ground and those ingrained in their communities. As such, they identify the normative importance of the local citizen who is familiar with the people and customs of a certain community while also connecting calls for water to a universalized human right to water, glocalizing the social movement in the process. Thus, parochialism or provincialism might be overcome by the plurality of voices contributing to the glocalization of such social movements for water, either in person (e.g., marches) or in writing (e.g., informally in blogs, or formally in legal or academic treatises). The voices of the people experiencing water injustice in these communities are sometimes conveyed through formal documents; for example, community voices are amplified in the Report of the Michigan Civil Rights Commission on the Flint water crisis. This powerful report details the systemic racism that perpetuates water injustice against Black people by white-centric water distribution, that is, distribution manifested in clean water for the 'visible' (i.e., political clout), predominately wealthy white populace and unclean, expensive water for racialized persons (i.e., those without political clout).[54] As social scientist Ingrid Waldron has evinced in her influential work *There's Something in the Water*, systemically racist water injustices perpetuate WASH issues and racialization in Black and Indigenous communities.[55] In the words of Rev. Roslyn Bouier of the Brightmore Connection Food pantry in Detroit, 'The highest proportion of shut-offs is among Black women. Women of colour with babies'.[56] For activists such as Rev. Bouier, denying water to those who cannot pay their water bills is not only a matter of health but of 'dignity'.[57]

Social movements for water justice thus work to build dignity by strengthening community ties especially between and amongst women.[58] It is women who have been at the forefront of many anti-privatization and anti-commodification resistances.[59] Indeed, as Federici asserts, 'In the face of a new process of primitive accumulation, women are the main social force standing in the way of a complete commercialization of nature' by strengthening trust and building community through recommoning.[60] This may be done by forming autonomous spaces of action in the face of water 'enclosures' referenced earlier in Chapters 2 and 3. For instance, Monica Lewis-Patrick (executive director of the water justice organization We the People of Detroit), Elin Betanzo (owner of Safe Water Engineering in Detroit) and Jill Ryan (executive director of Freshwater Future) collaborate to test for lead in drinking water in high-risk areas of Detroit, expanding the sphere of democracy beyond political deliberation to scientific fields, as citizen science, too.[61]

Communities that democratically work through different social movements do not so much create new ties as strengthen already existing ones at the expense of anti- and undemocratic water injustice. Despite the enclosure of water by commodification, social movements for water justice disclose, as *aletheia*, the political harms of water injustice as structural impediments. Such movements, in Kolers' words, '[reveal] attitudes ... [alert] others to genuine social problems and [spur] creativity' to understand water injustice as not only a problem of distribution, but of political harms such as domination and anti-democracy.[62] In doing so, movements unfurl a world that water commodifiers are epistemologically blind towards. As will be seen in the following cases in Cochabamba, Grenoble and India, democracy brings much needed transparency to water injustices: an increase in democracy (i.e., water justice) lays bare the sutures of undemocratic water governance and makes clear the need for recommoning as the normative and ideological force behind activism and the instantiation of water justice itself.

5.2.2.3 Cochabamba, Bolivia

The 'water wars' in Cochabamba, Bolivia, embody the struggle and reversal of water commodification through recommoning, as well as the vital role of locally situated popular movements against water injustice. In Cochabamba in 2000, the IMF and World Bank hastened the privatization of water (by way of privatizing the city's municipal water company, SEMAPA, with an aggressive partnership and bid from Aguas del Tunari, or Bechtel) which resulted in massive inequality in water access. Cochabamba illustrates a clear-cut instance of the commodification of water, and the subsequent public resistance engaged bottom-up and participatorily with diverse stakeholders. Cochabamba also shows the effectiveness of such resistance.

Activist Oscar Olivera's *Coordinadora* (working people, the majority) successfully reversed water commodification in Cochabamba by promoting the normative power of recommoning water – the *right* of water. Olivera and Alvaro Garcia Linera's Bolivian intellectual collective *Comuna* proved to their fellow Bolivians how commodification is controlling and alienating. Their resistances were of the 'multitude-form' instead of the 'union-form', the multitude-form being a flexible and diverse connection of similar groups in society. Olivera, Linera and anti-water commodification activists effectively fought against water injustice by acting contrary to those private actors; *they acted in another way* and made real their convictions and philosophies. Furthermore, the sacredness of water – a significant intrinsic value – for those anti-commodification activists in Cochabamba played a crucial role in unifying the movement.⁶³ For Linera, the *Coordinadora* is a Habermasian 'network of communicative action'; the actions and interactions of its members who struggle against water commodification form the network.⁶⁴

In March 2000, the *Coordinadora* organized a *consulta popular* (popular referendum) to vote against Agua del Tunari's takeover of SEMAPA and change Law 2029 (which enabled the prospective water privatization in Cochabamba). More than 50,000 people voluntarily voted as an act of participatory and deliberative democratic defiance against water commodification, revealing the disconnect between citizens and their elected representatives. The *Coordinadora* brought a mosaic of Bolivians together against a common enemy – water commodifiers – which not only built but instantiated trust that persists well after the water wars through constituent assemblies of non-establishment and non-political actors, where people discuss water issues outside of formal forums.

Olivera's movement enabled public workers and peasants alike to form and be active. Behind such activity was the trust and confidence in fellow citizens to mobilize and challenge water commodification. Such mass protests and organized community participants argued for transparent governance and compelled the transferring of power from the state government to the local populace. The Cochabamba water wars were, then, not only activism against water commodification but 'representative' government as well. Olivera writes,

> What is happening more and more today is that *democracy is becoming confused with elections*. At one time democracy – at least to us – meant participation in the distribution of wealth; collective decision-making on issues that affect us all; and pressure and mobilization in order to influence state policies. Now the only acceptable meaning of 'democracy' seems to be *competition in the electoral market*.⁶⁵

The *Coordinadora* and similar water activists mobilized against the passivity of representation through marches, protests, blockades and building occupations; these are direct acts at the people's disposal.

Olivera himself, the *de facto* leader of anti-water commodification activism in Cochabamba, summarizes the movement and what was learned:

> First, it is ordinary working people who achieved justice. Second, all of our individualism, isolation, and fear evaporated into a spirit of solidarity.

During the worst confrontations, there were people who brought water, who handed out food, who gave rides, who took care of communications. These are elements of a well-organized resistance. People lost their fear of the bullets; they lost their fear of repression. The ghosts of past times of terror were defeated on the blockades. The third thing we learned is that we want democracy. We want a government that takes our views into account – not the interests of the international financial institutions and their neoliberal politicians.[66]

In Cochabamba, a coalition of those most affected by water injustice developed and practiced, in Olivera's words, solidarity and the erasure of fear. Water was the fulcrum for the movement, and the activism itself brought people closer together and solidified their movement. Activism for recommoning is a defiant act of diverse citizenship and living democracy.

In Guelph-Wellington, Detroit, Baltimore, Flint, Cochabamba, Grenoble and India, water activism is the socioenvironmental actualization of water justice; in other words, activism is not merely an instrumental means to achieve water justice, it is intrinsically the practice of water justice itself. The very way social movements *act* for water activism – in their demands for recommoning water and transparency of water governance – has value separate from instrumental effects.

Although water activism has the obvious instrumental value of bringing forth concrete steps to make water commonly owned and democratic, there is intrinsic value in such activism embodying communal democracy: deliberation and participation amongst citizens, gathering together to push for common goals. The philosophical values entrusted to the spirit of democracy – trust in fellow citizens as well as those in power, transparency of those actors, institutions, and systems which govern, all while being held in check by a populace's participation – are given life by water activists who gather together to demand different and new systems and institutions.

5.2.2.4 Grenoble, France

Social movements for water justice demand trust, confidence, transparency, citizen participation and democratic decision-making in water governance. The call for recommoning is a common thread through different locations and contexts of water injustice. Let us look further into struggles against water commodification similar to that resisted and reversed in Cochabamba, such as in Grenoble, France, in the 1980s and 1990s. Activist Raymond Avrillier offers a first-hand account of the struggle in Grenoble against water privatization by the company Lyonnaise des Eaux.

Avrillier stresses that social movements which criticize and attempt to undo water commodification, and work to instil public water governance, must make transparent information and independent analyses of the role of the private sector. Furthermore, public and private sectors work together and 'essential work is provided by the public administration and other services are provided by the private sector through public procurement'.[67] The dissemination of water information (i.e., data on water usage, sources and distribution) fomented cogent policy discussions and informed voting in Grenoble. After recommoning water in Grenoble, quality has improved, costs have lowered (to some of the most inexpensive water for any city in France with more than 100,000 people), sustainability has improved, and decisions are more transparent because information has been publicized.

Avrillier and his fellow water activists used rights-based language to claim water as a right for all that should, therefore, be held as an essential public service to achieve water recommoning. To reclaim water for the public, these activists took a long-term view of the pitfalls of privatization and commodification by critiquing a proposed PPP and analysing money flows from Lyonnaise des Eaux and other water companies.[68] The campaign to recommon Grenoble's water used a variety of strategies:

1 Collective action to fight against commodification;
2 Legal action in administrative, financial and judicial courts;
3 Action in positions of authority; and
4 Actions in groups (different types of movements and forums).

This holistic yet variegated approach had the common strategy of bringing to light access to information, pluralist analyses and 'the choices of public policy, management and engagement [presented in] open public debate'.[69] Again, water commodification was successfully reversed because activists took advantage of formal *and* informal settings for participation and discursive democracy. A deliberative democratic assembly of local users now control the water utility in Grenoble, making decisions for their community.

5.2.2.5 Kerala, India

Activism in India elucidates the glocal and diverse power of communal social movements for water justice in their successes and failures. Activism against water injustices in India focuses on dams and water commodification; for instance, local and transnational resistance successfully defeated the big dam Silent Valley Project in Kerala in the 1970s. Globalization and governance scholar Sanjeev Khagram identifies this successful resistance as resulting from widespread democratic protests, connecting human rights issues with democratic separation of powers (i.e., an independent judiciary) as well as the transnational alignment of movements such as Indigenous rights groups and environmentalist organizations.[70]

Khagram identifies big dams and rights to water as inherently connected; he writes, 'The prioritizing of the provision of drinking water and the creation of a National Drinking Water Mission [in India] in 1986, as well as the formulation of a National Water Policy [in India] in 1987, and subsequent debates over it, were clearly influenced by criticisms of big dam building'.[71] This struggle for rights to water contributed to 'the foundation of a collective set of understandings' and unified water activist groups.[72] These social movements consistently fight for water as a human right through a glocal lens. For example, anti-water commodification movements against Coca-Cola in Plachimada, Kerala, promoted the human right to water and educated local citizens of the global harms of water commodification, successfully communicating these issues as glocal harms. Further, social movements such as the Right to Water Campaign and Citizen's Front for Water Democracy have used global examples to communicate the deleterious effects of water commodification in Manila, Philippines; Cochabamba and La Paz, Bolivia; San Juan, Puerto Rico; and Johannesburg, South Africa.

It is important to recognize that bottom-up water struggles are not merely localized reactions to specific water injustices, such as damming, but rather are genuine social movements in the sense of articulating a vision of social change centred on ideas of community-led development, the commons and citizen governance. According to sociologist Krista Bywater, the success of these movements against Coca-Cola in Plachimada, Kerala, was in 'integrating human-rights discourse, conceptions of water commons, and cultural understandings of water into campaigns [that] can advance claims to the right of water'.[73] Subramaniam, too, argues that the intertwined strategy of promoting water as a human right *and* the participatory, democratic bolstering of water activism through informal forums led to success in India. For example, the water activism in Plachimada and the Arvari Sansad (parliament) stressed 'the need to define water as a common property resource and the right to water as a human right, rejecting the economic commodification as well as any form of public–private partnership in managing water resources'.[74] Moreover, Tarun Bharat Sangh, an Indian NGO, uses water parliaments – informal gatherings of local people – to discuss water governance.

The alternative to big dams, commodification and water injustice in general is a turn towards recommoning water and buttressing community water management. In Olavanna, Kerala, community-managed water has improved water delivery for all citizens, not only the richest or the poorest.[75] Participation of citizens in discursive democracy in Kerala, through a formalized People's Plan policy, led to more efficient use of water with improved distribution and maintenance. In addition, the *polis* voted on budgets, participated in planning, construction, management and maintenance, and communities supplemented public funds. Balanyá and colleagues argue that this ingratiation of the public into water management fostered a sense of ownership amongst the populace which contributed to sustainability improvements.[76]

Local governments and political parties supported the success of water activism in Kerala, such as the fomenting of deeper ties between participatory local movements and water governance, unlike other water activist movements (e.g., Cochabamba). However, the state, either at the level of municipal government or within certain political parties, is not, and should not be, the end-all-be-all for protecting rights to water. In Section 5.2, I proffered that the recommoning of water, as shown in the cases presented in this chapter, is a common argument in social movements for water which is consistent with discursive democratic principles. Moreover, in this section, I put forward that popular social movements play a distinct and necessary role in hastening water justice – a role that governments and state or regulatory institutions cannot supplant. Furthermore, the recommoning of water actualizes the socioenvironmental water justice that I have argued for in Chapter 4 and is imbued with philosophical ideas of trust, confidence, transparency, participatory development and democracy. In the next section, I explain how the decentralization of power and actualization of recommoning can face strong opposition from entrenched private and undemocratic actors.

5.3 Resistance and violence

The cases of grassroots inspired social movements in this chapter exemplify a 'human rights from below' approach that sees human rights as needing to be claimed and instantiated in newly envisioned, 'glocal' democratic processes. This process is transformative, and the above cases show the philosophical ideas necessary – the normative importance and support – for recommoning water. However, I would be remiss to not address the possibility of violence when examining water justice and anti-water commodification movements. Are social movements that use tactics of violence against property or persons warranted in doing so as a means to achieve recommoning and water justice generally? I must acknowledge that I cannot do justice in one section to the extensive debate in political science as to whether violence is an effective means to achieve ends in social movements, nor to the debate in normative political theory regarding the permissibility (or not) of violence as a means to meeting objectives. I raise the issue of violence because I want to briefly explore the question of the moral justifiability of violence in water justice movements with a view to establishing some minimal or partial criteria for such permissibility.

To begin, political theorist Simon Caney argues that a right of resistance, complemented and supported by a 'human rights from below' approach, overcomes the lack of entitlements of those suffering water injustice. In addition, deliberative democracy is key to effectively resist global injustices. Caney states that agents should engage in resistance which forces reflection on

> (a) the values that underlie the society to which we are aspiring (say one committed to freedom, equality, reciprocity and democratic decision-making governed by norms of reasonableness), and also (b) facts about the nature of the existing situation ... facts about the extent to which the *status quo* has just civil and political procedures, facts about people's openness to argument, and facts about their willingness to use force to silence dissent.[77]

Therefore, social movements can be reflexive and discursive not only concerning water justice, but justice itself. By this I mean that ends are decided by movements over time. Furthermore, these movements must identify what (a) a just society is and the values behind it, along with (b) the political constraints the society is under. The structural political constraints and injustices to which social movements respond generally motivate their members to create new, more just structures of water. To add, new structures might be created through discussion, reflexivity, action and participation, and the fulfilment of the protection of water rights through formal (i.e., legal-institutional) and informal (i.e., communal, non-state forums, recommoning) institutions. I do not think it is quixotic to argue that community-based social movements can build and maintain regulatory institutions with the support of a state apparatus, as long as this process is bottom-up initiated; in fact, there is much proof that local communities can build and create thriving institutions that regulate natural resources.[78]

The process of recommoning itself, though, might face resistance from the state and water commodifiers. How should social movements act in the face of violent resistance? Without question, violence against the human body is antithetical to the broader goal of developing widely inclusive democratic institutions against the backdrop of political stability and peace. What about violence against property? Caney considers this question and argues that we cannot totally prohibit violence because toleration of injustice might be worse than the violence that resists injustice.[79]

Political theorist Sharon Krause clarifies that violence may take the form of environmental domination made manifest in the violent exploitation of natural resources and 'blind domination'. Violence, in turn, may be a response to such domination. She writes:

> 'Blind domination' of the masses [occurs] in affluent democracies, who are captivated more than coerced into a system that gratifies many of their desires even as it subjects them to unchecked power and exploitation. Their participation makes them complicit in their own domination as well as the domination of nature and other people, but it is a forced complicity that attenuates the type and degree of responsibility they bear.[80]

Here, injustice is a rote, slow violence without discursively democratic, reflexive or participatory mechanisms for the populace to express itself or build trust, confidence and transparency. This type of violence is not usually overt; instead, it mimics surreptitious path dependencies that were explained in Chapters 2 and 3.

Along this rationale, violence may be morally permissible as direct action against property because such action might cleave new epistemic, deliberative paths that illuminate the harms and injustice of water commodification. Political theorist Jennifer Dodge argues that such actions exist as 'frontiers of disagreement' arising from political gridlock of discursiveness. In Dodge's terms, the ways in which disagreements are framed serve a 'discursive function' in deliberative democracy which 'can illuminate the relationship between conflict and reflexivity in deliberative policy-making'.[81] The conventional understanding amongst democratic theorists is that more conflict leads to less deliberation and, therefore, more gridlock.[82] On the other hand, Dodge argues (with reference to research of civil society organizations in the State of New York for and against hydraulic fracturing) that greater conflict can lead to more reflexivity in the sense that more avenues for discussion are opened.[83] In deliberative democracy, reflexivity sometimes comes about through conflict, formed from the external and internal criticality of assessing the language of demands; for instance, groups construct claims and counterclaims for access to clean fresh water or against water commodification, and through contestation and conflict (i.e., gridlock) there is reflection and, then, the victory of political power and norms.[84]

Such a quasi-Hegelian dialectic necessarily involves conflict, but it *does not* necessarily have to be violence against the body to actualize water justice.[85] For example, participatory action against property and institutions, such as the 'Struggle Plumbers' who illegally open water pipes or wells to those without water in Soweto, is a part of a dialectic.[86] The dialectic is the very mechanism that builds trust, confidence and transparency between members of a movement, as well as between a movement and its antagonists. The truly deliberative democratic movement embodies the values of democracy as a meta-principle, being that which it works to instantiate. This direct action, as a dialectic which includes civil disobedience and direct action, is undertaken by movement members who are communicating with words and actions.

Direct action can bring about productive tension not only between water justice proponents and opponents, but within water justice movements themselves. Tully writes succinctly about the untenability of violence in relation to such action and social movements:

> Distrust and violence beget distrust and violence and from the history of non-violence that there is another more powerful way that leads to peace. [Alternative social movements] start from the simple premise that humans in all civilizations are already familiar with proto-civic and civicizing relationships, even imperialistic Westerners, and thus already able to recognize and enter into others…Democratization cannot be spread by imposing institutional preconditions because non-violent grass roots democratic relationships are the preconditions of democratization. Consequently, peace cannot be the end of a long historical process of war and the spread of Western institutions. Peace is the *way*.[87]

For Tully, to act non-violently is to act counter to the established colonial tradition, to forge through discussion and reflection a different structure from the remnants of past injustice.

It is important to note that of all the examples of water justice movements in this book, not one involved physical violence initiated by water justice activist groups against others; instead, the social movements worked to protect rights to water and build structures of water justice through deliberative democracy, reflexivity and participatory activism. Intrinsically, violence does not embody the meta-value of recommoning, the normative values that make democracy something to be valued in the first place. This violence that I denounce – ruptures community and democracy, two pillars of recommoning.

5.4 Conclusion

Social movements play a crucial role in the protection of water rights; additionally, these movements pressure states for more transformative forms of water justice, as well as build community structures to support a social vision of recommoning. Diverse yet unified water justice activists reinvigorate deliberative democracy through reflexive deliberation and participatory philosophy. Furthermore, they rebuild weakened democratic institutions through their activism, first, and then formalize their work through laws. The social movements and water justice actors comparatively examined in this chapter, in Guelph-Wellington, Detroit, Flint, Baltimore, Cochabamba, Grenoble and Kerala, overcome the 'ambivalence' of the state because they construct new, bottom-up structures welded together by 'glocal' alternate arguments of non-anthropocentric water rights and co-operation between transnational, non-state, anti-water commodification organizations. Yes, there are myriad existing international and transnational water agreements; however, as I first broached in Section 3.2.1, their global scope dilutes community power and freedom, and so they may only provide a guiding, broad framework for glocalized policies.

Recommoning water ought to be the focus of social movements for water justice. Recommoning aligns with discursive democratic principles and actualizes socioenvironmental justice because it can be fostered by local- and community-led participation and the building of trust, confidence, transparency, participation and democracy amongst citizens and between citizens and the government. Bottom-up community water activism is, thus, a normatively meaningful resistance to water injustice. Although such resistance is instrumentally valuable, social activism for recommoning instantiates water justice as intrinsically valuable too.

6

Conclusion

The political harms identified and explicated in this book should elicit a limbic panic in those of us concerned about water justice. The erosion of democratic institutions and principles, locally and globally, in recent years makes it likely that disasters of water access will grow worse before they abate. However, this sobering realization should not tarry action or wilt resolve – it should steel action for water justice and expanded democracy. As I have argued, political and legal obligations and mechanisms that are intentionally spurred and led by 'glocal' social activism can transform water governance.

In this concluding chapter, I will first recap the central arguments and claims from Chapters 1-5 and explain where in the current literature – the contemporary water ethics and justice conversation – this book is placed, now that my arguments are fully fleshed. Secondly, I will explain that my research progresses the field of philosophical water ethics and justice by illuminating the fact that environmentalists (theorists and practitioners) need to be as concerned about deepening *democratic* processes and governance as they are about the moral arguments around environmental degradation. Deliberative democracy is, thus, indispensable in any normative environmental work. I will argue that the next steps for the academic field of environmental justice and sub-discipline of water ethics and justice involves deeper collaboration between academics and non-academics, and that ethicists and political philosophers must meld engaged philosophy with non-ideal theory. Thirdly, I will draw out the implications of my research and explain where normative thinking about water justice should lead by asking questions about water governance, ethics and justice, specifically in relation to the case of the Canada Water Agency.

I have presented non-ideal, yet normative, arguments in the philosophical field of water ethics and justice. My own arguments have built on the social and political philosophy of Iris Marion Young and David Schlosberg, the philosophy of property of Avery Kolers, Anna Stilz and Mathias Risse, and the environmental political theory of Tim Hayward. It is my hope that my insights will be taken up in academic and policy circles.

6.1 Synopsis of arguments and conclusions

The Ethics of Water: From Commodification to Common Ownership aims to make normative philosophy a living theory, and to influence theory, arguments and activism for water ethics and justice. As such, I drew useful arguments from existing environmental and political philosophy, critically analysed said arguments, and connected my own arguments with examples of water justice movements in the world to show real-world importance and applicability. Above all, I identified the various political harms against water justice understood in a broader framework of socioenvironmental justice, argued that water should be a commonly governed communal resource, and put forth the idea that social movements for water are themselves the actualization of democracy and water justice, with the goal being the recommoning of water.

I began with an examination of the rights to water in Chapter 1. I presented the scene for the contemporary debate on human rights to natural resources, noting egalitarian, cosmopolitan, nationalist and capabilities approaches. Moreover, I explicated arguments skeptical of human rights from Karen Bakker and Radha D'Souza, with the reason being the anthropocentrism and Western-centrism of such a right possibly doing more harm than good for ensuring uncommodified water. I moved to acknowledge the trouble with anthropocentrism but argued against the drastic measure of not endorsing the human right to water; instead, I identified water as a right with both anthropocentric and non-anthropocentric importance as a socioenvironmental right and, setting up arguments in Chapters 2 and 3, as 'territory' and not 'property'.

In Chapter 2, I explicated prominent arguments for water as a public or private good, the ownership and governance of water, as well as the harms of commodification and identifying water as 'property'. I conceded that 'rights talk' concerning water can be harmful if done haphazardly but held firm that a robust deliberative democracy can make environmental rights an extension of human rights to undergird people's ability to access clean fresh water equitably and justly. Next, I concluded that water should be held as a public good which intersects with democratic norms and institutions. Furthermore, I identified the harms of commodification, namely the erosion of democracy by way of citizens being viewed only as consumers; moreover, this harm is engendered through the same instrumental lens that considers water as 'property' and values as only economic or neoliberal. Finally, I began the argument (which continued into subsequent chapters) that commodification is anti-democratic because it signals domination (i.e., lack of citizens' recognition, participation and deliberation in water governance). Such harms are stated explicitly as the consequences of commodification and the framing of water as property, instead of territory.

I examined the distinction between property and territory in Chapter 3. Ultimately, I situated my argument between Mathias Risse's 'common ownership of the earth' argument and Avery Kolers' delineations between property and territory. I supported arguments that water should be a common territory because ideals of stewardship (explained in Chapter 2) are only within the idea of territory, not property; moreover, commonly owned water aligns best with deliberative democratic principles and does not reduce humanity to profit or merely a consumer base. Schlosberg's work on recognition and participation helped to bridge my eventual argument for water recommoning with Risse's Egalitarian Ownership approach to common ownership of the earth by making explicit larger political and justice-related issues connected to normativity and water. My position was distinctive, however, in that I saw common ownership and territory as the necessary antidote to pathological path dependencies, and I expanded the sphere of deliberative democracy with help from Anna Stilz's broad characterization of the state (*contra* nation-state). I argued that deliberative democracy at the local and then the state level (what was, in later chapters, referred to as a 'glocal' strategy), a bottom-up approach to democracy and the support of human rights, should initiate just water governance which breaks such path dependencies.

After having given an account of current arguments around water ownership, ethics and justice, and having argued that common ownership of water as common territory aligns with deliberative democracy, I moved into the more normative labour of explaining the political harms of water injustice in Chapter 4. First, I argued that water justice is best understood in the framework of socioenvironmental justice (i.e., political water norms which are both anthropocentric and non-anthropocentric), the justice that leading theorists such as Schlosberg do not explicitly connect with water because his theory is not dual (anthropocentrism and non-anthropocentrism) focused. The identification of socioenvironmental justice was important because it provided support for the claim that water should be commonly owned territory, something Hayward and Schlosberg do not capture, and sets the stage for the political, democratic reinvigoration spurred by the recommoning of water.

The type of democratic governance I argued for requires extensive citizen participation and ecological reflexivity; as such, it best aligns with the normative ideals advanced by theorists of deliberative democracy. This led me, in a departure from leading theorists about property and ownership of natural resources (e.g., Risse), to argue that water injustice was a marker of a dearth of democracy, of a weakening of democratic rights and institutions, and that water commodification further erodes our democratic rights vis-á-vis what should be common entitlements. As a political harm, water injustice is a consequence of a democratic deficit and, subsequently, domination. A lack of decision-making by citizens and democratic governance speak to an absence of participation (i.e., recognition and inclusion), communicating the political harms of water commodification identified in Chapters 2 and 3.

Up to Chapter 5, I elucidated contemporary debates in water ethics and justice while developing my own arguments within important social and political theory (e.g., deliberative democracy), property (e.g., the political harms of property connected to commodification), and environmental philosophy (e.g., normative value of water). I argued that the political harms of commodification in the service of establishing water injustice are social as well as environmental injustices, and I identified why it is the case that water justice requires far-reaching changes to resource ownership and governance. I focused on debates within political philosophy then pivoted to discuss social movements in Chapter 5, where I used normative analyses of social movements for water justice to shed light on real-world social movements. I discussed social movements for water justice (e.g., Guelph-Wellington, Detroit,

Cochabamba, Grenoble and Kerala) to show the global importance of these movements – the issues of water ethics and justice broadly – while explaining the struggles, warts and all. The road to water justice is fraught with failure, but I posited that the very act of protest, as reflected in social movements, can bring transformative change with recommoning of water as the endpoint of movements. Recommoning embodies the normative values of such movements and should be the impetus for water justice activism. Social movements that work for recommoning concretized philosophical ideas of trust, confidence, transparency, participatory development and democracy.

6.2 Water ethics and justice going forward

This book fills gaps in the multi- and interdisciplinary study of water ethics and justice by offering normative analyses of water governance and social movements. In addition, it provides an analytical scaffolding for the normative relationship between politics – namely deliberative democracy – and water. In this section, I will explain that this research aligns with political and environmental philosophy, utilizing non-ideal, normative theory that is under the wider umbrella of engaged philosophy as explained by Jonathan Wolff. Engaged environmental ethics and justice is an exciting and growing field, and my research fits within the field while forging its own path in the philosophically neglected area of water ethics and justice, specifically.

As a work of hybrid engaged philosophy, this book asks normative questions about access to, and ownership and governance of, water. As such, it contributes to the relatively nascent academic philosophical field of water ethics and justice by working in the philosophical focuses of environmental and political philosophy, and property. Further, it examines, explains, utilizes and critiques research from sociology, human geography and political science while, also, connecting with real-world cases.

Academic water ethics and justice can continue to move forward by embracing multi-, inter- and transdisciplinarity. Ethical analysis of commodification can bring to light the full range of harms wrought by water commodification, and political theorizing about the anti-democracy of commodification can spotlight why these practices are morally objectionable.[1] Then, such questions can be brought into the world with actionable philosophy (which I postulated in Chapter 5), political science, hard sciences (e.g., hydrology and water engineering), and other descriptive research (e.g., human geography).[2] Such academic areas should not be in competition but in co-operation, commingling their research to reach out to policymakers, politicians and non-experts and non-technical actors who all play roles in the deliberative democratic interplay of water.[3]

Academic research in water ethics and justice is, in my opinion, merely one aspect of what it means to work in water ethics and justice. The activist and community elements of water ethics are what makes this field alive – they complement theory with practice – and it is important to acknowledge those scholar-activists lighting the way in academic environmental and water ethics and justice, such as Aimée Craft, Deborah McGregor, Ingrid Waldron and Kyle Whyte. Academic researchers in water ethics and justice should look outside the academy, as well, to those who have experienced water injustice first-hand and mobilized communities to resist and act differently against injustice. For example, outside of the academy and within their communities, Josephine Mandamin, from Wiikwemkoong Unceded Territory who founded the Mother Earth Water Walk, walked 17,000 km around all five Great Lakes to bring awareness and change to pollution in rivers and lakes; Mandamin devoted her life to realizing water ethics and justice. Autumn Peltier, also from Wiikwemkoong First Nation and Mandamin's great-niece, fights for clean fresh water locally and globally, making water ethics and justice a *praxis*. Such efforts by scholars and activists embedded in communities experiencing water injustice should be amplified above more privileged academic voices, such as my own, whose analysis is not directly informed by these lived injustices. These scholars and activists have developed and actualized norms which researchers should look to for leadership both inside academia, and outside of it when thinking of their own day-to-day activism.

I have tried to present a more nuanced account of the political harms of commodification as anti-democratic, and I hope that this more fleshed-out account can bolster the arguments of those who seek to reform water governance structures. We must now consider some central questions in water ethics and justice moving forward. Afterwards, I will conclude this section by briefly analysing proposed and extant policies and struggles for water justice and their potential for transformative, engaged change.

6.2.1 Questions for water ethicists and political theorists

Philosophers and political theorists working in water ethics and justice have much opportunity to work within and amongst organizations and movements explicated throughout this book, and such researchers will inevitably ponder about water governance. It is crucial that researchers not only do descriptive work – to describe the reality of water ethics justice, and governance – but to also contest long-held norms that play a role in water tragedies (e.g., the nature and validity of private property and the pervasiveness or ambivalence of the state). As I explained in the early sections of Chapter 1, researchers ought to embrace non-ideal theory and engaged philosophy. Researchers in water ethics and justice inevitably speak about how governance of water affects life, so questions must be appropriately incisive, dynamic and interdisciplinary.

Researchers should consider counterfactuals to the importance of deliberative democracy and posit questions that weigh deliberative democracy against non-anthropocentric water concerns. Does deliberative democratic theory provide sufficiently far-reaching ideals in response to non-democratic models of governance and water? Should we look to more radical traditions for sufficient normative support to contest the bases of private property? Crucially, are the academic ideas of common property and common territory compatible with Indigenous sovereignty claims over water? Arsenault et al. make clear that grounded, local, Indigenous knowledge and experience of water governance and research methods, such as the 'Two-Eyed Seeing' philosophy – an approach that braids Indigenous research methods with Western approaches – are necessary to decolonize water research.[4] Theories of territory should not override Indigenous claims of water sovereignty.

Philosophers working in water ethics and justice, and political theorists, should also reckon with scientific advancements in hydrology, water engineering, and specifically desalination. Cheaper, more broadly available desalination technology will bring more water to water-scarce regions.[5] Normative theorists must anticipate the environmental consequences (and subsequent sociopolitical ramifications) of such technology. What moral calculus should we perform to weigh the production of clean fresh water and the production of harmful post-desalination brine?[6] If desalination technology makes clean fresh water readily available, yet is privately funded and controlled, how can citizens wrest democratic control of water? How can we best democratize desalination companies (and water companies in general), the state, and citizens? Is the democracy-commons-water nexus even a concern if such technology makes clean fresh water readily and cheaply available?

Finally, I view the important questions above in relation to deliberative democratic systems between individuals, communities and states in the midst of climate change. Moving forward, the overarching question for ethicists and political theorists in water should revolve around the importance of water in such systems. In my view, there are essential characteristics of water that could be leveraged to strengthen bonds in a world of fracturing environmental systems, hastened by anthropogenic environmental destruction. The role of communal and state institutions for supporting deliberative democratic systems thinking might be secured through, for example, the recently created Canada Water Agency (CWA), a relationship that I will explore in the next section.

6.2.2 *Practical policies and real-world water struggles*

I will now briefly discuss practical agencies and policies that could embody water justice and end the section by positing important water governance questions going forward. In Chapter 5, I provided examples of important water justice activism in Canada and globally; of movements that are glocal in their ambitions, philosophies and strategies. I want to now shine a light on an agency of the Canadian federal government that may be an example of the kinds of institutions that bridge the divide between local water governance and the state. The agency might be used as an example of good water governance for other states; moreover, such an agency might connect academic water research and engaged public water movements.

The CWA could adopt, as working norms, the research done by those academics in water ethics and justice.[7] The CWA might act effectively as a mediating bridge between federal (the state) and local communities; indeed, the creation of the federal water agency aims to integrate a plurality of worldviews (local and federal, Indigenous and Western) into the foundation of the agency by doing joint programming of integrating Western science and Indigenous traditional knowledge.

The steps taken to formalize and realize the CWA were participatory and instantiate co-governance of water.[8] Furthermore, as I have argued throughout this book, actualizing water justice means to act differently, to forge a new and separate morality that is unlike dominant neoliberal and instrumental water ownership and government. This method of policy development, with potential agents of change in water issues, can foment pathways of change that are 'dynamically feasible' and co-created. I am cautiously optimistic that the method employed in the consultation and creation of the CWA can be woven into the fabric of its mandate because of the level of participation from the public, community water leaders and water researchers from different disciplines.

In addition to the CWA, there are organizations and movements all over the world that support communal and democratic water. Besides the host of case studies of organizations and social movements in Chapter 5, a few examples of dynamic people-led water organizations include Eau de Paris[9] (a publicly owned company fighting for cleaner, cheaper water in Paris, France), Agua Para Todos[10] (fighting privatization and climate change in Cochabamba, Bolivia) and Observatorio del Agua de Terrassa[11] (fighting for democratic governance of water in Catalonia). Such organizations can provide opportunities for future water ethicists and political theorists to be engaged with movements, and to respectfully change and be changed, themselves, by those who live injustice yet work to ameliorate water governance.

6.3 Final thoughts

My research has addressed real-world problems of water ethics and justice. It does not merely focus on distribution; it considers, and answers, normative questions of fresh water centred on political philosophy, policy agreements, democracy and freedom. Furthermore, this project provided a normative assessment and development of the water ethics landscape. I built on existing contemporary theories of property (e.g., Avery Kolers' distinction between property and territory, Anna Stilz's identification of territorial sovereignty and the state, and Mathias Risse's 'common ownership of the earth'), deliberative democracy (e.g., research from John Dryzek and James Tully), environmental political theory (e.g., Tim Hayward's 'ecological space') and structural injustice (e.g., models provided by Iris Marion Young and David Schlosberg) to explicate the nexus of water ethics, justice, property and democratic theory. I provided insight into political harms of water injustice (i.e., commodification), the relationship between discursive democracy and water, and the normative power of social movements themselves.

I wanted to contribute to the water ethics and justice debate in a way that is normative first, instead of strictly descriptive, because it is those first philosophical questions – those questions I have asked at the beginning of each chapter – that inform the very field of action in water policy. Thus, this project enlightens and reframes the traditionally non-philosophical study of freshwater resource governance with a new innovative approach based on normative questions concerning democracy and freedom, supported by ideas of community-led models of policy-making and social activism.

Notes

Chapter 1

1 I use the terms 'water ethics' and 'water justice' to include strictly *freshwater* issues and concerns. Going forward in this book, 'water' and 'fresh water/freshwater' are to be taken synonymously. In the interest of scope, this book does not cover all the ethical issues of water. To elaborate, water ethics and justice pertain to water allocation, of course, but also flooding and water quality; thus, the term 'water ethics' includes the ethics of flooding and flood prevention, the ethical aspects of water quality, and water, sanitation and hygiene (WASH), topics which fall largely outside the scope of this book.

2 Robeyns, Ingrid, 'Ideal Theory in Theory and Practice', *Social Theory and Practice* 34.3 (2008): 347.

3 In addition to these positions, I have held the position of Policy Analyst in the Canada Water Agency Transition Office at Environment and Climate Change Canada (ECCC). Note that this book is a product of my research before I worked for ECCC and does not necessarily represent the views of the Government of Canada.

4 Caney, Simon, 'Responding to Global Injustice: On the Right of Resistance', *Social Philosophy and Policy* 32.1 (2015): 51–73.

5 Shue, Henry, *Climate Justice: Vulnerability and Protection*, Oxford: Oxford University Press, 2014.

6 Mills, Charles W. '"Ideal Theory" as Ideology', *Hypatia* 20.3 (2005): 165–84; Pateman, Carole and Charles Mills, *Contract and Domination*, Cambridge, UK: Polity Press, 2007; Green, Fergus and Eric Brandstedt, 'Engaged Climate Ethics', *Journal of Political Philosophy* 0.0 (2020): 5.

7 Balanyá, Belén, Brid Brennan, Olivier Hoedeman, Satoko Kishimoto and Phillip Terhorst, 'Empowering Public Water – Ways Forward', in *Reclaiming Public Water: Achievements, Struggles and Visions from Around the World*, eds Belén Balanyá, Brid Brennan, Olivier Hoedeman, Satoko Kishimoto and Philipp Terhorst; Transnational Institute (TNI) & Corporate Europe Observatory (CEO), 2005, 252.

8 Stafford, Katrease, 'Controversial water shutoffs could hit 17,461 Detroit households', *Detroit Free Press*, 26 Mar. 2018. Web, 14 Nov. 2018.

9 Swaine, Jon, 'Detroit residents fight back over water shutoff: "It's a life-or-death situation."' *The Guardian*, 21 July 2014. Web, 14 Nov. 2018.
10 'Ontario allowing bottled water companies to take 7.6M litres a day on expired permits', *CBC News*, 26 Nov. 2017. Web, 14 Nov. 2018.
11 Stemplowska, Zofia, 'What's Ideal About Ideal Theory?', *Social Theory and Practice* 34.3 (2008): 326.
12 O'Neill, Onora. *Towards Justice and Virtue*, Cambridge, UK: Cambridge University Press, 1996, 40–1.
13 Mills, '"Ideal Theory" as Ideology'.
14 Cohen, G. A., *Rescuing Justice and Equality*, Cambridge, MA: Harvard University Press, 2008.
15 Stemplowska, 'What's Ideal About Ideal Theory?', 319–40.
16 Valentini, Laura, 'Ideal vs. Non-ideal theory: A conceptual map', *Philosophy Compass* 7.9 (2012): 654–64; Valentini, Laura, 'On the Apparent Paradox of Ideal Theory', *Political Philosophy* 17.3 (2009): 332–55.
17 Hamlin, Alan and Zofia Stemplowska, 'Theory, Ideal Theory, and the Theory of Ideal', *Political Studies Review* 10 (2012): 48–62; O'Neill, Onora, *Towards Justice and Virtue*.
18 Gilabert, Pablo, 'Comparative Assessments of Justice, Political Feasibility, and Ideal Theory', *Ethical Theory & Moral Practice* 15 (2012): 51.
19 Stemplowska, 'What's Ideal About Ideal Theory?', 319–40; Valentini, 'On the Apparent Paradox of Ideal Theory'.
20 Mills, '"Ideal Theory" as Ideology'.
21 Swift, Adam, 'The Value of Philosophy in Nonideal Circumstances', *Social Theory and Practice* 34.3 (2008): 363.
22 Khader, Serene, 'Transnational Feminisms, Nonideal Theory, and "Other" Women's Power', *Feminist Philosophy Quarterly* 3.1 (2017): Article 1 doi:10.5206/fpq/2016.3.1; Khader, Serene, *Decolonizing Universalism: A Transnational Feminist Ethic*, Oxford: Oxford University Press, 2018.
23 Swift, Adam, 'The Value of Philosophy in Nonideal Circumstances', 363–87.
24 Cohen, G. A., *Rescuing Justice and Equality*.
25 Shelby, Tommie, *Dark Ghettos: Injustice, Dissent, and Reform*, Cambridge, MA: Harvard University Press, 2016.
26 Laurence, Ben, 'The Question of the Agent of Change', *Journal of Political Philosophy* 28.4 (2020): 355–77.
27 Ibid., 375.
28 Brandstedt, Eric, 'Non-ideal Climate Justice', *Critical Review of International Social and Political Philosophy* 22.2 (2019): 221–34; Green and Brandstedt, 'Engaged Climate Ethics', 24; Laurence, 'The Question of the Agent of Change', 363, 375.

29 Green and Brandstedt, 'Engaged Climate Ethics', 24; Herzog, Lisa and Bernardo Zacka, 'Fieldwork in Political Theory: Five Arguments for an Ethnographic Sensibility', *British Journal of Political Science* 49 (2019): 778–80.
30 Mills, '"Ideal Theory" as Ideology'.
31 Montag, Coty, *Water/Color: A Study of Race and the Water Affordability Crisis in America's Cities*. New York: NAACP Legal Defense and Educational Fund, Inc. (LDF) (2019); Waldron, Ingrid, *There's Something in the Water: Environmental Racism in Indigenous and Black Communities*, Winnipeg and Black Point, Nova Scotia: Fernwood Publishing, 2018.
32 Robeyns, Ingrid, 'Ideal Theory in Theory and Practice', *Social Theory and Practice* 34.3 (2008): 344–5.
33 Ibid., 341–62; Brandstedt, 'Non-ideal Climate Justice'; Green and Brandstedt, 'Engaged Climate Ethics'. 1–15.
34 Wolff, Jonathan, 'Method in Philosophy and Public Policy: Applied Philosophy versus Engaged Philosophy', in *The Routledge Handbook of Ethics and Public Policy*, eds Annabelle Lever and Andrei Poama, New York: Routledge, 2019, 17.
35 Ibid., 19.
36 Ibid., 14–16.
37 Ibid., 14–17.
38 Wolff, 'Method in Philosophy and Public Policy', 17.
39 Ibid., 23.
40 Ibid., 22.
41 Wolff, 'Method in Philosophy and Public Policy', 21.
42 Ackerly, Brooke, Luis Cabrera, Fonna Forman, Genevieve Fuji Johnson, Chris Tenove and Antje Wiener, 'Unearthing Grounded Normative Theory: Practices and Commitments of Empirical Research in Political Theory', *Critical Review of International Social & Political Philosophy* (2021): 1–27.
43 Along these lines, I consider this book to be in the same vein of environmental political philosophy as political and moral philosopher Leif Wenar's book *Blood Oil: Tyrants, Violence, and the Rules that Run the World* (2017). Although Wenar focuses on oil and does not provide many solutions to conflicts, he does write about environmental injustices from a similar interdisciplinary, grounded and non-ideal perspective.
44 Swift, 'The Value of Philosophy in Nonideal Circumstances', 363–87.
45 Clark, Cristy, 'Water Justice Struggles as a Process of Commoning', *Community Development Journal* 54.1 (2018): 81–2.
46 Harvey, David, *The New Imperialism*, Oxford: Oxford University Press, 2003.
47 Bächtiger, Andre, John S. Dryzek, Jane Mansbridge and Mark Warren, 'Deliberative Democracy: An Introduction', in *The Oxford Handbook of Deliberative Democracy*,

eds Andre Bächtiger, John S. Dryzek, Jane Mansbridge and Mark Warren, Oxford; Oxford University Press, 2018, 2.
48 Ibid.
49 Ibid.
50 My understanding of the human right to water is the same as the right to water recognized in international human rights law.
51 UN General Assembly, 'The human right to water and sanitation: resolution/adopted by the General Assembly.' 3 Aug. 2010, A/RES/64/292, 14 Nov. 2018, 2.
52 UN General Assembly, 'Transforming our world: the 2030 Agenda for Sustainable Development.' 21 Oct. 2015, A/RES/70/1, 14 Nov. 2018, 14.
53 Armstrong, Chris, *Justice and Natural Resources: An Egalitarian Theory*, Oxford: Oxford University Press, 2017, 15.
54 Ibid.; Armstrong, Chris, 'Land, Resources and Inequality', *Journal of Social Philosophy* 52.1 (2021): 10–16. I will explain Armstrong's egalitarian theory of ownership in Chapter 2.
55 Risse, Mathias, 'Common Ownership of the Earth as a Non-parochial Standpoint: A Contingent Derivation of Human Rights', *European Journal of Philosophy* 17.2 (2009a): 277–304; Risse, Mathias, 'The Right to Relocation: Disappearing Island Nations and Common Ownership of the Earth', *Ethics & International Affairs* 23.3 (2009b): 281–99; Risse, Mathias, 'The Human Right to Water and Common Ownership of the Earth', *Journal of Political Philosophy* 22 (2014): 178–203. I will explain Risse's theory of common ownership of the earth fully in Chapters 2 and 3.
56 See Risse 2009a; 2009b; 2014.
57 Beitz, Charles, *Political Theory and International Relations*, Princeton, NJ: Princeton University Press, 1979.
58 Caney, Simon, 'Responding to Global Injustice: On the Right of Resistance', *Social Philosophy and Policy* 32.1 (2015): 51–73; I explicate Caney's theory of the right of resistance in Chapter 5.3.
59 Miller, David, 'Territorial Rights: Concept and Justification', *Political Studies* 60.2 (2011): 252–68.
60 Hayward, Tim, *Constitutional Environmental Rights*, New York: Oxford University Press, 2005.
61 Hayward, Tim, 'Global Justice and the Distribution of Natural Resources', *Political Studies* 54.2 (2006): 359; Hayward, Tim, 'Human Rights Versus Emissions Rights: Climate Justice and the Equitable Distribution of Ecological Space', *Ethics & International Affairs* 21.4 (2007): 445. I will explain Hayward's theories pertaining to water rights and ecological space later in this section and in Chapter 4.

62 Nussbaum, Martha, *Women and Human Development: The Capabilities Approach*, Cambridge and New York: Cambridge University Press, 2000.
63 Sen, Amartya, *Development as Freedom*, New York: Knopf, 1999; see Section 3.3 for a discussion of Sen's conception of 'Public Reason' in relation to deliberative democracy.
64 Schlosberg, David, 'Reconceiving Environmental Justice: Global Movements and Political Theories', *Environmental Politics* 13.3 (2004): 517–40; Schlosberg, David, *Defining Environmental Justice*, New York: Oxford University Press, 2007; Schlosberg, David, 'Theorising Environmental Justice: The Expanding Sphere of a Discourse', *Environmental Politics* 22.1 (2013): 37–55. I will explicate Schlosberg's conceptions of political and environmental justice and governance in Chapter 4.
65 Bakker, Karen, 'The "Commons" Versus the "Commodity": Alter-globalization, Anti-privatization and the Human Right to Water in the Global South", *Antipode* 39 (2007): 439.
66 Bakker, Karen, *Privatizing Water: Governance Failure and the World's Urban Water Crisis*, Ithaca, NY: Cornell University Press, 2010, 150, 158.
67 Ibid., 159. Also see Bakker, Karen, 'Commons versus Commodities: Debating the Human Right to Water', *The Right to Water: Politics, Governance and Social Struggles*, eds Farhana Sultana and Alex Loftus, New York: Earthscan, 2012.
68 D'Souza, Radha, 'Liberal Theory, Human Rights and Water-Justice: Back to Square One?', *Law, Social Justice & Global Development* 46 (2008): 11.
69 Ibid.
70 Harvey, David, *Justice, Nature, and the Geography of Difference*, Oxford: Blackwell, 1996, 401.
71 Clark, Cristy, 'Of What Use is a Deradicalized Human Right to Water?', *Human Rights Law Review* 17 (2017): 231–60.
72 Stilz, Anna, *Territorial Sovereignty: A Philosophical Exploration*,. New York: Oxford University Press, 2019, 229.
73 Ibid. See Section 3.2.2.1 for a fuller explication of Stilz's theory of territorial sovereignty.
74 Kolers, Avery, *Land, Conflict, and Justice: A Political Theory*, New York: Cambridge University Press, 2009.
75 Alfred, Taiaiake, *Peace, Power, Righteousness: An Indigenous Manifesto*, Don Mills: Oxford University Press, 2009.
76 McGregor, Deborah, 'Traditional Knowledge and Water Governance: The Ethic of Responsibility', *AlterNative: International Journal of Indigenous Peoples* 10 (2014): 493–507; McGregor, Deborah, Steven Whitaker and Mahisha Sritharan. 'Indigenous Environmental Justice and Sustainability', *Current Opinion in Environmental Sustainability* 43 (2020): 35–40.

77 Craft, Aimée, 'Navigating our Ongoing Sacred Legal Relationship with Nibi (Water)', *UNDRIP Implementation, More Reflections on the Braiding of International, Domestic and Indigenous Laws*, Centre for International Governance Innovation, 2018, 53–61.
78 Kolers, *Land, Conflict, and Justice*, 27–8.
79 Ibid., 29.
80 Ibid.
81 Ibid., 107.
82 Ibid., 78.
83 Alfred, *Peace, Power, Righteousness*, 84.
84 Ibid., 45.
85 Ibid., 66.
86 Hayward, Tim, *Constitutional Environmental Rights*, 65–6.
87 Ibid., 66.
88 Hayward, Tim, 'Human Rights Versus Emissions Rights, 445.
89 Hayward, Tim, 'Global Justice and the Distribution of Natural Resources', 357, 368.
90 Ibid., 445.
91 Hayward, 'Human Rights Versus Emissions Rights', 445.
92 Ibid., 360.
93 Hayward, Tim, 'A Global Right of Water', *Midwest Studies in Philosophy* 40.1 (2016), 218.
94 Ibid., 220.
95 Ibid., 220–1.
96 Young, Iris Marion, *Responsibility for Justice*, New York: Oxford University Press, Inc., 2011, 44.
97 Ibid., 45.
98 Ibid., 52.
99 Ibid.
100 Ibid., 62.
101 Ibid.
102 Ibid., 63.
103 Ibid., 151.
104 Kolers investigates the relationship between deliberative democracy and social movements, noting that a critic (Young, 2001) might contend that social movements violate basic deliberative norms because not all people can participate in them (2016, 585). I am in accordance with his insight that deliberative democrats, such as myself, might overcome this tension by the necessary role of 'contestation', of dispersed disputation and argument (2016,

585). See Sections 3.1, 4.1.2 and 5.3 for deeper exploration of the relationship between deliberative democracy and contestation.
105 I elaborate on this in Chapter 5.
106 Risse, 'The Human Right to Water and Common Ownership of the Earth', 178–203.
107 Risse, 'The Right to Relocation', 283.
108 Schlosberg, 'Theorising Environmental Justice', 42.

Chapter 2

1 As will be explained further in Chapter 5, this collective, bottom-up activism is a resistance to commodification and an inherent proponent of human rights to water.
2 Water issues in Flint (Michigan Civil Rights Commission, 2017), Detroit (Stafford 2018; Swaine 2018), Bolivia (Balanyá, 2005), and Indigenous communities in Canada (Human Rights Watch, 2015) are a few examples which attest to this. Globally, 2.1 billion people do not have access to clean and continuously available drinking water, and racialized and minoritized people are more likely to lack access to clean drinking water (see 2019 UNESCO Report 'Leaving No One Behind'). Poor people pay *more* than rich people to receive *less* water of *lower* quality: people in low- and middle-income countries spend between 5% and 25% of their income on water, buying from trucks, kiosks or other vendors; people in certain parts of Madagascar and Papua New Guinea spend over 50% of their income on water (2019 UNESCO Report, 49).
3 Bakker, Karen, 'The "Commons" Versus the "Commodity": Alter-globalization, Anti-privatization and the Human Right to Water in the Global South', *Antipode* 39 (2007): 435.
4 Bakker notes that the privatization of the water supply industry in England and Wales in 1989 did not entail commodification or marketization of water (2007, 434). Regardless of having not been commodified or marketized, privatization in England has still been harmful. In 2019 alone, raw sewage was discharged 200,000 times into England's rivers (Laville and McIntyre, 2020). Moreover, privatization has proved lucrative, as England's private water companies have paid out £57 billion or $97 billion (CAD) in dividends since 1991 (Laville and McIntyre, 2020).
5 Bakker, 'The "Commons" Versus the "Commodity"', 432.
6 Broome, John, *Climate Matters: Ethics in a Warming World*, New York: W.W. Norton and Company, 2012.

7 Smith, Adam, *An Inquiry into the Nature and Causes of The Wealth of Nations*, Hampshire, UK: Harriman House Ltd., 2007.
8 Nordhaus, William, 'The Ethics of Efficient Markets and Commons Tragedies: A Review of John Broome's "Climate Matters: Ethics in a Warming World"', *Journal of Economic Literature* 52.4 (2014): 1136; Stern, N. H., *The Economics of Climate Change: The Stern Review*, Cambridge, UK: Cambridge University Press, 2007.
9 Broome, *Climate Matters*.
10 Sen, Amartya, 'Utilitarianism and Welfarism', *Journal of Philosophy* 76.9 (1979): 463–89.
11 Smith, *An Inquiry into the Nature and Causes of The Wealth of Nations*, 293. I will explain in Section 2.4.1, though, that market environmentalism's focus and strength concerning individual consumption/distribution and epistemological efficiency are to its detriment, making citizens 'remote' from water, abstracting them from knowledge of the resource.
12 Nordhaus, 'The Ethics of Efficient Markets and Commons Tragedies', 1137.
13 Ibid., 1138.
14 Smith, *An Inquiry into the Nature and Causes of The Wealth of Nations*, 9–10.
15 Michael Sandel (2012), Debra Satz (2012), and Elizabeth Anderson (2012) will more fully illuminate this point regarding the amorality of markets as an unfair, corruptive force behind commodification in Section 2.3.
16 Nordhaus, 'The Ethics of Efficient Markets and Commons Tragedies', 1138–9.
17 Ibid., 1139.
18 Bakker, 'The "Commons" Versus the "Commodity"', 432.
19 Ibid.
20 Ibid., 437.
21 Bayliss, Kate, 'The Financialization of Water', *Review of Radical Political Economies* 46 (2014): 294.
22 Ibid., 296.
23 Ibid., 305; see examples that Bayliss lists: Poteete et al. (2010); Walljasper (2010).
24 Ibid., 305.
25 As I will proffer in Chapter 4, justice demands more than the egalitarian distribution of natural resources, but, of course, natural resources still play a role in egalitarian justice. The tangible structural changes of political reforms will be seen, in Chapter 5, to be water recommoning supported by deliberative democracy.
26 Armstrong, Chris, *Justice and Natural Resources: An Egalitarian Theory*, Oxford: Oxford University Press, 2017, 81–2.
27 Ibid., 13.
28 Ibid., 15.

29 Ibid.
30 Ibid., 18.
31 Ibid., 19.
32 Ibid., 41–2.
33 Ibid.
34 Miller, David, 'Territorial Rights: Concept and Justification', *Political Studies* 60.2 (2011): 252–68.
35 A thorough explication of Risse's theory is given in Chapter 3.
36 Armstrong, *Justice and Natural Resources*, 44.
37 Risse, Mathias. 'The Human Right to Water and Common Ownership of the Earth', *Journal of Political Philosophy* 22 (2014): 188.
38 Ibid., 191.
39 Kolers, Avery, *Land, Conflict, and Justice: A Political Theory*, New York: Cambridge University Press, 2009, 10.
40 Ibid., 8.
41 Ibid., 23.
42 Ibid., 5. In Kolers' words, 'A territorial right exists if and only if an ethnogeographic community demonstrably achieves plenitude in a juridical territory; this right grounds independent statehood only if there is no competing right and the territory is a country' (5). To clarify terms: 'Ethnography' pertains to culturally specific conceptions of a land and the intimate relationship between a people and land (3–4); 'Ethnogeographic community' is the people themselves who have a strong bond – an intimate working relationship – with the land (through use) (3–4). Territorial rights are privileged towards these people instead of other cultures or nations; 'Plenitude' means 'fullness' of a land's use, as either empirical or intentional; the term is also attached to 'settlement' of a land. It is intentional (actual) plenitude – intentional (actual) use – of a territory that determines territorial rights (and defines what makes a natural resource what it is). Along with plenitude, a land must also be 'resilient' in order to be considered territory (4); 'juridical territory' means lands bound by rules of law and governed.
43 McGregor, Deborah, 'Traditional Knowledge and Water Governance: The Ethic of Responsibility', *AlterNative: International Journal of Indigenous Peoples* 10 (2014): 501.
44 McGregor, Deborah, Steven Whitaker and Mahisha Sritharan, 'Indigenous Environmental Justice and Sustainability', *Current Opinion in Environmental Sustainability* 43 (2020): 35.
45 Poelina, Anne, Katherine S. Taylor and Ian Perdrisat, 'Martuwarra Fitzroy River Council: An Indigenous Cultural Approach to Collaborative Water Governance', *Australasian Journal of Environmental Management* 26.3 (2019): 236–54.

46 Chiblow, Susan, 'Anishinabek Women's Nibi Giikendaaswin (Water Knowledge)', *Water* 11.2 (2019), 209: 1–14; Craft, Aimée, 'Giving and Receiving Life from Anishinaabe Nibi Inaakonigewin (Our Water Law) Research', in *Methodological Challenges in Nature-Culture and Environmental History Research*, eds Jocelyn Thorpe, Stephanie Rutherford and L. Anders Sandberg, New York: Routledge, 2017: 105–19; Wilson, Nicole J., Leila M. Harris, Angie Joseph-Rear, Jody Beaumont and Terre Satterfield, 'Water is Medicine: Reimagining Water Security through Tr'ondëk Hwëch'in Relationships to Treated and Traditional Water Sources in Yukon, Canada', *Water* 11.3 (2019), 624: 1–19.

47 Craft, Aimée, 'Navigating Our Ongoing Sacred Legal Relationship with Nibi (Water)', *UNDRIP Implementation, More Reflections on the Braiding of International, Domestic and Indigenous Laws*, Centre for International Governance Innovation, 2018, 53–61.

48 Alfred, Taiaiake, *Peace, Power, Righteousness: An Indigenous Manifesto*, Don Mills: Oxford University Press, 2009, 29.

49 Ibid., 45.

50 Ibid., 84.

51 Ibid., 45.

52 Ibid., 45.

53 Bakker, 'The "Commons" Versus the "Commodity"', 430–455; Bakker, Karen, *Privatizing Water: Governance Failure and the World's Urban Water Crisis*, Ithaca, NY: Cornell University Press, 2010; D'Souza, Radha, 'Liberal Theory, Human Rights and Water-Justice: Back to Square One?', *Law, Social Justice & Global Development* 46 (2008): 1–15; McGregor, 'Traditional Knowledge and Water Governance', 493–507; McGregor et al., 'Indigenous Environmental Justice and Sustainability', 35–40.

54 Nikolakis, William and R. Quentin Grafton, 'Law versus Justice: The Strategic Aboriginal Water Reserve in the Northern Territory, Australia', *International Journal of Water Resources Development* (2021): 1–19.

55 Nikolakis and Grafton are dubious about the SAWR because it 'codifies, but also restricts, First Peoples' water rights' (2021, 14). The SAWR privileges economic rights and codifies the value of water as overwhelmingly commercial, and it 'does not embody holistic Indigenous views of water and the spiritual and cultural values of water' (2021, 14). In this case, rights are problematic because the SAWR was formed without meaningful deliberative democratic principles (i.e., recognition, participation and deference to Indigenous peoples).

56 UN General Assembly, 'United Nations Declaration on the Rights of Indigenous Peoples: resolution / adopted by the General Assembly.' 2 Oct. 2007, A/RES/61/295, 22 April 2021.

57 Taylor, Katherine S., Sheri Longboat and R. Quentin Grafton, 'Whose Rules? Principles of Water Governance, Rights of Indigenous Peoples, and Water Justice', *Water* 11.4 (2019), 809: 1–19; Taylor, Katherine S., Sheri Longboat and R. Quentin Grafton, 'Water Governance Frameworks Need to Harmonise with United Nations Declaration on the Rights of Indigenous Peoples', *Global Water Forum*, 18 June 2020, Web 22 April 2021.
58 Taylor, Longboat and Grafton, 'Water Governance Frameworks Need to Harmonise'.
59 Sandel, Michael J., 'How Markets Crowd Out Morals', *Boston Review*, 1 May 2012, Web 26 June 2019.
60 Ibid.
61 Ibid.
62 Satz, Debra, 'The Egalitarian Intuition', *Boston Review*, 25 June 2012, Web 26 June 2019.
63 Anderson, Elizabeth, 'For-Profit Corruption', *Boston Review*, 25 June 2012, Web 26 June 2019.
64 Ibid.
65 Ibid.
66 Plumwood, Val, *Environmental Culture: The Ecological Crisis of Reason*, New York: Routledge, 2002, 144.
67 This hearkens to Locke's 'Second Treatise of Government' from *Two Treatises of Government* (1764), the progenitor of rational instrumentalism through classical liberalism.
68 Plumwood, *Environmental Culture*, 71.
69 Human Rights Council, 'Climate change and poverty: Report of the Special Rapporteur on extreme poverty and human rights', 25 June 2019, A/HRC/41/39, 26 June 2019, 14.
70 Plumwood, *Environmental Culture*, 71.
71 Ibid., 81.
72 Ibid., 85.
73 Ibid.
74 Ibid., 86.
75 Ibid.
76 Ibid.
77 Ibid., 87.
78 Ibid., 146. Note the non-anthropocentrism of Plumwood's stance, characteristic of deep ecology literature.
79 Bakker, *Privatizing Water*, 150, 158; Bakker, 'The "Commons" Versus the "Commodity"', 436.

80 Bakker, 'The "Commons" Versus the "Commodity"', 436.
81 Ibid., 438.
82 Ibid., 438–9.
83 Ibid., 439.
84 Ibid., 440.
85 Ibid., 442.
86 Ibid., 446.
87 Bayliss, 'The Financialization of Water', 292.
88 Ibid., 294.
89 Bakker, 'The "Commons" Versus the "Commodity"', 441.
90 Lövbrand, Eva and Jamil Khan, 'The Deliberative Turn in Green Political Theory', in *Environmental Politics and Deliberative Democracy: Examining the Promise of New Modes of Governance*, eds Karin Bäckstrand, Jamil Khan, Annica Kronsell and Eva Lövbrand, Northhampton, MA: Edward Elgar Publishing Inc., 2010, 48. Also see O'Neill, John, *Markets, Deliberation and Environment*, London: Routledge, 2007.
91 Bayliss, 'The Financialization of Water', 293.
92 Shiva, Vandana, *Globalization's New Wars*, New Delhi: Women Unlimited, 2005.
93 Schlosberg, David, 'Reconceiving Environmental Justice: Global Movements and Political Theories', *Environmental Politics* 13.3 (2004): 524.
94 Federici, Silvia, *Caliban and the Witch: Women, the Body and Primitive Accumulation*, Brooklyn, NY: Autonomedia, 2004, 84.
95 Ibid., 71.
96 Balanyá, Belén, Brid Brennan, Olivier Hoedeman, Satoko Kishimoto and Phillip Terhorst, 'Empowering Public Water – Ways Forward', in *Reclaiming Public Water: Achievements, Struggles and Visions from Around the World*, eds Belén Balanyá, Brid Brennan, Olivier Hoedeman, Satoko Kishimoto and Philipp Terhorst, Transnational Institute (TNI) & Corporate Europe Observatory (CEO), 2005, 252.
97 Bayliss, 'The Financialization of Water', 304.
98 Nordhaus, 'The Ethics of Efficient Markets and Commons Tragedies', 1137.
99 Avrillier, Raymond, 'A Return to the Source – Re-Municipalisation of Water Services in Grenoble, France', in *Reclaiming Public Water*, eds Belén Balanyá et al., 66.
100 Ibid., 66.
101 Ibid.
102 Ibid., 70.
103 D'Souza, Radha, 'Liberal Theory, Human Rights and Water-Justice: Back to Square One?', *Law, Social Justice & Global Development* 46 (2008): 10–11; Wood, E. M., *Democracy against Capitalism: Renewing Historical Materialism*, New York: Cambridge University Press, 1995.

Chapter 3

1. Macpherson, C. B., *The Political Theory of Possessive Individualism: Hobbes to Locke*, New York: Oxford University Press, 1962.
2. Dryzek, John S. and Jonathan Pickering, *The Politics of the Anthropocene*, Oxford: Oxford University Press, 2018, 22.
3. Dryzek and Pickering, *The Politics of the Anthropocene*, 27.
4. To wit, the government of Ontario continued to allow bottling of water, despite two-thirds of the public supporting an end to water-extraction permits for bottling; See Nagy, Mike and Maude Barlow, 'Time for Ontario to Protect its Water Supplies', *The Hamilton Spectator*, 11 May 2017. Web 8 Nov. 2019.
5. Whyte, Kyle, 'Settler Colonialism, Ecology, and Environmental Injustice', *Environment and Society* 9 (2018): 131, 137–8.
6. Dryzek and Pickering, *The Politics of the Anthropocene*, 28.
7. McGregor, Deborah, Steven Whitaker and Mahisha Sritharan, 'Indigenous Environmental Justice and Sustainability', *Current Opinion in Environmental Sustainability* 43 (2020): 36.
8. Ibid.
9. Ibid., 37.
10. Ibid., 35–40; Whyte, Kyle, 'The Dakota Access Pipeline, Environmental Injustice, and U.S. Colonialism', *RED INK: An International Journal of Indigenous Literature, Arts, & Humanities* 19.1 (2017): 154–69.
11. Whyte, 'The Dakota access pipeline', 154–69.
12. Perkins, Tom, 'The fight to stop Nestlé from taking America's water to sell in plastic bottles', *The Guardian*, 29 Oct. 2019. Web 8 Nov. 2019.
13. See 'Consolidated Financial Statements of the Nestlé Group 2018'.
14. Perkins, 'The fight to stop Nestlé'.
15. Glinza, Jessica, 'Nestlé pays $200 a year to bottle water near Flint – where water is undrinkable', *The Guardian*, 29 Sept. 2017. Web 8 Nov. 2019.
16. Kurth, Joel, 'In Detroit, surviving without running water has become a way of life', *Bridge Magazine*, 24 Oct. 2018. Web 8 Nov. 2019.
17. Doremus, Holly, 'Groundwater and the public trust doctrine, California style.' Legal Planet – Insight & Analysis: Environmental Law and Policy. Berkley Law, UCLA Law, 21 July 2014. Web 8 Nov. 2019.
18. Latimer, Kendall, 'Regina homeowners grapple with untainted water', *CBC News*, 4 Nov. 2019. Web 8 Nov. 2019.
19. 'Make it Safe. Canada's Obligation to End the First Nations Water Crisis', *Human Rights Watch*, 7 June 2015. Web 26 June 2019.

20 Risse, Mathias, 'Common Ownership of the Earth as a Non-parochial Standpoint: A Contingent Derivation of Human Rights', *European Journal of Philosophy* 17.2 (2009a): 285.
21 Ibid., 285–6.
22 Risse, Mathias, *Global Political Philosophy*, New York: Palgrave MacMillan, 2012, 127.
23 Risse, Mathias, 'The Right to Relocation: Disappearing Island Nations and Common Ownership of the Earth', *Ethics and International Affairs* 23.3 (2009b): 283.
24 Ibid.
25 Ibid., 292.
26 Risse, 'Common Ownership of the Earth as a Non-parochial Standpoint', 293.
27 Risse, *Global Political Philosophy*, 34.
28 I use 'common ownership' and 'collective ownership' synonymously, as Risse does (2014, 190). Risse explains that 'Common Ownership' in upper-case denotes 'names of interpretations of Egalitarian Ownership', whereas in lower-case ('common ownership') names are 'general forms of ownership of anything' (2009b, 286); I follow this specification and convention.
29 Risse, Mathias, 'The Human Right to Water and Common Ownership of the Earth', *Journal of Political Philosophy* 22 (2014): 188.
30 Common ownership is contrasted by four different conceptions of community ownership which could be discussed by relevant discursive actors: negative community, inclusive positive community, divisible positive community, and joint positive community. See A. John Simmons' seminal work on Lockean property rights, *The Lockean Theory of Rights* (1992, 238), for descriptions and explanations of types of ownership which contrast common ownership. Lockean property, as a mixing of one's labour with a resource to create private property, is a refutation of common ownership and common territory which may be broached in a deliberative democracy. In positive community, taking more than one's fair share hurts no one else in one's community, and so no prior consent is needed. Simmons writes that Locke is 'committed to the idea that lawful appropriation from the common must be limited to what we can use and what is no more than our fair share', but Locke wrote in a time where water was a virtually infinite resource, so plentiful that he considered it, in fact, *worthless*. Moreover, Locke and classical liberalist discourse on water ownership are use-rights and distribution-focused with little regard for normative and non-instrumental value of water. Such discourse is, also, heavily anthropocentric.
31 Risse, *Global Political Philosophy*, 34.
32 Risse, 'The Human Right to Water and Common Ownership of the Earth', 197.

33 Bächtiger, A., S. Niemeyer, M. Neblo, M. R. Steenbergen and J. Steiner. 'Disentangling Diversity in Deliberative Democracy: Competing Theories, their Blind Spots and Complementarities', *Journal of Political Philosophy* 18 (2010): 32–63; Owen, D. and G. Smith, 'Survey Article: Deliberation, Democracy, and the Systemic Turn', *Journal of Political Philosophy* 23 (2015): 218; Elstub, S., S. Ercan and R. F. Mendoça, 'The Fourth Generation of Deliberative Democracy', *Critical Policy Studies* 10 (2016): 146; Brown, Mark B, 'Deliberation and Representation', in *The Oxford Handbook of Deliberative Democracy*, eds Andre Bächtiger, John S. Dryzek, Jane Mansbridge and Mark Warren, Oxford: Oxford University Press, 2018, 181.
34 See Stevenson, Hayley and John S. Dryzek, 'The Discursive Democratisation of Global Climate Governance', *Environmental Politics* 21.2 (2012): 189–210; Stevenson, Hayley and John S. Dryzek, *Democratizing Global Climate Governance*, New York: Cambridge University Press, 2014; Dryzek and Pickering, *The Politics of the Anthropocene*.
35 Schlosberg, David, 'Reconceiving Environmental Justice: Global Movements and Political Theories', *Environmental Politics* 13.3 (2004): 518.
36 Dryzek and Pickering, *The Politics of the Anthropocene*, 36.
37 Risse, 'The Human Right to Water and Common Ownership of the Earth', 198.
38 Dryzek and Pickering, *The Politics of the Anthropocene*, 87.
39 Stuart-Ulin, Chloe Rose, 'Quebec's Magpie River becomes first in Canada to be granted legal personhood', *Canada's National Observer*, 24 Feb. 2021. Web 26 Feb. 2021.
40 Dryzek and Pickering, *The Politics of the Anthropocene*, 72.
41 Safi, Michael, 'Ganges and Yamuna rivers granted same legal rights as human beings', *The Guardian*, 21 March 2017. Web 8 Nov. 2019.
42 See Lake Erie Bill of Rights, *City of Toledo*, Web 8 Nov. 2019.
43 Proffitt, James, 'Struck Down: Federal court rules Lake Erie Bill of Right unconstitutional', *Great Lakes Now*, 6 March 2020. Web 6 March 2020.
44 Johnson, Baylor L., 'Ethical Obligations in a Tragedy of the Commons', *Environmental Values* 12.3 (2003): 271–87; Kahn, Elizabeth, 'The Tragedy of the Commons as an Essentially Aggregative Harm', *Journal of Applied Philosophy* 31.3 (2014): 223–36.
45 Hardin, Garrett, 'The Tragedy of the Commons', *Science* 13 (1968): 1243–48.
46 Ostrom defines a CPR as 'a natural or man-made resource system that is sufficiently large as to make it costly (but not impossible) to exclude potential beneficiaries from obtaining benefits from its use' (1990, 30).
47 Ostrom, Elinor, *Governing the Commons: The Evolution of Institutions for Collective Action*, Cambridge: Cambridge University Press, 1990, 182.
48 Ostrom, *Governing the Commons*, 60.
49 Ibid.

50 Ibid.
51 Ibid.
52 At the beginning of Chapter 5, I term the dynamic of these organizations as an 'ouroboros', circularly making and unmaking each other through deliberation and action.
53 Ostrom, *Governing the Commons*, 60.
54 Ibid., 64.
55 Ibid., 69.
56 Ibid., 71.
57 Ibid.
58 Ibid., 72.
59 Ibid.
60 Maass, A. and R. L. Anderson. . . . *and the desert shall rejoice: Conflict, growth, and justice in arid environments*. Malabar, FL: R. E. Krieger, 1986, 117.
61 Ostrom, *Governing the Commons*, 80.
62 Ibid., 82.
63 Ibid., 107–8.
64 Ibid., 108.
65 Ibid., 116.
66 Ibid.
67 Ibid., 125.
68 Ibid.
69 Ibid., 149.
70 Ibid., 33.
71 Ostrom's eclectic examples, explained above, focus largely on farmer communities, and so are not clear-cut examples of recommoning; therefore, I use her framework to broaden democratic governance to entire (glocal) communities and to clean freshwater consumption, not only irrigation.
72 Johnson, 'Ethical Obligations in a Tragedy of the Commons', 271.
73 Ibid., 284.
74 Ibid., 273, 277, 284.
75 Johnson, 'Ethical Obligations in a Tragedy of the Commons', 274.
76 Ibid.
77 Armstrong, Chris, 'Land, Resources and Inequality', *Journal of Social Philosophy* 52.1 (2021): 10–16.
78 Johnson, 'Ethical Obligations in a Tragedy of the Commons', 272.
79 Stilz, Anna, *Territorial Sovereignty: A Philosophical Exploration*, New York: Oxford University Press, 2019, 10. Basic justice requires the existence of states' legal systems, property and contracts, courts, police, and other institutions, as Stilz

writes, 'States are essential to securing justice among us' (2019, 10). Collective self-determination gives us moral reason, in Stilz's rationale, to favour the state system.
80 Ibid., 10.
81 Ibid., 22.
82 Ibid., 11.
83 Ibid., 12–14.
84 Ibid., 169.
85 Ibid., 229; Stilz's delineation between jurisdiction and ownership is derived from Cara Nine's distinction in her book *Global Justice and Territory* (2012, 9).
86 Stilz, *Territorial Sovereignty*, 232.
87 Ibid., 240.
88 Bächtiger, Andre, John S. Dryzek, Jane Mansbridge and Mark Warren, 'Deliberative Democracy: An Introduction', in *The Oxford Handbook of Deliberative Democracy*, eds Andre Bächtiger, John S. Dryzek, Jane Mansbridge and Mark Warren, Oxford: Oxford University Press, 2018, 2.
89 Brown, Mark B., 'Deliberation and Representation', in *The Oxford Handbook of Deliberative Democracy*, 172.
90 Armstrong, Chris, *Justice and Natural Resources: An Egalitarian Theory*, Oxford: Oxford University Press, 2017; Armstrong, 'Land, Resources and Inequality'.
91 Dryzek and Pickering, *The Politics of the Anthropocene*, 36.
92 Pirsoul, Nicolas and Maria Armoudian, 'Deliberative Democracy and Water Management in New Zealand: a Critical Approach to Collaborative Governance and Co-Management Initiatives', *Water Resources Management* 33 (2019): 4821–34.
93 Hurlbert, Margot and Evan Andrews, 'Deliberative Democracy in Canadian Watershed Governance', *Water Alternatives* 11.1 (2018): 163–86.
94 Elstub, Stephen, 'Deliberative and Participatory Democracy', in *The Oxford Handbook of Deliberative Democracy*, 189.
95 Brown, 'Deliberation and Representation', 172. Also see Walzer, M., 'Deliberation, and What Else?', in *Deliberative Politics: Essays on Democracy and Disagreement*, ed. S. Macedo, New York: Oxford University Press, 1999, 58–69.
96 Vitale, D., 'Between Deliberative and Participatory Democracy: A Contribution on Habermas', *Philosophy and Social Criticism* 32 (2006): 739–66; Della Porta, D., *Can Democracy Be Saved?*, Cambridge: Polity Press, 2013; Davidson, S. and S. Elstub, 'Deliberative and Participatory Democracy in the UK', *British Journal of Politics and International Relations* 16 (2014): 367–85; Elstub, 'Deliberative and Participatory Democracy', in *The Oxford Handbook of Deliberative Democracy*, 187–202.

97 Niemeyer, Simon, 'Deliberation and Ecological Democracy: From Citizen to Global System', *Journal of Environmental Policy and Planning* 22.1 (2020): 20–1. Also see Warren, M. E. and J. Gastil, 'Can Deliberative Minipublics Address the Cognitive Challenges of Democratic Citizenship?' *Journal of Politics* 77.2 (2015): 562–74.

98 Niemeyer, 'Deliberation and Ecological Democracy', 21.

99 Ostrom, Elinor, 'A General Framework for Analyzing Sustainability of Social-Ecological Systems', *Science* 325 (2009): 419.

100 Ostrom, *Governing the Commons*; Ostrom, 'A General Framework for Analyzing Sustainability of Social-Ecological Systems', 419–22.

101 Ostrom, 'A General Framework for Analyzing Sustainability of Social-Ecological Systems', 419. Also see National Research Council, *The Drama of the Commons*, Washington, DC: National Academies Press, 2002; Pritchett, Lant and Michael Woolcock, 'Solutions When the Solution is the Problem: Arraying the Disarray in Development', *World Development* 32 (2004): 191–212.

102 Ostrom, 'A General Framework for Analyzing Sustainability of Social-Ecological Systems', 419.

103 Ibid.

104 See Ostrom (2009: 421) for a lengthy and trenchant set of criteria for assessing SESs and self-governance.

105 Ostrom, 'A General Framework for Analyzing Sustainability of Social-Ecological Systems', 420–1.

106 Robertson, Roland, 'Glocalization: Time-space and Homogeneity-heterogeneity', in *Global Modernities*, eds Mike Featherstone, Scott Lash and Roland Robertson, London: Sage, 1995; Tully, James, 'On Global Citizenship', in *On Global Citizenship: James Tully In Dialogue*, London: Bloomsbury Academic, 2014, 3–100.

107 Hardin, Garrett, 'The Tragedy of the Commons', 1243–8.

108 Johnson, Baylor L., 'Ethical Obligations in a Tragedy of the Commons', *Environmental Values* 12.3 (2003): 276.

109 Johnson, 'Ethical Obligations in a Tragedy of the Commons', 277.

110 Ibid.

111 Ibid., 284.

112 Stevenson and Dryzek, *Democratizing Global Climate Governance*, 27.

113 Ercan, Selen A., Carolyn M. Hendriks and John S. Dryzek, 'Public Deliberation in an Era of Communicative Plenty', *Policy and Politics* 47.1 (2019): 19–36.

114 Ibid., 27.

115 'Agreement to prevent unregulated high seas fisheries in the central Arctic Ocean.' Government of Canada, 3 Oct. 2018, Web 8 Nov. 2019. http://www.dfo-mpo.gc.ca/international/agreement-accord-eng.htm. This agreement is

intra-state (between peoples in Canada) and international (between Canada and other nations).

116 Bakker, Karen, Rosie Simms, Nadia Joe and Leila Harris, 'Indigenous Peoples and Water Governance in Canada: Regulatory Injustice and Prospects for Reform', in *Water Justice*, eds Rutgerd Boelens, Tom Perreault and Jeroen Vos, Cambridge: Cambridge University Press, 2018, 204.

117 Note that all relevant discourses need to be engaged within a deliberative democratic system, but this does not mean all discourses are included. As Dryzek and Pickering (2018) write, relevant discourses are those capable of critical reflection and change, so discourses that obfuscate issues, and are rigid, passive and uncritical are excluded.

118 Recall from Section 3.2.1 that this conception of reflexivity aligns with Dryzek and Pickering's explanation (2018, 36).

119 Global High-Level Panel on Water and Peace (2017). *A Matter of Survival* (Report). Geneva: Geneva Water Hub, 14.

120 Allouche, J., Nicol, A., Mehta, L. and Srivastava, S., 'Water Securities and the Individual: Challenges From Human Security to Consumerism', *Handbook on Water Security*, 2016, 60–1; Wolf, Aaron, 'Conflict and Cooperation Along International Waterways', *Water Policy* 1.2 (1998): 251–65.

121 See Innes, J. E. and D. E. Booher, 'Collaborative Policymaking: Governance through Dialogue', in *Deliberative Policy Analysis: Understanding Governance in the Network Society*, eds Maarten A. Hajer and Hendrik Wagenaar, Cambridge: Cambridge University Press, 2003, 33–59.

122 Niemeyer, 'Deliberation and Ecological Democracy', 16. Also see Dryzek, John S. 'Institutions for the Anthropocene: Governance in a Changing Earth System', *British Journal of Political Science* 46.4 (2014): 937–56.

123 Dryzek, John S., 'Institutions for the Anthropocene'. Also see Niemeyer, 'Deliberation and Ecological Democracy', 18.

124 Pirsoul and Armoudian, 'Deliberative Democracy and Water Management in New Zealand', 4831.

125 Ibid., 4823.

126 Jenkins (2018) gives a thorough examination of water management in New Zealand's Canterbury region.

127 Bächtiger, Andre and John Parkinson, *Mapping and Measuring Deliberation: Towards a New Deliberative Quality*. Oxford: Oxford University Press, 2019, 82.

128 Mackenzie, Michael K. and Mark E. Warren, 'Two Trust-based Uses of Minipublics in Democratic Systems', in *Deliberative Systems: Deliberative Democracy at the Large Scale*, eds Jane Mansbridge and John Parkinson, Cambridge: Cambridge University Press, 2012, 96.

129 Dryzek, John S., 'The Forum, the System, and the Polity: Three Varieties of Democratic Theory', *Political Theory* 45.5 (2017): 613.
130 Hurlbert, Margot and Evan Andrews, 'Deliberative Democracy in Canadian Watershed Governance', *Water Alternatives* 11.1 (2018): 175.
131 Ibid., 177.
132 Ibid.
133 Ibid., 178.
134 Stevenson and Dryzek, *Democratizing Global Climate Governance*, 118.
135 Ibid., 120.
136 Sen, Amartya. *Development as Freedom*, New York: Knopf, 1999.
137 Sen, Amartya, *The Idea of Justice*, Cambridge, MA: Belknap Press, 2009.
138 Stevenson, Hayley and John S. Dryzek, 'The Discursive Democratisation of Global Climate Governance', *Environmental Politics* 21.2 (2012): 197.
139 Hayward, Tim, 'Global Justice and the Distribution of Natural Resources', *Political Studies* 54.2 (2006): 356.
140 Ibid., 349–69.
141 Ibid., 362. See Miller (2011) concerning territory and ownership through a nationalist frame.

Chapter 4

1 *Coping with Water scarcity. Challenge of the Twenty-first Century*. UN-Water, FAO, 2007, 10.
2 Mekonnen, Mesfin M. and Arjen Y. Hoekstra, 'Four Million People Facing Severe Water Scarcity', *Sciences Advances* 2.2 (2016): 1–6.
3 Tully, James, 'On Global Citizenship', in *On Global Citizenship: James Tully In Dialogue*, London: Bloomsbury Academic, 2014, 7, 8, 11–14, 32. Roland Robertson coined the term 'glocal', so consult his work (1995) for a foundational explanation of the term. Tully's idea of the 'glocal' builds on the work of social scientist Subhabrata Bobby Banerjee (2011), who endorses the power of 'translocal' movements. To my mind, Tully provides a more critical analysis of glocal movements – movements focused on the local level, yet with global scope and support – than is given for translocal movements. However, Tully owes a debt to the base that Banerjee sets with 'translocality', the 'specific local spaces that are distributed across multiple nation states involving particular configurations of actors, resources, territory, authority, rights and relationships of power' (Banerjee,

2011, 331). Translocal activism is local, yet also globally networked and participatory, and in discourse with other movements.
4 Young, Iris Marion, *Justice and the Politics of Difference*, Princeton, NJ: Princeton University Press, 1990; Young, Iris Marion, *Responsibility for Justice*, New York: Oxford University Press, Inc., 2011.
5 Schlosberg, David, 'Reconceiving Environmental Justice: Global Movements and Political Theories', *Environmental Politics* 13.3 (2004): 517–40; Schlosberg, David, *Defining Environmental Justice*, New York: Oxford University Press, 2007; Schlosberg, David, 'Theorising Environmental Justice: The Expanding Sphere of a Discourse', *Environmental Politics* 22.1 (2013): 37–55.
6 Khagram (2004) explains this point in light of the local and transnational resistance against the massive Sardar Sarovar Dam on the Narmada River in India.
7 Schlosberg, 'Reconceiving Environmental Justice', 517.
8 The traditional liberal justice theory of distribution stems from Rawls who explained that, in an initial position as rational beings, we would all, under a veil of ignorance, make choices so everyone had equal political rights, and economic and social inequality should benefit everyone, especially those worst off (1999). However, the traditional liberal justice view, highlighted with capitalist mechanisms, misses much of actual justice: goods are not static because they are influenced by social and institutional relations. Moreover, social, cultural, symbolic and institutional conditions underlie poor distribution. Theories of environmental justice have focused too much on distribution to the disbenefit of recognition and participation. As Young (1990) and Schlosberg (2004, 518) have argued, 'injustice is not based solely on inequitable distribution'.
9 Bakker, Karen, Rosie Simms, Nadia Joe and Leila Harris, 'Indigenous Peoples and Water Governance in Canada: Regulatory Injustice and Prospects for Reform', in *Water Justice*, eds Rutgerd Boelens, Tom Perreault and Jeroen Vos, Cambridge, MA: Cambridge University Press, 2018, 202.
10 Ibid.
11 Ibid.
12 Ibid., 197–8.
13 Ibid., 200.
14 Ibid.
15 Baber, Walter F. and Robert V. Bartlett, *Consensus and Global Environmental Governance: Deliberative Democracy in Nature's Regime*, Cambridge, MA: The MIT Press, 2015, 111. I will explain in Chapter 5 this reflexivity of deliberative democracy – its imprimatur on us as we, in turn, actualize water justice as recommoning – by way of 'glocal' case studies.

16 Sunstein, Cass R., *Going to Extremes: How Like Minds Unite and Divide*, New York: Oxford University Press, 2009, 152.
17 In the latter half of Chapter 5, I provide further explanation of these neo-Hegelian 'frontiers of disagreement', in political theorist Jennifer Dodge's (2015) terminology.
18 Lam, Steven, Michelle Thompson, Kathleen Johnson, Cameron Fioret and Sarah Hargreaves, 'Toward Community Food Security through Transdisciplinary Action Research', *Action Research* 19.4 (2019): 656–73.
19 Lam et al. (2019) offer a strategy that is reflexive, looking back at ecological, democratized farming and farmer-led research. Furthermore, Fioret et al. (2018) have developed a guidebook on farmer-led research, which Lam et al. reflect upon.
20 D'Souza, Radha, 'Liberal Theory, Human Rights and Water-Justice: Back to Square One?', *Law, Social Justice & Global Development* 46 (2008): 4–5.
21 Ibid., 4.
22 Ibid., 7.
23 Ibid., 8.
24 Rob Nixon's (2011) idea of 'slow violence' is applicable to the study of water injustice, as will be made evident in Section 4.2.1.
25 Young, *Responsibility for Justice*, 52.
26 Krause, Sharon R., 'Environmental Domination', *Political Theory* 48.4 (2020): 444–5.
27 Ibid., 446.
28 Ibid.; Krause's point is exemplified by cases in Chapter 5, most starkly in Detroit, Flint and Baltimore, United States; Cochabamba, Bolivia; and Kerala, India.
29 Ibid., 456.
30 Ibid., 445.
31 Ibid., 449.
32 Stevenson, Hayley and John S. Dryzek, *Democratizing Global Climate Governance*, New York: Cambridge University Press, 2014, 109.
33 Neither commodification nor authoritarianism do a better job of handling and improving environmental issues than democracy; in fact, there is evidence that authoritarianism does worse (Li and Reuveny, 2006). This appeal to utilitarianism against authoritarianism, though, should not overshadow the political, social and normative violence of authoritarianism. Some argue, as James Lovelock has, that 'democracy must be put on hold' to address climate change (Hickman, 2010); however, it is naïve to believe that authoritatians would concede power to a democratic system once already in power, not to mention the type of society worth maintaining only in an authoritarian state. Authoritarianism is inherently without meaningful, reflexive socioenvironmental dialogue that engages all

relevant actors in water discourse, so we cannot turn to it for justice. Authoritarianism is bereft of widespread engagement with diverse discourses.

34 Smee, Ben, 'Queensland school runs out of water as commercial bottlers harvest local supplies', *The Guardian*, 12 Dec. 2019, Web 13 Dec. 2019. Democratic inequalities can be exacerbated when the state opens water to private control in PPPs; see Miraftab (2004).
35 Young, *Justice and the Politics of Difference*, 38.
36 Forst, Rainer, 'Transnational Justice and Non-Domination, a Discourse-Theoretical Approach', in *Domination and Global Political Justice: Conceptual, Historical and Institutional Perspectives*, eds Barbara Buckinx, Jonathan Trejo-Mathys and Timothy Waligore, New York, Routledge (Taylor & Francis), 2015, 88–110.
37 Young, *Justice and the Politics of Difference*, 55.
38 Ibid., 57.
39 See definition provided in Section 3.2.3.
40 Stilz, Anna, *Territorial Sovereignty: A Philosophical Exploration*, New York: Oxford University Press, 2019, 14.
41 Deveaux, Monique, 'Poor-Led Social Movements and Global Justice', *Political Theory* 46.5 (2018): 712.
42 Clark, Cristy, 'Water Justice Struggles as a Process of Commoning', *Community Development Journal* 54.1 (2018): 84.
43 Ibid., 85.
44 Tully, 'On Global Citizenship'. 38.
45 Ibid., 41, 50.
46 Plumwood, Val, *Environmental Culture: The Ecological Crisis of Reason*, New York: Routledge, 2002, 86; Schlosberg, David, 'Reconceiving Environmental Justice: Global Movements and Political Theories', *Environmental Politics* 13.3 (2004): 524.
47 Tully, 'On Global Citizenship', 7.
48 Ibid., 7–8.
49 Ibid., 50.
50 Ibid., 7.
51 Ibid., 73–80.
52 Ibid., 8.
53 Ibid.
54 Ibid.
55 Ibid., 13.
56 Ibid.
57 The economic historian and social philosopher Karl Polanyi identified privatization as power from above, where the private realm placed limits on democratic participation in the economic realm of society. In *The Great*

Transformation: The Political and Economic Origins of Our Time, Polanyi notes that privatization makes human production and consumption commodities all their own, so that social and even environmental relationships become competitive 'free-market' endeavours. Essentially, in the case of water, commodifiers place limits on the democracy that can be allowed in the water ownership and distribution process; these limits enable path dependencies. Furthermore, Polanyi notes that commodification of natural resources, such as water, rips the resource from its ecological relationships and makes it into an abstract, instrumental object and supplicant of profit. As Polanyi and Tully argue, peaceful non-compliance is a strong response to ossified systems of modern citizenship and liberal capitalist theory (Polanyi, 2004; Tully, 2014, 90–1).
58 Nixon, Rob, *Slow Violence and the Environmentalism of the Poor*, Cambridge, MA: Harvard University Press, 2011, 141.
59 Allen, Amy, 'Power and the Politics of Difference: Oppression, Empowerment, and Transnational Justice', *Hypatia* 23.3 (2008): 167.
60 Ibid.
61 Switzer, David, and Manuel P. Teodoro, 'Class, Race, Ethnicity, and Justice in Safe Drinking Water Compliance', *Social Science Quarterly* 99.2 (2018): 524–35.
62 https://detroitwaterproject.org; https://www.coc-guelph.org.
63 Balanyá, Belén, Brid Brennan, Olivier Hoedeman, Satoko Kishimoto, and Phillip Terhorst, 'Empowering Public Water – Ways Forward', in *Reclaiming Public Water: Achievements, Struggles and Visions from Around the World*, eds. Belén Balanyá, Brid Brennan, Olivier Hoedeman, Satoko Kishimoto and Philipp Terhorst, Transnational Institute (TNI) & Corporate Europe Observatory (CEO), 2005, 275.
64 Van Harten and Křístková (2018) provide an explanation of the deleterious effects that ISDS has on democracy and judiciary independence.

Chapter 5

1 Bakker, Karen, *Privatizing Water: Governance Failure and the World's Urban Water Crisis*, Ithaca, NY: Cornell University Press, 2010.
2 Robinson, Joanna, *Contested Water: The Struggle Against Water Privatization in the United States and Canada*, Cambridge, MA: The MIT Press, 2013.
3 Subramaniam, Mangala, *Contesting Water Rights: Local, State, and Global Struggles*, Cham, Switzerland: Springer, 2018.
4 Sultana, Farhana and Alex Loftus, 'The Right to Water: Prospects and Possibilities', in *The Right to Water: Politics, Governance and Social Struggles*, eds Farhana

Sultana and Alex Loftus, New York: Earthscan, 2012, 1-18; Sultana, Farhana and AlexLoftus, *Water Politics: Governance, Justice and the Right to Water*, London: Routledge, 2019.

5 I consider my term 'recommoning' (of water) more accurate than 'commoning', the term scholars such as Karen Bakker (2007), Patrick Bond (2002, 2012), Cristy Clark (2018), and Farhana Sultana and Alex Loftus (2012) use, because private interests have made significant inroads commodifying water the world-over, and the protection of rights to water through law, politics and social movements ought to have the goal of taking water back from private control, of '*re*commoning' water.

6 Clark, Cristy, 'Water Justice Struggles as a Process of Commoning', *Community Development Journal* 54.1 (2018): 95.

7 Ercan, Selen A. and John Dryzek, 'The Reach of Deliberative Democracy', *Policy Studies* 36.3 (2015): 242.

8 Deliberative democracy is a normative theory that is transformative and always happens 'in degrees; as such, deliberative democracy 'is not an additional "model" of democracy that can be "verified" or "falsified" based on empirical inquiry' (Ercan and Dryzek, 2015, 243). Importantly, through critical inquiry, normative theory shows the incompleteness of democracy and the limits of democratic exclusion (Ercan and Gagnon, 2014; Ercan and Dryzek, 2015). This is the aim of the forthcoming analyses of transnational water agreements, policies and local social movements for water justice, to show the gaps and incompleteness of democracy and identify where they might be coming up short.

9 Flynn, Sean and Kathryn Boudouris, 'Democratising the Regulation and Governance of Water in the US', *Reclaiming Public Water: Achievements, Struggles and Visions from Around the World*, eds Belén Balanyá, Brid Brennan, Olivier Hoedeman, Satoko Kishimoto and Philipp Terhorst, Transnational Institute (TNI) & Corporate Europe Observatory (CEO), 2005, 82.

10 Ibid., 81.

11 Bakker, *Privatizing Water*, 43.

12 Robinson, Joanna, *Contested Water: The Struggle Against Water Privatization in the United States and Canada*, Cambridge, MA: The MIT Press, 2013, 2-7, 34-8.

13 Ibid., 102.

14 Subramaniam notes that a tension with local communities – and I see no reason to not extend this observation to the level of the state – lies in being 'constituted around social politics of gender, caste, and class which influence decision-making processes' (2018, 33-4).

15 Subramaniam, *Contesting Water Rights*, 33–4.

16 Ibid., 91.

17 Madlingozi, Tshepo, 'Post-Apartheid Social Movements and Legal Mobilisation', in *Socio Economic Rights in South Africa: Symbols or Substance?*, eds M. Langford, B. Cousins, J. Dugard and T. Madlingozi, Cambridge: Cambridge University Press, 2013, 92–130.
18 Kolers, Avery, 'Social Movements', *Philosophy Compass* 11/10 (2016): 582.
19 Ibid., 582.
20 Ibid., 584.
21 Some researchers of water-focused social movements, such as Caitlin Schroering, rightly connect such forums with a 'right to the city' approach of social movements 'organizing to claim a collective right, working to generate something new that does not yet exist' (2019, 30).
22 See La Via Campesina, *Struggles of La Via Campesina For Agrarian Reform and the Defense of Life, Land and Territories* (2017) for a trenchant analysis of the grassroots, glocal and collaborative work done by La Via Campesina, in their own words.
23 Young, Iris Marion, *Inclusion and Democracy*, New York: Oxford University Press, 2000, 274.
24 Griffiths, John, 'What is Legal Pluralism?', *Journal of Legal Pluralism and Unofficial Law* 24 (1986): 1–55.
25 Rajagopal, Balakrishnan, 'Counter-hegemonic International Law: Rethinking Human Rights and Development as a Third World Strategy', *Third World Quarterly* 27.5 (2006): 767.
26 Global High-Level Panel on Water and Peace, *A Matter of Survival* (Report), Geneva: Geneva Water Hub, 2017.
27 Ibid.
28 Federici, Silvia, *Caliban and the Witch: Women, the Body and Primitive Accumulation*, Brooklyn, NY: Autonomedia, 2004, 105.
29 See *A Matter of Survival* (Report) (2017) for more information on these presented water agreements.
30 Clark, 'Water Justice Struggles as a Process of Commoning', 81–2.
31 Haiven, Max, 'Reimagining Our Collective Powers Against Austerity', *Roar Magazine*, 5 June 2015, Web 1 March 2021; Clark, 'Water Justice Struggles as a Process of Commoning', 80–99.
32 Clark, 'Water Justice Struggles as a Process of Commoning', 93; Haiven, 'Reimagining Our Collective Powers Against Austerity'.
33 Perera, Verónica, 'Engaged Universals and Community Economies: The (Human) Right to Water in Colombia', *Antipode* 47.1 (2015): 197.
34 Ostrom, Elinor, *Governing the Commons: The Evolution of Institutions for Collective Action*, Cambridge: Cambridge University Press, 1990, 90.

35 Shiva, Vandana, *Water Wars: Privatization, Pollution and Profit*, Cambridge, MA: South End Press, 2002.
36 Ostrom, *Governing the Commons*, 80, 107–10, 116.
37 Harvey, David, *Rebel Cities*, London: Verso, 2012, 87; Pithouse (2014), in the same vein as Harvey, also argues for a 'double-edged' attack with reference to urban squatter movements in South Africa. In this way, Pithouse argues that the state might be a crucial proponent against commodification.
38 Fletcher, Heelsum and Roggeband (2018: https://www.tandfonline.com/doi/full/10.1080/1774 8689.2018.1496308) found that those in Ireland most motivated to protest against water commodification and for water justice and water as a human right had high instrumental motivation and low ideological motivation, a combination of motivations that does not lead to success.
39 'Recommoning' is equivalent to 'remunicipalization'. Here, I use the term 'recommoning' to connect this term and idea more explicitly with water as commonly owned territory.
40 'Ontario allowing bottled water companies to take 7.6M litres a day on expired permits', *CBC News*, 26 Nov. 2017. Web 14 Nov. 2018.
41 Barlow, Maude, 'Making Water a Human Right', in *Water Consciousness: How We All Have to Change to Protect Our Most Critical Resources*, ed. Tara Lohan, San Francisco, CA: AlterNet Books, 2008, 181. In *Blue Gold: The Fight to Stop the Corporate Theft of the World's Water* (2002), Barlow and Tony Clarke give a thorough yet accessible explanation of, and argument against, water commodification from the perspective of veteran water justice activists.
42 Patterson, Brent, 'Guelph Chapter Presents to City Council on Nestle Water-Takings', *Council of Canadians*, 28 Nov. 2016. Web 20 July 2020.
43 Karunananthan, Meera and Satoko Kishimoto, '(Re)municipalization of Water – the Right Way Towards Achieving SDG 6', in *Exploring New Policy pathways: How to Overcome Obstacles and Contradictions in the Implementation of the 2030 Agenda. Report by the Civil Society Reflection Group on the 2030 Agenda for Sustainable Development*, eds Barbara Adams, Roberto Bissio, Chee Yoke Ling, Kate Donald, Jens Martens, Stefano Prato and Sandra Vermuyten, Civil Society Reflection Group on the 2030 Agenda for Sustainable Development, 2018, 123-5; Barlow, Maude, *Whose Water Is It Anyway? Taking Water Protection Into Public Hands*, Toronto: ECW Press, 2019.
44 Dodge, Jennifer, 'The Deliberative Potential of Civil Society Organizations: Framing Hydraulic Fracturing in New York', *Policy Studies* 36.3 (2015): 252.
45 Ercan, Selen A., Carolyn M. Hendriks and John S. Dryzek, 'Public Deliberation in an Era of Communicative Plenty', *Policy and Politics* 47.1 (2019): 19–36.
46 Ibid., 30-1.

47 Dryzek, John S, 'The Forum, the System, and the Polity: Three Varieties of Democratic Theory', *Political Theory* 45.5 (2017): 611.
48 The WATER Act of 2019 would create a WATER Trust Fund of $35 billion for water infrastructure improvements in the United States. Representatives Brenda Lawrence and Ro Khanna first brought the legislation to Congress, and Senator Bernie Sanders introduced companion legislation to the Senate.
49 Stafford, Katrease, 'Controversial water shutoffs could hit 17,461 Detroit households', *Detroit Free Press*, 26 March 2018, Web 14 Nov. 2018.
50 Swaine, Jon, 'Detroit residents fight back over water shutoff: "It's a life-or-death situation".' *The Guardian*, 21 July 2014, Web 14 Nov. 2018.
51 See http://detroitwaterbrigade.org, https://detroitwaterproject.org, and https://www.wethepeopleofdetroit.com.
52 Biron, Carey L., 'Baltimore votes to become first large U.S. city to ban water privatization', *Reuters*, 7 Nov. 2018, Web 14 Nov. 2018.
53 Gwynn, Alvin, 'Baltimore ban on privatizing water system was the right thing to do', *The Baltimore Sun*, 10 Feb. 2020, Web 16 June 2018.
54 The Flint water crisis: Systemic racism through the lens of Flint, *Report of the Michigan Civil Rights Commission*, Detroit: Michigan Civil Rights Commission (2017).
55 Waldron, Ingrid, *There's Something in the Water: Environmental Racism in Indigenous and Black Communities*, Winnipeg and Black Point, Nova Scotia: Fernwood Publishing, 2018.
56 Maqbool, Aleem, 'Coronavirus: "I can't wash my hands – my water was cut off".' BBC News, 24 April 2020, Web 16 June 2020; Mosley, Elizabeth A., Cortney K. Bouse and Kelli Stidham Hall, 'Water, Human Rights, and Reproductive Justice: Implication for Women in Detroit and Monrovia', *Environmental Justice* 8.3 (2015): 78–85.
57 Maqbool, 'Coronavirus'.
58 These injustices in Flint and Baltimore speak to the difficulty of democratizing water, especially due to the systemic nature of water injustice. It is a slow, agonizing process to recommon water; indeed, to use the term 'recommon' is to acknowledge that a formerly common resource has been privatized despite protestations and struggles. Social movements might struggle internally, and they certainly struggle against external factors such as private actors. The road to water justice is not straight.
59 Federici, Silvia, 'Feminism and the Politics of the Commons in an Era of Primitive Accumulation', in *Re-enchanting the World: Feminism and the Politics of the Commons*, Oakland, CA: PM Press/Kairos, 2018, 107; also see Shiva (1989).

60 Ibid., 107.
61 Great Big Story, 'The Woman Fighting for Detroit's Water', *YouTube*, uploaded by Great Big Story, 18 Sept. 2017, https://www.youtube.com/watch?v=q9D4ysxbGao; Smith, Rhonda J., '3 "women water warriors" testing lead in Detroit drinking water', *Detour Detroit*, 12 Nov. 2020, Web 19 March 2021.
62 Kolers, 'Social Movements', 582.
63 Bakker, *Privatizing Water*, 167.
64 Olivera, Oscar and Tom Lewis, *Cochabamba!: Water War in Bolivia*, Cambridge, MA: South End Press, 2004, 72.
65 Ibid., 20.
66 Ibid., 50.
67 Avrillier, Raymond, 'A Return to the Source – Re-Municipalisation of Water Services in Grenoble, France', in *Reclaiming Public Water: Achievements, Struggles and Visions from Around the World*, eds Belén Balanyá, Brid Brennan, Olivier Hoedeman, Satoko Kishimoto and Philipp Terhorst, Transnational Institute (TNI) & Corporate Europe Observatory (CEO), 2005, 63.
68 Ibid., 66.
69 Ibid., 67.
70 Khagram, Sanjeev, *Dams and Development: Transnational Struggles for Water and Power*, Ithaca, NY: Cornell University Press, 2004, 25, 42.
71 Ibid., 62.
72 Ibid., 113.
73 Bywater, Krista, 'Anti-privatization Struggles and the Right to Water in India: Engendering Cultures of Opposition', in *The Right to Water: Politics, Governance and Social Struggles*, eds Farhana Sultana and Alex Loftus, New York: Earthscan, 2012, 207.
74 Subramaniam, *Contesting Water Rights*, 77.
75 See Balanyá et al. (2005, 247) for an explanation about people-centred water solutions around the world. Public utility co-operatives in Porto Alegre (Brazil), Santa Cruz (Bolivia) and Penang (Malaysia); public-centred delivery models in Caracas (Venezuela), Harrismith (South Africa) and the province of Buenos Aires (Argentina); and community-management in Olavanna (Kerala, India) and Savelugu (Ghana) improved water delivery as compared to private, non-people-centred water schemes and attest to the power of recommoning.
76 Balanyá, Belén, Brid Brennan, Olivier Hoedeman, Satoko Kishimoto, and Philip & Terhorst, 'Empowering Public Water – Ways Forward', in *Reclaiming Public Water*, eds Belén Balanyá, et al., 251.
77 Caney, Simon, 'Responding to Global Injustice: On the Right of Resistance', *Social Philosophy and Policy* 32.1 (2015): 65.

78 Dryzek, John S. and Jonathan Pickering, *The Politics of the Anthropocene*, Oxford: Oxford University Press, 2018; Ostrom, *Governing the Commons*, Ostrom, Elinor, 'A General Framework for Analyzing Sustainability of Social-ecological Systems', *Science* 325 (2009): 419–22; Scott, James C., *Seeing Like a State: How Certain Schemes to Improve the Human Condition Have Failed*, New Haven: Yale University Press, 1998; Scott, James C., *Against the Grain: A Deep History of the Earliest States*, New Haven: Yale University Press, 2017; Taylor, Charles, Patrizia Nanz and Madeleine Beaubien Taylor, *Reconstructing Democracy: How Citizens Are Building from the Ground Up*, Cambridge, MA: Harvard University Press, 2020.

79 Caney, 'Responding to Global Injustice', 67.

80 Krause, Sharon R., 'Environmental Domination', *Political Theory* 48.4 (2020): 451.

81 Dodge, 'The Deliberative Potential of Civil Society Organizations', 250.

82 Calvert, A. and M. E. Warren, 'Deliberative Democracy and Framing Effects: Why Frames are a Problem and How Deliberative Mini-Publics Might Overcome Them', in *Deliberative Mini-Publics: Involving Citizens in the Democratic Process*, eds Kimmo Grönlund, André Bächtiger and Maija Setälä, Colchester: ECPR Press, 2014.

83 Dodge, 'The Deliberative Potential of Civil Society Organizations', 251.

84 Norval, Aletta, 'Deliberative, Agonistic and Aversive Grammars of Democracy: The Question of Criteria', in *Practices of Freedom: Decentered Governance, Conflict and Democratic Participation*, eds S. Griggs, A. J. Norval and H. Wagenaar, New York: Cambridge University Press, 2014, 74.

85 I note the Hegelian nature of this discursive conflict as derivative. Dodge terms the discursive positions as the 'act' (the actor arguing for a particular way of framing an issue, i.e., the thesis), the 'interact' (other actors react to the issue and its framing, i.e., the antithesis), and the 'double interact' (actors adjust their framing in reaction to challenges, i.e., the synthesis). However, violence as war (or some such physical conflict) is not inherent in the schema.

86 Clark, 'Water Justice Struggles as a Process of Commoning', 85.

87 Tully, James, 'On Global Citizenship', In *On Global Citizenship: James Tully In Dialogue*, London: Bloomsbury Academic, 2014, 67.

Chapter 6

1 The very same questions I have asked in this book concerning property, community politics and ethics.

2 Fioret, Cameron, 'Complimentary Intersections? Water Commodification through the Lens of Philosophy and Geography', *Geoforum* 86 (2017): 16–19.

3 Nagabhatla and Fioret (2020), Nagabhatla et al. (2020), and Nagabhatla, Fioret and Pouramin (2021) provide examples of such co-operative and diverse water governance research.
4 Arsenault, Rachel, Sibyl Diver, Deborah McGregor, Aaron Witham and Carrie Bourassa, 'Shifting the Framework of Canadian Water Governance through Indigenous Research Methods: Acknowledging the Past with an Eye on the Future', *Water* 10.1 (2018): 1–18.
5 Culp, Tyler E. et al., 'Nanoscale Control of Internal Inhomogeneity Enhances Water Transport in Desalination Membranes', *Science* 371.6524 (2021): 72–5.
6 Jones et al. (2019: https://doi.org/10.1126/science.abb8518) provide an exhaustive breakdown of the current global state of desalination technology and brine production.
7 In December 2019, Canadian Prime Minister Justin Trudeau appointed Member of Parliament Terry Duguid as Parliamentary Secretary to the Minister of Environment and Climate Change, in charge of leading the effort to establish the CWA; see 'Prime Minister welcomes new parliamentary secretaries', *Government of Canada*, for a formal announcement of the appointment and initiative.
8 For further detail on the public consultation process in service to formalizing and creating the Canada Water Agency, consult 'Toward the Creation of a Canada Water Agency: Discussion Paper' and 'Toward the Creation of a Canada Water Agency: Stakeholder and Public Engagement – What We Heard' reports from Environment and Climate Change Canada.
9 http://www.eaudeparis.fr.
10 https://sustainabledevelopment.un.org/partnership/?p=2213.
11 Planas, Míriam and Juan Martínez, 'Water should be a public good, not a commodity. Catalonia is showing how', *openDemocracy*, 30 April 2020, Web. 10 Dec. 2020.

Bibliography

Ackerly, Brooke, Luis Cabrera, Fonna Forman, Genevieve Fuji Johnson, Chris Tenove and Antje Wiener. 'Unearthing Grounded Normative Theory: Practices and Commitments of Empirical Research in Political Theory.' *Critical Review of International Social & Political Philosophy* (2021): 1–27.

'Agreement to prevent unregulated high seas fisheries in the central Arctic Ocean.' Government of Canada, 3 Oct. 2018. Web 8 Nov. 2019: <http://www.dfo-mpo.gc.ca/international/agreement-accord-eng.htm>

Alfred, Taiaiake. *Peace, Power, Righteousness: An Indigenous Manifesto*. Don Mills: Oxford University Press, 2009.

Allen, Amy. 'Power and the Politics of Difference: Oppression, Empowerment, and Transnational Justice.' *Hypatia* 23.3 (2008): 156–72.

Allouche, J., Nicol A., Mehta, L. and Srivastava, S. 'Water Securities and the Individual: Challenges from Human Security to Consumerism.' *Handbook on Water Security*, 2016, 60–1.

Anderson, Elizabeth. 'For-Profit Corruption.' *Boston Review*, 25 June 2012. Web 26 June 2019: <http://bostonreview.net/anderson-for-profit-corruption>

Armstrong, Chris. *Justice and Natural Resources: An Egalitarian Theory*. Oxford: Oxford University Press, 2017.

Armstrong, Chris. 'Land, Resources and Inequality.' *Journal of Social Philosophy* 52.1 (2021): 10–16.

Arsenault, Rachel, Sibyl Diver, Deborah McGregor, Aaron Witham and Carrie Bourassa. 'Shifting the Framework of Canadian Water Governance through Indigenous Research Methods: Acknowledging the Past with an Eye on the Future.' *Water* 10.1 (2018): 1–18.

Avrillier, Raymond. 'A Return to the Source – Re-Municipalisation of Water Services in Grenoble, France.' In *Reclaiming Public Water: Achievements, Struggles and Visions from Around the World*, eds Belén Balanyá, Brid Brennan, Olivier Hoedeman, Satoko Kishimoto and Philipp Terhorst, Transnational Institute (TNI) & Corporate Europe Observatory (CEO), 2005, 63–72.

Baber, Walter F. and Robert V. Bartlett. *Consensus and Global Environmental Governance: Deliberative Democracy in Nature's Regime*. Cambridge, MA: The MIT Press, 2015.

Bächtiger, Andre and John Parkinson. *Mapping and Measuring Deliberation: Towards a New Deliberative Quality*. Oxford: Oxford University Press, 2019.

Bächtiger, Andre, John S. Dryzek, Jane Mansbridge and Mark Warren. 'Deliberative Democracy: An Introduction.' In *The Oxford Handbook of Deliberative Democracy*, eds Andre Bächtiger, John S. Dryzek, Jane Mansbridge and Mark Warren, Oxford: Oxford University Press, 2018, 1–34.

Bächtiger, A., S. Niemeyer, M. Neblo, M. R. Steenbergen and J. Steiner. 'Disentangling Diversity in Deliberative Democracy: Competing Theories, their Blind Spots and Complementarities.' *Journal of Political Philosophy* 18 (2010): 32–63.

Bächtiger, A., S. Niemeyer, M. Neblo, M. R. Steenbergen and J. Steiner. 'The "Commons" Versus the "Commodity": Alter-globalization, Anti-privatization and the Human Right to Water in the Global South.' *Antipode* 39 (2007): 430–55.

Bächtiger, A., S. Niemeyer, M. Neblo, M. R. Steenbergen and J. Steiner. *Privatizing Water: Governance Failure and the World's Urban Water Crisis*. Ithaca, NY: Cornell University Press, 2010.

Bakker, Karen, 'Commons versus Commodities: Debating the Human Right to Water.' In *The Right to Water: Politics, Governance and Social Struggles*, eds Farhana Sultana and Alex Loftus, New York: Earthscan, 2012.

Bakker, Karen, Rosie Simms, Nadia Joe and Leila Harris. 'Indigenous Peoples and Water Governance in Canada: Regulatory Injustice and Prospects for Reform.' In *Water Justice*, eds Rutgerd Boelens, Tom Perreault and Jeroen Vos, Cambridge: Cambridge University Press, 2018, 193–209.

Balanyá, Belén, Brid Brennan, Olivier Hoedeman, Satoko Kishimoto and Philipp Terhorst. 'Empowering Public Water – Ways Forward.' In *Reclaiming Public Water: Achievements, Struggles and Visions from Around the World*, eds Belén Balanyá, Brid Brennan, Olivier Hoedeman, Satoko Kishimoto and Philipp Terhorst, Transnational Institute (TNI) & Corporate Europe Observatory (CEO), 2005, 247–75.

Banerjee, Subhabrata Bobby. 'Voices of the Governed: Towards a Theory of the Translocal.' *Organization* 18.3 (2011): 323–44.

Barlow, Maude. 'Making Water a Human Right.' In *Water Consciousness: How We All Have to Change to Protect Our Most Critical Resources*, ed. Tara Lohan, San Francisco, CA: AlterNet Books, 2008, 177–85.

Barlow, Maude. *Whose Water Is It Anyway? Taking Water Protection Into Public Hands*. Toronto: ECW Press, 2019.

Barlow, Maude and Tony Clarke. *Blue Gold: The Fight to Stop the Corporate Theft of the World's Water*. New York: New Press, 2002.

Bayliss, Kate. 'The Financialization of Water.' *Review of Radical Political Economies* 46 (2014): 292–307.

Beitz, Charles. *Political Theory and International Relations*. Princeton, NJ: Princeton University Press, 1979.

Biron, Carey L. 'Baltimore votes to become first large U.S. city to ban water privatization.' *Reuters*, 7 Nov. 2018. Web 14 Nov. 2018.

Biron, Carey L. *Unsustainable South Africa*. London: Merlin Press, 2002.

Bond, Patrick. 'The Right to the City and the Eco-Social Commoning of Water: Discursive and political lessons from South Africa.' In *The Right to Water: Politics, Governance and Social Struggles*, eds. Farhana Sultana and Alex Loftus, New York: Earthscan, 2012, 190–205.

Brandstedt, Eric. 'Non-ideal Climate Justice.' *Critical Review of International Social and Political Philosophy* 22.2 (2019): 221–34.

Broome, John. *Climate Matters: Ethics in a Warming World*. New York: W.W. Norton and Company, 2012.

Brown, Mark B. 'Deliberation and Representation.' In *The Oxford Handbook of Deliberative Democracy*, eds Andre Bächtiger, John S. Dryzek, Jane Mansbridge and Mark Warren, Oxford: Oxford University Press, 2018, 171–86.

Bywater, Krista. 'Anti-privatization Struggles and the Right to Water in India: Engendering Cultures of Opposition.' In *The Right to Water: Politics, Governance and Social Struggles*, eds Farhana Sultana and Alex Loftus, New York: Earthscan, 2012, 206–22.

Calvert, A. and M. E. Warren. 'Deliberative Democracy and Framing Effects: Why Frames are a Problem and How Deliberative Mini-Publics Might Overcome Them.' In *Deliberative Mini-Publics: Involving Citizens in the Democratic Process*, eds Kimmo Grönlund, André Bächtiger and Maija Setälä. Colchester: ECPR Press, 2014.

Caney, Simon. 'Responding to Global Injustice: On the Right of Resistance.' *Social Philosophy and Policy* 32.1 (2015): 51–73.

Chiblow, Susan. 'Anishinabek women's Nibi Giikendaaswin (Water knowledge).' *Water* 11.2 (2019), 209: 1–14.

Clark, Cristy. 'Of What Use is a Deradicalized Human Right to Water?' *Human Rights Law Review* 17 (2017): 231–60.

Clark, Cristy. 'Water Justice Struggles as a Process of Commoning.' *Community Development Journal* 54.1 (2018): 80–99.

Cohen, G.A. *Rescuing Justice and Equality*. Cambridge, MA: Harvard University Press, 2008.

'Consolidated Financial Statements of the Nestlé Group 2018.' 152nd Financial Statements of Nestlé S.A. Web. 8 Nov. 2019: <https://www.nestle.com/sites/default/files/asset-library/documents/library/documents/financial_statements/2018-financial-statements-en.pdf>

Coping with Water Scarcity. Challenge of the Twenty-first Century. UN-Water, FAO, 2007. Available from: http://www.fao.org/3/a-aq444e.pdf

Craft, Aimée. 'Giving and Receiving Life from Anishinaabe Nibi Inaakonigewin (Our Water Law) research.' In *Methodological Challenges in Nature-Culture and Environmental History Research*, eds. Jocelyn Thorpe, Stephanie Rutherford and L. Anders Sandberg. New York: Routledge, 2017: 105–19.

Craft, Aimée. 'Navigating Our Ongoing Sacred Legal Relationship with Nibi (Water).' *UNDRIP Implementation, More Reflections on the Braiding of International, Domestic and Indigenous Laws*. Centre for International Governance Innovation, 2018, 53–61.

Culp, Tyler E. et al. 'Nanoscale Control of Internal Inhomogeneity Enhances Water Transport in Desalination Membranes.' *Science* 371.6524 (2021): 72–5.

Davidson, S. and S. Elstub. 'Deliberative and Participatory Democracy in the UK.' *British Journal of Politics and International Relations* 16 (2014): 367–85.

D'Souza, Radha. 'Liberal Theory, Human Rights and Water-Justice: Back to Square One?' *Law, Social Justice & Global Development* 46 (2008): 1–15.

Della Porta, D. *Can Democracy Be Saved?* Cambridge: Polity Press, 2013.

Deveaux, Monique. 'Poor-Led Social Movements and Global Justice.' *Political Theory* 46.5 (2018): 698–725.

Dodge, Jennifer. 'The Deliberative Potential of Civil Society Organizations: Framing Hydraulic Fracturing in New York.' *Policy Studies* 36.3 (2015): 249–66.

Doremus, Holly. 'Groundwater and the Public Trust Doctrine, California Style.' Legal Planet – Insight & Analysis: Environmental Law and Policy. Berkley Law, UCLA Law, 21 July 2014. Web 8 Nov. 2019: <https://legal-planet.org/2014/07/21/groundwater-and-the-public-trust-doctrine-california-style/>

Dryzek, John S. 'Institutions for the Anthropocene: Governance in a Changing Earth System.' *British Journal of Political Science* 46.4 (2014): 937–56.

Dryzek, John S. 'The Forum, the System, and the Polity: Three Varieties of Democratic Theory.' *Political Theory* 45.5 (2017): 610–36.

Dryzek, John S. and Jonathan Pickering. *The Politics of the Anthropocene*. Oxford: Oxford University Press, 2018.

Elstub, Stephen. 'Deliberative and Participatory Democracy.' In *The Oxford Handbook of Deliberative Democracy*, eds Andre Bächtiger, John S. Dryzek, Jane Mansbridge and Mark Warren. Oxford: Oxford University Press, 2018, 187–202.

Elstub, S., S. Ercan and R. F. Mendoça. 'The Fourth Generation of Deliberative Democracy.' *Critical Policy Studies* 10 (2016): 139–51.

Environment and Climate Change Canada, 'Toward the Creation of a Canada Water Agency: Discussion Paper.' Gatineau, Quebec, 2021. Available at: https://publications.gc.ca/site/eng/9.910347/publication.html

Environment and Climate Change Canada, 'Toward the Creation of a Canada Water Agency: Stakeholder and Public Engagement – What We Heard.' Gatineau, Quebec, 2021. Available at: https://publications.gc.ca/site/eng/9.900082/publication.html; ISBN: 9780660390062

Ercan, Selen A. and John S. Dryzek. 'The Reach of Deliberative Democracy.' *Policy Studies* 36.3 (2015): 241–8.

Ercan, Selen A. and Jean-Paul Gagnon. 'The Crisis of Democracy: Which Crisis? Which Democracy?' *Democratic Theory* 1.2 (2014): 1–10.

Ercan, Selen A., Carolyn M. Hendriks and John S. Dryzek. 'Public Deliberation in an Era of Communicative Plenty.' *Policy and Politics* 47.1 (2019): 19–36.

Federici, Silvia. *Caliban and the Witch: Women, the Body and Primitive Accumulation.* Brooklyn, NY: Autonomedia, 2004.

Federici, Silvia. *Re-enchanting the World: Feminism and the Politics of the Commons.* Oakland, CA: PM Press/Kairos, 2018.

Fioret, Cameron. 'Complimentary Intersections? Water Commodification through the Lens of Philosophy and Geography.' *Geoforum* 86 (2017): 16–19.

Fioret Cameron, Kathleen Johnson, Steven Lam, Michelle Thompson and Sarah Hargreaves. *Towards Farmer-led Research: A Guidebook.* Ecological Farmers Association of Ontario, Guelph, Ontario, 2018.

Flynn, Sean and Kathryn Boudouris. 'Democratising the Regulation and Governance of Water in the US.' In *Reclaiming Public Water: Achievements, Struggles and Visions from Around the World*, eds. Belén Balanyá, Brid Brennan, Olivier Hoedeman, Satoko Kishimoto and Philipp Terhorst, Transnational Institute (TNI) & Corporate Europe Observatory (CEO), 2005, 73–84.

Forst, Rainer. 'Transnational Justice and Non-Domination, a Discourse-Theoretical Approach.' In *Domination and Global Political Justice: Conceptual, Historical and Institutional Perspectives*, eds. Barbara Buckinx, Jonathan Trejo-Mathys and Timothy Waligore. New York: Routledge (Taylor & Francis), 2015, 88–110.

Gilabert, Pablo. 'Comparative Assessments of Justice, Political Feasibility, and Ideal Theory.' *Ethical Theory & Moral Practice* 15 (2012): 39–56.

Glinza, Jessica. 'Nestlé pays $200 a year to bottle water near Flint – where water is undrinkable.' *The Guardian*, 29 Sept. 2017. Web 8 Nov. 2019: <https://www.theguardian.com/us-news/2017/sep/29/nestle-pays-200-a-year-to-bottle-water-near-flint-where-water-is-undrinkable>

Global High-Level Panel on Water and Peace. *A Matter of Survival* (Report). Geneva: Geneva Water Hub, 2017.

Great Big Story. 'The Woman Fighting for Detroit's Water.' *Youtube*, uploaded by Great Big Story, 18 Sept. 2017, https://www.youtube.com/watch?v=q9D4ysxbGao

Green, Fergus and Eric Brandstedt. 'Engaged Climate Ethics.' *Journal of Political Philosophy* 0.0 (2020): 1–15.

Griffiths, John. 'What is Legal Pluralism?' *Journal of Legal Pluralism and Unofficial Law* 24 (1986): 1–55.

Gwynn, Alvin. 'Baltimore ban on privatizing water system was the right thing to do.' *The Baltimore Sun*, 10 Feb. 2020. Web 16 June 2018.

Habermas, Jürgen. *Between Facts and Norms*, trans. William Rehg. Cambridge: Polity Press, 1997.

Haiven, Max. 'Reimagining Our Collective Powers Against Austerity.' *Roar Magazine*, 5 June 2015. Web 1 March 2021: <https://roarmag.org/essays/max-haiven-common-austerity/>

Hamlin, Alan and Zofia Stemplowska. 'Theory, Ideal Theory, and the Theory of Ideal.' *Political Studies Review* 10 (2012): 48–62.

Hardin, Garrett. 'The Tragedy of the Commons.' *Science* 13 (1968): 1243–8.

Hardin, Garrett. *Justice, Nature, and the Geography of Difference*. Oxford, Blackwell, 1996.

Harvey, David. *The New Imperialism*. Oxford: Oxford University Press, 2003.

Harvey, David. *Rebel Cities*. London: Verso, 2012.

Harvey, David. *Constitutional Environmental Rights*. New York: Oxford University Press, 2005.

Harvey, David. 'Global Justice and the Distribution of Natural Resources.' *Political Studies* 54.2 (2006): 349–69.

Harvey, David. 'Human Rights Versus Emissions Rights: Climate Justice and the Equitable Distribution of Ecological Space.' *Ethics & International Affairs* 21.4 (2007): 431–50.

Hayward, Tim. 'A Global Right of Water.' *Midwest Studies in Philosophy* 40.1 (2016): 217–33.

Herzog, Lisa and Bernardo Zacka. 'Fieldwork in Political Theory: Five Arguments for an Ethnographic Sensibility.' *British Journal of Political Science* 49 (2019): 763–84.

Hickman, Leo. 'James Lovelock: Humans are too stupid to prevent climate change.' *The Guardian*, 29 March 2010. Web 13 Dec. 2019.

Horkheimer, Max and Theodor W. Adorno. *Dialectic of Enlightenment*. New York: Continuum, 2002.

Hurlbert, Margot and Evan Andrews. 'Deliberative Democracy in Canadian Watershed Governance.' *Water Alternatives* 11.1 (2018): 163–86.

Human Rights Council. 'Climate change and poverty: Report of the Special Rapporteur on extreme poverty and human rights.' 25 June 2019, A/HRC/41/39, 26 June 2019.

Innes, J. E. and D. E. Booher. 'Collaborative Policymaking: Governance through Dialogue.' In *Deliberative Policy Analysis: Understanding Governance in the Network Society*, eds Maarten A. Hajer and Hendrik Wagenaar. Cambridge: Cambridge University Press, 2003, 33–59.

Jenkins, B. *Water Management in New Zealand's Canterbury Region: A Sustainability Framework*. Dordrecht: Springer.

Johnson, Baylor L. 'Ethical Obligations in a Tragedy of the Commons.' *Environmental Values* 12.3 (2003): 271–87.

Jones, Edward, Manzoor Qadir, Michelle T. H. van Vliet, Vladimir Smakhtin and Seong-mu Kang. 'The State of Desalination and Brine Production: a Global Outlook.' *Science of the Total Environment* 657 (2019): 1343–56.

Kahn, Elizabeth. 'The Tragedy of the Commons as an Essentially Aggregative Harm.' *Journal of Applied Philosophy* 31.3 (2014): 223–36.

Karunananthan, Meera and Satoko Kishimoto. '(Re)municipalization of Water – the Right Way Towards Achieving SDG 6.' In *Exploring New Policy Pathways: How to Overcome Obstacles and Contradictions in the Implementation of the 2030 Agenda. Report by the Civil Society Reflection Group on the 2030 Agenda for Sustainable Development*, eds Barbara Adams, Roberto Bissio, Chee Yoke Ling, Kate Donald, Jens Martens, Stefano Prato and Sandra Vermuyten, Civil Society Reflection Group on the 2030 Agenda for Sustainable Development, 2018, 123–5.

Karunananthan, Meera and Satoko Kishimoto. 'Transnational Feminisms, Nonideal Theory, and "Other" Women's Power.' *Feminist Philosophy Quarterly* 3.1 (2017): Article 1 doi:10.5206/fpq/2016.3.1.

Khader, Serene. *Decolonizing Universalism: A Transnational Feminist Ethic*. Oxford: Oxford University Press, 2018.

Khagram, Sanjeev. *Dams and Development: Transnational Struggles for Water and Power*. Ithaca, NY: Cornell University Press, 2004.

Kolers, Avery. *Land, Conflict, and Justice: A Political Theory*. New York: Cambridge University Press, 2009.

Kolers, Avery. 'Social Movements.' *Philosophy Compass* 11/10 (2016): 580–90.

Krause, Sharon R. 'Environmental Domination.' *Political Theory* 48.4 (2020): 443–68.

Kurth, Joel. 'In Detroit, surviving without running water has become a way of life.' *Bridge Magazine*, 24 Oct. 2018. Web 8 Nov. 2019: <https://www.bridgemi.com/detroit/detroit-surviving-without-running-water-has-become-way-life>

La Via Campesina. *Struggles of La Via Campesina For Agrarian Reform and the Defense of Life, Land and Territories*. Harare: La Via Campesina, 2017.

Lake Erie Bill of Rights. *City of Toledo*. Web 8 Nov. 2019: <https://beyondpesticides.org/assets/media/documents/LakeErieBillofRights.pdf>

Lam, Steven, Michelle Thompson, Kathleen Johnson, Cameron Fioret and Sarah Hargreaves. 'Toward Community Food Security through Transdisciplinary Action Research.' *Action Research* 19.4 (2019): 656–73.

Latimer, Kendall. 'Regina homeowners grapple with untainted water.' *CBC News*, 4 Nov. 2019. Web 8 Nov. 2019: <https://www.cbc.ca/news/canada/saskatchewan/regina-lead-levels-in-tap-water-1.5347705>

Laurence, Ben. 'The Question of the Agent of Change.' *Journal of Political Philosophy* 28.4 (2020): 355–77.

Laville, Sandra. 'England's privatised water firms paid £57bn in dividends since 1991.' *The Guardian*, 1 July 2020. Web. 1 July 2020: <https://www.theguardian.com/environment/2020/jul/01/england-privatised-water-firms-dividends-shareholders>

Laville, Sandra and Niamh McIntyre. 'Exclusive: water firms dumped raw sewage into England's rivers 200,000 times in 2019.' *The Guardian*, 1 July 2020. Web 1 July 2020: <https://www.theguardian.com/environment/2020/jul/01/water-firms-raw-sewage-england-rivers>

Li, Quan and Rafael Reuveny. 'Democracy and Environmental Degradation.' *International Studies Quarterly* 50.4 (2006): 935–56.

Locke, John. *Two Treatises of Government*, ed. Thomas Hollis. London: A. Miller et al., 1764.

Lövbrand, Eva and Jamil Khan. 'The Deliberative Turn in Green Political Theory.' In *Environmental Politics and Deliberative Democracy: Examining the Promise of New Modes of Governance*, eds Karin Bäckstrand, Jamil Khan, Annica Kronsell and Eva Lövbrand. Northampton, MA: Edward Elgar Publishing Inc., 2010, 47–64.

Maass, A. and R. L. Anderson. *... and the desert shall rejoice: Conflict, growth, and justice in arid environments*. Malabar, FL: R. E. Krieger, 1986.

Mackenzie, Michael K. and Mark E. Warren. 'Two Trust-based Uses of Minipublics in Democratic Systems.' In *Deliberative Systems: Deliberative Democracy at the Large Scale*, eds Jane Mansbridge and John Parkinson. Cambridge: Cambridge University Press, 2012, 95–124.

Madlingozi, Tshepo. 'Post-Apartheid Social Movements and Legal Mobilisation.' In *Socio Economic Rights in South Africa: Symbols or Substance?*, eds M. Langford, B. Cousins, J. Dugard and T. Madlingozi. Cambridge: Cambridge University Press, 2013, 92–130.

'Make it Safe. Canada's Obligation to End the First Nations Water Crisis.' *Human Rights Watch*, 7 June 2015. Web 26 June 2019: <https://www.hrw.org/report/2016/06/07/make-it-safe/canadas-obligation-end-firstnations-water-crisis#page>

Maqbool, Aleem. 'Coronavirus: "I can't wash my hands – my water was cut off."' *BBC News*, 24 April 2020. Web 16 June 2020.

McGregor, Deborah. 'Traditional Knowledge and Water Governance: The Ethic of Responsibility.' *AlterNative: International Journal of Indigenous Peoples* 10 (2014): 493–507.

McGregor, Deborah, Steven Whitaker and Mahisha Sritharan. 'Indigenous Environmental Justice and Sustainability.' *Current Opinion in Environmental Sustainability* 43 (2020): 35–40.

Mekonnen, Mesfin M. and Arjen Y. Hoekstra. 'Four Million People Facing Severe Water Scarcity.' *Sciences Advances* 2.2 (2016): 1–6. DOI: 10.1126/sciadv.1500323.

Miller, David. 'Territorial Rights: Concept and Justification.' *Political Studies* 60.2 (2011): 252–68.

Mills, Charles W. '"Ideal Theory" as Ideology.' *Hypatia* 20.3 (2005): 165–84.

Miraftab, Faranak. 'Public-private Partnerships: the Trojan Horse of Neoliberal Development?' *Journal of Planning, Education and Research* 24 (2004): 89–101.

Montag, Coty. *Water/Color: A Study of Race and the Water Affordability Crisis in America's Cities* (2019). New York: NAACP Legal Defense and Educational Fund, Inc. (LDF).

Mosley, Elizabeth A., Cortney K. Bouse and Kelli Stidham Hall. 'Water, Human Rights, and Reproductive Justice: Implication for Women in Detroit and Monrovia.' *Environmental Justice* 8.3 (2015): 78–85.

Nagabhatla, N. and C. Fioret. 'The Water-Migration Nexus: An Analysis of Causalities and Response Mechanisms with a Focus on the Global South.' In *Regional Integration and Migration Governance in the Global South*, eds G. Rayp, I. Ruyssen and K. Marchand. Springer Nature Switzerland AG: Cham, Switzerland, 2020, 85–115.

Nagabhatla, N., C. Fioret and P. Pouramin. 'Water-Migration-Peace Nexus: Challenges and Opportunities.' In *Encyclopedia of UN Sustainable Development Goals: Peace, Justice and Strong Institutions*, eds W. L. Filho, A. M. Azul, L. Brandil, A. L. Salvia, P. G. Özuyer and T. Wall. Springer Nature Switzerland AG: Cham, Switzerland, 2021 (forthcoming).

Nagabhatla, N., Pouramin, P., Brahmbhatt, R., Fioret, C., Glickman, T., Newbold, K. B. and Smakhtin, V. 2020. *Water and Migration: A Global Overview*. UNU-INWEH Report Series, Issue 10. United Nations University Institute for Water, Environment and Health, Hamilton, Canada.

Nagy, Mike and Maude Barlow. 'Time for Ontario to Protect its Water Supplies.' *The Hamilton Spectator*, 11 May 2017. Web 8 Nov. 2019: <https://www.thespec.com/opinion-story/7309925-time-for-ontario-to-protect-its-water-supplies/>

National Research Council, *The Drama of the Commons*. Washington, DC: National Academies Press, 2002.

Niemeyer, Simon. 'Deliberation and Ecological Democracy: From Citizen to Global System.' *Journal of Environmental Policy and Planning* 22.1 (2020): 16–29.

Nikolakis, William and R. Quentin Grafton. 'Law versus Justice: the Strategic Aboriginal Water Reserve in the Northern Territory, Australia.' *International Journal of Water Resources Development* (2021): 1–19.

Nine, Cara. *Global Justice and Territory*. Oxford: Oxford University Press, 2012.

Nixon, Rob. *Slow Violence and the Environmentalism of the Poor*. Cambridge, MA: Harvard University Press, 2011.

Nordhaus, William. 'The Ethics of Efficient Markets and Commons Tragedies: A Review of John Broome's "Climate Matters: Ethics in a Warming World"', *Journal of Economic Literature* 52.4 (2014): 1135–41.

Norval, Aletta. 'Deliberative, Agonistic and Aversive Grammars of Democracy: The Question of Criteria.' In *Practices of Freedom: Decentered Governance, Conflict and Democratic Participation*, eds S. Griggs, A. J. Norval and H. Wagenaar. New York: Cambridge University Press, 2014, 60–84.

Nussbaum, Martha. *Women and Human Development: The Capabilities Approach*. Cambridge and New York: Cambridge University Press, 2000.

O'Neill, John. *Markets, Deliberation and Environment*. London: Routledge, 2007.

O'Neill, Onora. *Towards Justice and Virtue*. Cambridge: Cambridge University Press, 1996.

Olivera, Oscar and Tom Lewis. *Cochabamba!: Water War in Bolivia*. Cambridge, MA: South End Press, 2004.

'Ontario allowing bottled water companies to take 7.6M litres a day on expired permits.' *CBC News*, 26 Nov. 2017. Web 14 Nov. 2018.

'Ontario allowing bottled water companies to take 7.6M litres a day on expired permits.' *Governing the Commons: The Evolution of Institutions for Collective Action*. Cambridge: Cambridge University Press, 1990.

'Ontario allowing bottled water companies to take 7.6M litres a day on expired permits.' 'Reformulating the Commons.' *Swiss Political Science Review* 6.1 (2000): 29–52.

Ostrom, Elinor. 'A General Framework for Analyzing Sustainability of Social-ecological Systems.' *Science* 325 (2009): 419–22.

Owen, D. and G. Smith. 'Survey Article: Deliberation, Democracy, and the Systemic Turn.' *Journal of Political Philosophy* 23 (2015): 213–34.

Pateman, Carole and Charles Mills. *Contract and Domination*. Cambridge: Polity Press, 2007.

Patterson, Brent. 'Guelph Chapter Presents to City Council on Nestle Water-Takings.' *The Council of Canadians*, 28 Nov. 2016, Web. 20 July 2020.

Perera, Verónica. 'Engaged Universals and Community Economies: The (Human) Right to Water in Colombia.' *Antipode* 47.1 (2015): 197–215.

Perkins, Tom. 'The fight to stop Nestlé from taking America's water to sell in plastic bottles.' *The Guardian*, 29 Oct. 2019. Web 8 Nov. 2019: <https://www.theguardian.com/environment/2019/oct/29/the-fight-over-water-how-nestle-dries-up-us-creeks-to-sell-water-in-plastic-bottles>

Pirsoul, Nicolas and Maria Armoudian. 'Deliberative Democracy and Water Management in New Zealand: a Critical Approach to Collaborative Governance and Co-Management Initiatives.' *Water Resources Management* 33 (2019): 4821–34.

Pithouse, Richard. 'An Urban Commons? Notes from South Africa.' *Community Development Journal* 49 (2014): i31–i43.

Planas, Míriam and Juan Martínez. 'Water should be a public good, not a commodity. Catalonia is showing how.' *openDemocracy*, 30 April 2020. Web 10 Dec. 2020.

Plumwood, Val. *Feminism and the Mastery of Nature*. New York: Routledge, 1993.

Plumwood, Val. *Environmental Culture: The Ecological Crisis of Reason*. New York: Routledge, 2002.

Poelina, Anne, Katherine S. Taylor and Ian Perdrisat. 'Martuwarra Fitzroy River Council: An Indigenous Cultural Approach to Collaborative Water Governance.' *Australasian Journal of Environmental Management* 26.3 (2019): 236–54.

Polanyi, Karl. *The Great Transformation: The Political and Economic Origins of Our Time*. Boston: Beacon Press, 2004.

Poteete, Amy, Marco Janssen and Elinor Ostrom. *Working Together: Collective Action, the Commons and Multiple Methods in Practice*. Princeton, NJ: Princeton University Press, 2010.

Pritchett, Lant and Michael Woolcock. 'Solutions When the Solution is the Problem: Arraying the Disarray in Development.' *World Development* 32 (2004): 191–212.

'Prime Minister welcomes new parliamentary secretaries.' *Government of Canada*, 12 Dec. 2019. Web 19 Nov. 2020: <https://pm.gc.ca/en/news/news-releases/2019/12/12/prime-minister-welcomes-new-parliamentary-secretaries>

Proffitt, James. 'Struck Down: Federal Court Rules Lake Erie Bill of Right Unconstitutional.' *Great Lakes Now*, 6 March 2020. Web 6 March 2020: <https://www.greatlakesnow.org/2020/03/lake-erie-bill-rights-federal-court-unconstitutional/>

Rajagopal, Balakrishnan. 'Counter-hegemonic International Law: Rethinking Human Rights and Development as a Third World Strategy.' *Third World Quarterly* 27.5 (2006): 767–83.

Rawls, John. *A Theory of Justice*. Cambridge, MA: Belknap Press of Harvard University Press, 1999.

Risse, Mathias. 'Common Ownership of the Earth as a Non-parochial Standpoint: A Contingent Derivation of Human Rights', *European Journal of Philosophy* 17.2 (2009a): 277–304.

Risse, Mathias. 'The Right to Relocation: Disappearing Island Nations and Common Ownership of the Earth', *Ethics and International Affairs* 23.3 (2009b): 281–99.

Risse, Mathias. *Global Political Philosophy*. New York: Palgrave MacMillan, 2012.

Risse, Mathias. 'The Human Right to Water and Common Ownership of the Earth', *Journal of Political Philosophy* 22 (2014): 178–203.

Robertson, Roland. 'Glocalization: Time-Space and Homogeneity-Heterogeneity.' In *Global Modernities*, eds Mike Featherstone, Scott Lash and Roland Robertson. London: Sage, 1995.

Robeyns, Ingrid. 'Ideal Theory in Theory and Practice.' *Social Theory and Practice* 34.3 (2008): 341–62.

Robinson, Joanna. *Contested Water: The Struggle Against Water Privatization in the United States and Canada*. Cambridge, MA: The MIT Press, 2013.

Safi, Michael. 'Ganges and Yamuna rivers granted same legal rights as human beings.' *The Guardian*, 21 March 2017. Web 8 Nov. 2019: <https://www.theguardian.com/world/2017/mar/21/ganges-and-yamuna-rivers-granted- same-legal-rights-as-human-beings>

Sandel, Michael J. 'How Markets Crowd Out Morals.' *Boston Review*, 1 May 2012. Web 26 June 2019: <https://bostonreview.net/forum-sandel-markets-morals>

Satz, Debra. 'The Egalitarian Intuition.' *Boston Review*, 25 June 2012. Web. 26 June 2019: <https://bostonreview.net/satz-egalitarian-response>

Satz, Debra. 'Reconceiving Environmental Justice: Global Movements and Political Theories.' *Environmental Politics* 13.3 (2004): 517–40.

Schlosberg, David. *Defining Environmental Justice*. New York: Oxford University Press, 2007.

Schlosberg, David. 'Theorising Environmental Justice: The Expanding Sphere of a Discourse.' *Environmental Politics* 22.1 (2013): 37–55.

Schroering, Caitlin. 'Water is a Human Right! Grassroots Resistance to Corporate Power.' *Journal of World-Systems Research* 25.1 (2019): 28–34. <https://doi.org/10.5195/jwsr.2019.899>

Schroering, Caitlin. *Seeing Like a State: How Certain Schemes to Improve the Human Condition Have Failed*. New Haven: Yale University Press, 1998.

Scott, James C. *Against the Grain: A Deep History of the Earliest States*. New Haven: Yale University Press, 2017.
Scott, James C. 'Utilitarianism and Welfarism.' *Journal of Philosophy* 76.9 (1979): 463–89.
Sen, Amartya. *Development as Freedom*. New York: Knopf, 1999.
Sen, Amartya. *The Idea of Justice*. Cambridge, MA: Belknap Press, 2009.
Shelby, Tommie. *Dark Ghettos: Injustice, Dissent, and Reform*. Cambridge, MA: Harvard University Press, 2016.
Shelby, Tommie. *Staying Alive: Women, Ecology and Development*. London: Zed Books, 1989.
Shelby, Tommie. *Water Wars: Privatization, Pollution and Profit*. Cambridge, MA: South End Press, 2002.
Shiva, Vandana. *Globalization's New Wars*. New Delhi: Women Unlimited, 2005.
Shue, Henry. *Climate Justice: Vulnerability and Protection*. Oxford: Oxford University Press, 2014.
Simmons, A. John. *The Lockean Theory of Rights*. Princeton, NJ: Princeton University Press, 1992.
Smee, Ben. 'Queensland school runs out of water as commercial bottlers harvest local supplies.' *The Guardian*, 12 Dec. 2019. Web 13 Dec. 2019.
Smith, Adam. *An Inquiry into the Nature and Causes of The Wealth of Nations*. Hampshire, UK: Harriman House Ltd., 2007.
Smith, Rhonda J. '3 "women water warriors" testing lead in Detroit drinking water.' *Detour Detroit*, 12 Nov. 2020, Web 19 March 2021.
Stafford, Katrease. 'Controversial water shutoffs could hit 17,461 Detroit households.' *Detroit Free Press*, 26 March 2018. Web 14 Nov. 2018.
Stemplowska, Zofia. 'What's Ideal About Ideal Theory?' *Social Theory and Practice* 34.3 (2008): 319–40.
Stern, N. H. *The Economics of Climate Change: The Stern Review*. Cambridge: Cambridge University Press, 2007.
Stern, N. H. 'The Discursive Democratisation of Global Climate Governance.' *Environmental Politics* 21.2 (2012): 189–210.
Stevenson, Hayley and John S. Dryzek. *Democratizing Global Climate Governance*. New York: Cambridge University Press, 2014.
Stilz, Anna. *Territorial Sovereignty: A Philosophical Exploration*. New York: Oxford University Press, 2019.
Stuart-Ulin, Chloe Rose. 'Quebec's Magpie River becomes first in Canada to be granted legal personhood.' *Canada's National Observer*, 24 Feb. 2021. Web 26 Feb. 2021: <https://www.nationalobserver.com/2021/02/24/news/quebecs-magpie-river-first-in- canada-granted-legal-personhood>

Subramaniam, Mangala. *Contesting Water Rights: Local, State, and Global Struggles.* Cham, Switzerland: Springer, 2018.

Sultana, Farhana and Alex Loftus. 'The Right to Water: Prospects and Possibilities.' In *The Right to Water: Politics, Governance and Social Struggles*, eds Farhana Sultana and Alex Loftus. New York: Earthscan, 2012, 1–18.

Sultana, Farhana and Alex Loftus. *Water Politics: Governance, Justice and the Right to Water.* London: Routledge, 2019.

Sunstein, Cass R. *Going to Extremes: How Like Minds Unite and Divide.* New York: Oxford University Press, 2009.

Swaine, Jon. 'Detroit residents fight back over water shutoff: "It's a life-or-death situation."' *The Guardian*, 21 July 2014. Web 14 Nov. 2018.

Switzer, David and Manuel P. Teodoro. 'Class, Race, Ethnicity, and Justice in Safe Drinking Water Compliance.' *Social Science Quarterly* 99.2 (2018): 524–35.

Swift, Adam. 'The Value of Philosophy in Nonideal Circumstances.' *Social Theory and Practice* 34.3 (2008): 363–87.

Taylor, Charles, Patrizia Nanz and Madeleine Beaubien Taylor. *Reconstructing Democracy: How Citizens Are Building from the Ground Up.* Cambridge, MA: Harvard University Press, 2020.

Taylor, Katherine S., Sheri Longboat and R. Quentin Grafton. 'Water Governance Frameworks Need to Harmonise with United Nations Declaration on the Rights of Indigenous Peoples.' *Global Water Forum*, 18 June 2020. Web 22 April 2021.

Taylor, Katherine S., Sheri Longboat and R. Quentin Grafton. 'Whose Rules? Principles of Water Governance, Rights of Indigenous Peoples, and Water Justice.' *Water* 11.4 (2019), 809: 1–19.

The Flint Water Crisis: Systemic Racism through the Lens of Flint. *Report of the Michigan Civil Rights Commission.* Detroit: Michigan Civil Rights Commission (2017).

Tully, James. 'On Global Citizenship.' In *On Global Citizenship: James Tully In Dialogue.* London: Bloomsbury Academic, 2014, 3–100.

UN General Assembly, 'The human right to water and sanitation: resolution/adopted by the General Assembly.' 3 Aug. 2010, A/RES/64/292, 14 Nov. 2018.

UN General Assembly, 'Transforming our world: the 2030 Agenda for Sustainable Development.' 21 Oct. 2015, A/RES/70/1, 14 Nov. 2018.

UN General Assembly, 'United Nations Declaration on the Rights of Indigenous Peoples: resolution / adopted by the General Assembly.' 2 Oct. 2007, A/RES/61/295, 22 April 2021.

UN General Assembly, 'On the Apparent Paradox of Ideal Theory.' *Political Philosophy* 17.3 (2009): 332–55.

Valentini, Laura. 'Ideal vs. Non-ideal Theory: A Conceptual Map.' *Philosophy Compass* 7.9 (2012): 654–64.
Van Harten, Gus and Pavla Křístková. 'Comments on Judicial Independence and Impartiality in ISDS': A Paper Prepared for the UNCITRAL Working Group III, 2018. Available at SSRN: https://ssrn.com/abstract=3323010 or http://dx.doi.org/10.2139/ssrn.3323010.
Vitale, D. 'Between Deliberative and Participatory Democracy: A Contribution on Habermas.' *Philosophy and Social Criticism* 32 (2006): 739–66.
Waldron, Ingrid. *There's Something in the Water: Environmental Racism in Indigenous and Black Communities*. Winnipeg and Black Point, Nova Scotia: Fernwood Publishing, 2018.
Walljasper, Jay. *All That We Share: A Field Guide to the Commons*. New York: The New Press, 2010.
Walzer, M. 'Deliberation, and What Else?' In *Deliberative Politics: Essays on Democracy and Disagreement*, ed. S. Macedo. New York: Oxford University Press, 1999, 58–69.
Warren, M. E. and J. Gastil. 'Can Deliberative Minipublics Address the Cognitive Challenges of Democratic Citizenship?' *Journal of Politics* 77.2 (2015): 562–74.
Wenar, Leif. *Blood Oil: Tyrants, Violence, and the Rules that Run the World*. New York: Oxford University Press, 2017.
Wenar, Leif. 'The Dakota Access Pipeline, Environmental Injustice, and U.S. Colonialism.' *RED INK: An International Journal of Indigenous Literature, Arts, & Humanities* 19.1 (2017): 154–69.
Whyte, Kyle. 'Settler Colonialism, Ecology, and Environmental Injustice,' *Environment and Society* 9 (2018): 125–44.
Wilson, Nicole J., Leila M. Harris, Angie Joseph-Rear, Jody Beaumont and Terre Satterfield. 'Water is Medicine: Reimagining Water Security through Tr'ondëk Hwëch'in Relationships to Treated and Traditional Water Sources in Yukon, Canada.' *Water* 11.3 (2019), 624: 1–19.
Wolf, Aaron. 'Conflict and Cooperation Along International Waterways.' *Water Policy* 1.2 (1998): 251–65.
Wolff, Jonathan. 'Method in Philosophy and Public Policy: Applied Philosophy versus Engaged Philosophy.' In *The Routledge Handbook of Ethics and Public Policy*, eds Annabelle Lever and Andrei Poama. New York: Routledge, 2019, 13–24.
Wood, E. M. *Democracy Against Capitalism: Renewing Historical Materialism*. New York: Cambridge University Press, 1995.
WWAP (UNESCO World Water Assessment Programme). The United Nations World Water Development Report 2019: 'Leaving No One Behind'. Paris, UNESCO.

WWAP (UNESCO World Water Assessment Programme). *Justice and the Politics of Difference*. Princeton, NJ: Princeton University Press, 1990.
WWAP (UNESCO World Water Assessment Programme). *Inclusion and Democracy*. New York: Oxford University Press, 2000.
Young, Iris Marion. 'Activist Challenges to Deliberative Democracy.' *Political Theory* 29 (2001): 670–90.
Young, Iris Marion. *Responsibility for Justice*. New York: Oxford University Press, Inc., 2011.

Index

Aberfoyle, Ontario 4, 124
academic research, in water justice 145–6
Ackerly, Brooke et al. 8
activism 23, 123, 131
  see also water justice movements
activists 128, 146
agreements, formal 116–19
Albufeira Agreement (1998) 118
Alfred, Taiaiake 17, 34–5
Alicante, Spain 66–7
Allen, Amy 104
Alston, Philip 41
alter-globalization 43, 44, 45, 121–2
Alternative World Water Forum (AAWF) 115
ambivalent states 113–14
Anderson, Elizabeth 40
Andrews, Evan 83–4
anthropocentrism 36, 142
  see also non-anthropocentrism
anti-privatization 43, 44
anti-water commodification activism 123
(anti)commodification language 43
applied philosophy 7–8
Armouidan, Maria 82
Armstrong, Chris 14, 30, 31, 32
Arsenault, Rachel 147
Australia 37
authoritarianism 98, 172–3 n.33
Avrillier, Raymond 50, 132

Baber, Walter 94
Bakker, Karen 15, 43, 44, 45, 92, 93
Balanyá, Belén 134
Baltimore, Maryland 127
Barlow, Maude 124
Bartlett, Robert 94
Bayliss, Kate 29, 30, 47
biophysical view 86–7
Bolivia 3–4, 49, 129–31
bottled water 56, 124, 163 n.4
bottom-up organizations 68–9
  see also social movements
Bouier, Roslyn 128
Brandstedt, Eric 6

Broome, John 27
buen vivir (living well) 55
Bywater, Krista 133

California, USA 56, 112, 113
Canada
  case studies of water activism 124–6
  Indigenous peoples and the democratic process 92–3
  Local Water Councils (LWCs) 83–4
  personhood granted to rivers 62
  social movements 113
Canada Water Agency (CWA) 148–9
Caney, Simon 135
Canterbury, New Zealand 82–3
capabilities approach 14
capitalism 48–9
citizens, harms of 46–50
citizenship 101–3
civic organizations 126
Clark, Cristy 101, 120
Coca-Cola 99, 133
Cochabamba, Bolivia 3–4, 49, 129–31
collective agreements 64, 69–70, 79–81
collective consumption movements 100–1
commodification
  arguments against 39–40
  commons vs commodity 43
  drawbacks of 29
  as an economic good 45
  harms of 41–2, 46–51, 97–9, 105, 143
  inequalities of 98–9
  moral dualism of 40–1, 42–3
  path dependencies 54–7
  and privatization 26, 29, 173–4 n.57
  social relations and 53
  strategies against 100–1
  undemocratic nature of 21, 121
common ownership
  vs community ownership 164 n.30
  deep ecology discourse and 40–1
  hoarding, concern of 71–4
  and human rights 32, 58–9
  Indigenous ideas and stewardship 34–5
  as a public good 45

theories of 14, 57–63
 and the tragedy of the commons 63–71
 and water stewardship 22
common pool resources (CPRs) 64–8, 76
common territory 81–2, 143
 see also territorial rights
commons vs commodity 43
community forums and boards 112
community ownership 164 n.30
conflict and water justice movements 135–8
constitutive corruption 40
consumption of water 51, 134
corporate sponsorship 56
corruption, by markets 39, 40
Costa Rica 118–19
Council of Canadians (CoC) 124–6
Craft, Aimée 34
critical framework of 'ecological space' 18
customers, harms of 46–50

dams 133–4
deep ecology discourse 40–1
deliberative democracy
 discussion of 84–5, 175 n.8
 examples of 82–4
 movement-based 36–7
 participation and representation in 75–6
 as a reflexive practice 94
 scale of 73–4
 and social movements 111–16
democracy
 harms of 42
 harms of undermining 50–2, 144
 Indigenous peoples and 36–8, 92–3
 introduction to 21–2
 and social movements 111–16
 state level 100
 and violence 137
 and water justice 36–7, 59–62
 weakening of 96–9
denial of water 3–4
desalination technology 147–8
Detroit, Michigan 4, 56, 127, 128
Deveaux, Monique 101
direct political actions 101
 see also activism; water justice movements
distribution 91, 171 n.8
diverse citizenship 101–3
Dodge, Jennifer 125, 137
domination 96–9
donations and sponsorship 56

Dryzek, John 54, 55, 62, 74, 80, 81, 83, 84, 85, 86, 98, 112, 125
D'Souza, Radha 15, 51, 95–6

ecological reflexivity 61, 62, 74, 81
ecological space 14, 18, 86, 87
Egalitarian Ownership 59
egalitarianism 14, 30, 32
élite actors 41–2, 49, 118
Elstub, Stephen 75
engaged philosophy 6–7, 8, 9, 147
environmental classism 41–2
environmental domination 97–8
environmental rights 14, 17–18
Ercan, Selen 112, 125
Erie, Lake 63
Erin, Ontario 4, 124

fair-use proviso 72
Federici, Silvia 48, 49, 118, 128
financialization 47, 48
First Nation activists 146
Flint, Michigan 56, 128
Food & Water Watch 126
formal water agreements 116–19
Forst, Rainer 99
France 50, 132
frontiers of disagreement 125

Georgescu-Roegen, Nicholas 86
Gilabert, Pablo 4–5
global compact on water 59, 61
glocal movements 121–2, 170–1 n.3
governance, cosmopolitan theories of 14
Grafton, R. Quentin 37, 38
Green Belt Movement (GBM) 104
Green, Fergus 6
Green Radicalism 86
Grenoble, France 50, 132
grounded normative theory (GNT) 8–9
Guelph, Canada 124–6
Gwynn, Alvin 127

Hardin, Garrett 63–4, 78–9
Harvey, David 15–16, 48
Hayward, Tim 14, 17–18, 86, 87
Hendriks, Carolyn M. 125
hoarding, concern of 71–4
huerta irrigation system 66, 67
human right to water *see* right to water
Hurlbert, Margot 83–4
hybrid engaged philosophy 9

ideal theory 4–5, 6
India 63, 133–4
Indigenous activists 146
Indigenous Environmental Justice (IEJ) 34, 55
Indigenous ideas
    Declaration on the Rights of Indigenous Peoples (UNDRIP) 37–8
    environmental justice 34
    philosophical ideas 35
    of property and territory 17
    stewardship of the natural world 34–5
Indigenous peoples, democracy and 36–8, 92–3
individual responsibility 69, 70
individualism 27
inequality, commodification and 40
injustice *see* water injustice
instrumental corruption 40
international agreements 117, 118
international declarations 13, 18
international development organizations 49
International Monetary Fund (IMF) 49
investor-state dispute settlements (ISDS) 106–7
invisible hand theorem 27–8
irrigation 66–7

Japan 65
Johnson, Baylor 63, 69, 70, 79
justice, idea of 85

Kahn, Elizabeth 63
Kenya 104
Kerala, India 133–4
Khagram, Sanjeev 133
Kolers, Avery 16–17, 31–2, 33, 34–5, 114–15
Krause, Sharon 97–8, 99, 136
Kyoto Protocol (1992) 26

La Via Campesina 115
Lam, Steven 94
Laurence, Ben 5
liberalism 42, 53
limited resource sovereignty 72–3
Linera, Alvaro Garcia 129, 130
living well 55
Local Water Councils (LWCs) 83–4
Locke, John 164 n.30
Longboat, Sheri 38
Los Angeles, California 67–8

Maathai, Wangari 104
Macpherson, C. B. 53
Mandamin, Anishinaabekwe Josephine 146
market environmentalism 26–9, 47–8, 49–50
McGregor, Deborah 34, 55
middle way of resource government 64–5
Miller, David 14, 32, 87
Mills, Charles 4, 5
minimalism 32
minimalist proviso 72
minipublic deliberation 76, 83
modern citizenship 101, 102–3
Mongolia 119
moral entitlement to water 13–14
mountain resources 65

natural features, personhood granted to 62–3
natural resources 30, 31–2
neo-Cartesianism 40–1, 42–3
Nepal 68–9
Nestlé 56, 124
New Zealand 62–3, 82–3
Niemeyer, Simon 76, 81
Nikolakis, William 37
Nixon, Rob 104
non-anthropocentrism 36, 55, 97
non-governmental organizations (NGOs) 95
non-ideal theory 2–3, 4–6, 9
non-violence 138
Nordhaus, William. 27, 28
Nussbaum, Martha 14

occupancy, right of 71–2
Olivera, Oscar 129, 130
O'Neill, Onora 4
Ostrom, Elinor 64–9, 76–8, 120–1

Paris Agreement (2016) 117
participation 75–6, 91–4
path dependencies 54–7
Peltier, Autumn 146
personhood, granted to natural features 62–3
philosophical ideas 7–9, 35, 147–8
Pickering, Jonathan 54, 55, 62, 74
Pirsoul, Nicolas 82
Plumwood, Val 40, 41, 42–3
Polanyi, Karl 173–4 n.57

political actions *see* direct political actions
political theories 13–14
privatization
    and commodification 26, 29, 173–4 n.57
    dependency on privatized water 56
    resistance to 21
    and water agreements 117–18
    see also anti-privatization; commodification; public–private partnerships (PPPs)
privileged groups 41–2
property, definitions of 16, 17, 22, 82
public–private partnerships (PPPs) 29–30, 50, 84–5

racism 128
Radebe, Silumko 101
Rajagopal, Balakrishnan 116
recognition and participation, rights of 14–15, 75–6, 91, 93
recommoning of water 119–23
    alter-globalization and 121–2
    benefits of 139
    definition of 11, 119, 175 n.5, 177 n.39
    hoarding, concern of 70–4
    principles for 120–1
    rights and 122
    roadmap for 122–3
    self-governance systems and 77–8
reduction of use 69
reflexive participation 81
remoteness 41–2, 48
representation 75–6, 93–4
resistance and water justice movements 135–8
resource collapse 76–7
    see also tragedy of the commons
resource sovereignty 72–3
right-libertarianism 32
right to water
    difficulties of 94–6
    existing literature 13–19
    introduction to 19–24
    legal frameworks and 43–4
    and recommoning 120, 122
    as a step towards water justice 106
    synopsis 142
Risse, Mathias 14, 22, 32, 57–62
river-basin agreements 118
rivers, personhood granted to 62, 63
Robeyns, Ingrid 6
Robinson, Joanna 113

Sandel, Michael 39
Satz, Debra 39–40
Sava River Basin Framework Agreement 118
Schlosberg, David 14, 23, 48, 60, 90–1
self-governance 74–5, 77–8
Sen, Amartya 14, 85
settler interests 36–7
Shelby, Tommie 5
Shiva, Vandana 121
slow violence 104
Smith, Adam 28
social collaborations 100–1
social-ecological systems (SESs) 76
social movements 110–19
    and ambivalent states 113–14
    community forums and boards 112
    and deliberative democracy 111–16
    and formal water agreements 116–19
    other examples 149
    transnational social movements 116
    see also water justice movements
socioenvironmental justice 90, 105, 144
South Africa 101, 114
Spain 66–7
sponsorship, corporate 56
Sritharan, Mahisha 34, 55
Stemplowska, Zofia 4
steps towards water justice 105–6
Stevenson, Hayley 80, 84, 85, 86, 98
stewardship of the natural world 34–5, 82
Stilz, Anna 16, 71–3, 100
Strategic Aboriginal Water Reserves (SAWR) 37, 160 n.55
strategies of water justice movements 123, 126, 129, 132, 133
structural injustice 20–1, 23–4, 90–1, 92
Subramaniam, Mangala 113–14, 134
Swift, Adam 5
Switzerland 65

Taylor, Katherine 38
territorial rights 16–17, 22, 33–4, 62–3, 159 n.42
    see also common territory
tragedy of the commons 63–71, 76–7, 78–9
transnational agreements *see* international agreements
transnational social movements 116
Tully, James 101–3, 138

United Nations
 Declaration on the Rights of Indigenous Peoples (UNDRIP) 37–8
 General Assembly Resolution 64/292 13, 43
 Paris Agreement (2016) 117
 Sustainable Development Goals 13
 Watercourses Convention (1997) 117
United States of America
 civic organizations 126
 groundwater rights 67–8
 natural features, personhood granted to 63
 Nestlé 56
 privatized water 4, 56, 112–13
 social movements 112, 113
 water justice movements 127–9

Valencia, Spain 66, 67
Valentini, Laura 4
value of water 30–2
Vancouver, Canada 113
violence 104, 135–8

Waldron, Ingrid 128
water agreements 116–19
water injustice 20–1, 157 n.2
water justice movements 104–5, 124–35
 Bolivia 129–31
 Canada 124–6
 France 50, 132
 goals of 12
 and human rights 95–6
 India 133–4
 United States of America 127–9
 and violence 135–8
 see also social movements
water justice, steps towards 105–6
water, sanitation and health (WASH) 126, 128
Water Sustainability Act (WSA) 92–3
water use, rates of 51, 134
water wars 81
Wellington, Canada 124–6
Wellington Water Watchers (WWW) 124–6
West Basin Water Association 67–8
Whitaker, Steven 34, 55
Whyte, Kyle 54–5
Wiikwemkoong First Nation activists 146
Wolff, Jonathan 6–7
women, activist role of 128
Wood, Ellen Meiksins 51
World Bank 49
World Trade Organization (WTO) 49

Young, Iris Marion 20–1, 23, 90–1, 96–7, 99, 116